THE HEALER

THE HEALING WORK OF MARY BAKER EDDY

CHRISTIAN HEALING WORK
THROUGH PRAYER
PERFORMED BY
MARY BAKER EDDY
FROM 1821 TO 1866
AND CHRISTIANLY SCIENTIFIC
HEALING WORK FROM 1866 TO 1910

A History of Documented Healing Work
and the Overcoming of Material Laws
by the Discoverer and Founder
of Christian Science
and Author of
Science and Health with Key to the Scriptures

Compiled and Arranged
with Notes
by
David Lawson Keyston

CROSS & CROWN
PUBLICATIONS

ACKNOWLEDGEMENTS

The compiler wishes to thank the
individuals and organizations that have
had the courage to publish and preserve the
accounts of Mrs. Eddy's healing work, and in
particular for the courage of Paul Smillie for his
public stand for Mary Baker Eddy. Their work has
helped to make this material easier to publish.

The compiler wishes also to express grateful
appreciation to the following individuals
and organizations for permission to
quote from certain publications:

Christian Science Board of Directors of
The First Church of Christ, Scientist
The Gethsemane Foundation
Doris Grekel
Richard Oakes
Dr. Robert C. Putnam, C.S.
Rare Book Company
Helen Wright

Library of Congress Catalogue Card Number: 94-75652
International Standard Book Number (ISBN)
Hardcover Trade: 0-9645803-0-6
Limited Edition: 0-9645803-1-4

First Edition
Privately Printed

Trial Edition—December, 1994
First Edition, first issue—May, 1995

Printed in the United States of America

...Faith, if it hath not works, is dead, being alone. Yea, a man may say, Thou hast faith, and I have works: shew me thy faith without thy works, and I will shew you my faith by my works.
    —JAMES (James 2:17, 18)

...If the Spirit of him that raised up Jesus from the dead dwell in you, he that raised up Christ from the dead shall also quicken your mortal bodies by his Spirit that dwelleth in you.
    —ST. PAUL (Romans 8:11)

When I have most clearly seen and sensibly felt that the infinite recognizes no disease, this has not separated me from God, but has so bound me to Him as to enable me instantaneously to heal a cancer which had eaten its way to the jugular vein.
    —MARY BAKER EDDY (Unity of Good, p. 7:8-12)

Ye shall know the truth, and the truth shall make you free.
    —CHRIST JESUS (John 8:32)

Healing the sick and reforming the sinner demonstrate Christian Science and nothing else can, does.
    —MARY BAKER EDDY

...if I cast out devils [evils] by the Spirit of God, then the kingdom of God is come unto you.
    —CHRIST JESUS (Matt. 12:28)

If this counsel or this work be of men, it will come to nought: But if it be of God, ye cannot overthrow it, lest haply ye be found even to fight against God.
    —GAMALIEL (Acts 5:38, 39)

PREFACE

It seems that whenever great figures of world history have left their imprint on mankind, there is some critical aspect of their lives that has not been properly addressed or completely recorded by history. Such is the case of the incredible healing work performed by Mary Baker Eddy.

The world for centuries has thought that spiritual healing is a mystical event performed by those exceedingly rare individuals that are in some mysterious way gifted, or that it is a dispensation now ended. Yet, we have the promise aforetime that "...these signs shall follow them that believe; In my name shall they cast out devils; they shall speak with new tongues; they shall take up serpents; and if they drink any deadly thing, it shall not hurt them; they shall lay hands on the sick, and they shall recover."[1] And, we have the promise, "Lo, I am with you alway, even unto the end of the world."[2]

When we hear of healing most of the secular world is naturally inclined to the medical profession and material methods along with the relatively inconsistent results that have followed this growth since the earliest times of the so-called healing practice. However, history fortunately provides us with a more reliable and permanent record of healing based in Spirit, not matter. This opposite starting point, this wholly different method, has a history since the time of Moses that provides one with a source for healing that has proven able to meet every ill mankind is heir to.

Nowhere in the Bible, either in the Old Testament or in the New, are the children of God advised to resort to drugs or medicines of any kind to cure their sicknesses and diseases. There is not one case on record in the Bible where one of the children of God was cured by doctors and drugs.

When Moses listened to God and the Israelites did as they were commanded through God's chosen messenger, God blessed and healed the Israelites. (see Exodus) When they failed to heed God's commands—when they worshipped their idols and relied on their material methods—they were afflicted and suffered.

When Naaman, the captain of the army of the king of Syria, went to be healed of his leprosy by Elisha, the prophet of the Lord, he at first went away in a rage because Elisha had only sent a messenger to him requesting him to perform a simple, perhaps menial act, in order to receive his healing. He had thought that Elisha would come out to meet him and perform some great feat for his benefit, in providing him with his needed miracle. Nonetheless, when Naaman humbled himself and dipped himself in the Jordan river seven times, he came away with "the flesh of a little child." And, although Elisha would take no payment for healing Naaman, Elisha's servant showed more interest in the things of this world and went after Naaman to solicit from him some of the things offered Elisha. When he returned to Elisha's house and was found to be disobedient, he was afflicted with the leprosy that Naaman had previously. (see II Kings 5)

This same pattern is repeated throughout the Bible and history. Whenever human will is asserted mankind suffers; whenever there is reliance on God mankind is blessed. When one obeys God's messenger to that age (Moses, Elijah, Christ Jesus, etc.), one is blessed, but suffering attends those who insist on pursuing their own paths or who choose to malign or disobey that one whom God has appointed to voice His Word in blessing mankind. (See Num. 12) Yet, even today, mankind continues to follow the path leading away from spiritual enlightenment and healing and toward that which promotes material remedies for their ills and often meeting with disappointment and destruction. The Pharisees and Saduccees of the church today are no different than they were 2000 years ago. The love of position and prominence still hates the Christ idea and still casts it out of the church, refusing to follow its inspired example.

Mary Baker Eddy always told her students to emulate the life and character of Jesus. At one time she told a student, "If you would be a good healer, study the life of Jesus." Jesus' life and unparalleled healing work were due to his consummate tenderness and compassion, his reflection of God's infinite Love.

Prior to her discovery of this Christianly scientific principle that Jesus practiced in his healing ministry, Mary Baker Eddy had proven unsatisfactory, many different popular remedies of the day. Included in these were methods of allopathy, homeopathy, manipulation, spiritualism and hypnotism. Much of her life as a young woman was spent in the study of the Scriptures. These methods never could provide the inspiration and solace she always found in the Bible, methods which had no permanence nor relation to the divine influence in the human experience, such as the Master practiced.

Those that followed Jesus' example and precepts were able to perform similar healing work as the Master did. It was their obedience to his example and understanding of his place in the prophecies of the Old Testament as the Son of God, coupled with their abiding acknowledgement of this fact, that enabled their healing work to succeed and for healing to continue as long as it did. When these most important points were lost sight of and his followers failed to stand by his example, the world saw a substantial decline in the quality and quantity of healings up to about the third century, when spiritual healing ceased altogether.

There is a direct parallel in Christian Science. Those that followed Mrs. Eddy's example and precept were able to perform healing work similar to that of Jesus and herself. Through their obedience to her example and understanding of her proper place in relation to healing and her church, Christian Scientists accomplished magnificent healing work. This is attested to by the millions of healings in Christian Science that took place prior to Mrs. Eddy's leaving the human scene.

Mary Baker Eddy found the divine principle back of the healing work accomplished by the early prophets and Christ Jesus. She proved her rule by her works, healing many before ever publishing her book *Science and Health with Key to the Scriptures*. She never once lost a case of healing.

Although many biographies of this grand woman chronicle isolated healings or specific healing work done by her throughout periods of her life, there has never been an exhaustive study of this most vital topic. We have the four Gospels that provide a wonderful insight into the spiritual poise and power exercised by the Master Christian in his marvelous healing ministry, as well as that of the disciples. We even have the other books of the New Testament illustrating the healing work of the early disciples and others—as comprehensive a history of spiritual healing as can be found.

However, no one since Christ Jesus has accomplished a fragment of what Mary Baker Eddy did during her lifework for the benefit of mankind in her healing ministry. Her explanation of the divine principle of spiritual healing in her published writings and in the establishment of her church has enabled millions of others to accomplish wonderful healings. Yet, few individuals outside of the Christian Science Church have any idea who Mary Baker Eddy is, let alone know of her incredible legacy of healing work. Her healing ability as a child presaged the awe-inspiring spiritual power she exercised in her demonstration of the divine Principle in continuing years and in the founding of her church.

Her clear perception of the truth contained in the Scriptures and her motherly expressions of love and compassion enabled her to heal hundreds of individuals, perhaps thousands, the way Christ Jesus had centuries previously. This was evidenced with such frequency in the early period of her healing work that children used to follow her when she lived in Lynn, Massachusetts, to see if she would walk on water (Lynn being on the coast). Mrs. Eddy confirms this healing ability in *The First Church of Christ Scientist and Miscellany*, where she states:

> It was the healing of the sick, the saving of sinners, the works even more than the words of Christ, Truth, which had of a verity stirred the people to search the Scriptures and to find in them man's only medicine for mind and body. This Æsculapius, defined Christianly and demonstrated scientifically, is the divine Principle whose rules demonstrated prove one's faith by his works. After my discovery of Christian Science, I healed consumption [tuberculosis] in its last stages, a case which the M.D.'s, by verdict of the stethoscope and the schools, declared incurable because the lungs were mostly consumed. I healed malignant diphther-ia and carious bones that could be dented by the finger, saving the limbs when the surgeon's instruments were lying on the table ready for their amputation. I have healed at one visit a cancer that had eaten the flesh of the neck and exposed the jugular vein so that it stood out like a cord. I have physically restored sight to the blind, hearing to the deaf, speech to the dumb, and have made the lame walk. Many were the desperate cases I instantly healed, 'without money and without price,' and in most instances without even an acknowledgement of the benefit.

Mary Baker Eddy founded a system of metaphysical healing based upon the reflection of divine intelligence. The term "metaphysics," or "metaphysical," has a negative connotation in todays religious environment. It is associated with oriental mysticism and New Age practices. However, Mrs. Eddy utilized this term from a purely Biblical basis long before it had garnered its current ubiquitous impression.

Noah Webster, the father of the American Language and originator of the first true American Dictionary, defines metaphysical as, "...the science of mind or intelligence." (See *American Dicitonary of the English Language*, 1828.)*

St. Paul has said, "Let this mind be in you, which was also in Christ Jesus..." Mrs. Eddy discovered the science of the Christ that enables us to do just that, and heal just as our beloved Master has done.

Mrs. Eddy relates in her *Message for 1901*:

> Had not my first demonstrations of Christian Science or metaphysical healing exceeded that of other methods, they would not have arrested public attention and started the great Cause that to-day commands the respect of our best thinkers. It was that I healed the deaf, the dumb, the lame, the last stages of consumption, pneumonia, etc., and restored the patients in from one to three interviews, that started the inquiry, What is it? And when the public sentiment would allow it, and I had overcome a difficult stage of the work, I would put patients into the hands of my students and retire from the comparative ease of healing to the next more difficult stage of action for our Cause.

The unique feature that sets Mary Baker Eddy apart from others is the fact she established a demonstrable method of Christian healing, wholly metaphysical, that can be proved by anyone who is willing to fast to sense and feast on Soul.† By revealing this understanding of man's relationship to God in her textbook, *Science and Health with Key to the Scriptures*, Mary Baker Eddy has enabled *millions* more to receive healings of myriad illnesses, diseases and other debilitating circumstances of mortal sense. History documents these facts. Through her writings she has brought this understanding of God, and man's relationship to his creator, to untold millions more, so that they are enabled to heal themselves and others. Why has the world not recognized this great lady's incomparable spiritual attainments that brought healing and regeneration to so many? Why should not the world know of this marvelous woman, her character and what she has done for mankind? Even detractors of her day acknowledged that she healed, but they declared that healing was of the devil, all the while preferring their own prejudicial interpretation over the facts.

This book will present an historical chronology of the inspiring healing work performed by Mrs. Eddy from the time she was a child through the time of her passing. There are also incidents that illustrate her ability in overcoming so-called physical or material laws, just as our dear Master performed. In virtually every instance there is a Biblical parallel confirming the Biblical principles involved. Scriptural selections or selections from Mrs. Eddy's writings are included to illustrate the Biblical basis of her healing work. (All scriptural excerpts are from the King James version, unless otherwise specified.) Mrs. Eddy states in her textbook, *Science and Health with Key to the Scriptures*:

> I have demonstrated through Mind [God] the effects of Truth on the health, longevity, and morals of men; and I have found nothing in ancient or in modern systems on which to found my own, except the teachings and demonstrations of our great Master and the lives of the prophets and apostles. The Bible has been my only authority. I have had no other guide in 'the straight and narrow way' of Truth.

The incidents related here are by no means comprehensive. There are certainly many, many more examples of Mrs. Eddy's healing ability that are contained in the Archives of The Mother Church, The First Church of Christ, Scientist in Boston, Massachusetts. However, with respect to examples of Mrs. Eddy's healing ability and other demonstrations of spiritual insight that are in the public domain, the attempt has been to compile as complete a record as possible.

There are countless instances where "miracles" to human sense of one sort or another were performed in direct opposition to every material law concerning the progress, organization and affairs of her church. A whole volume could be written regarding these demonstrations of divine law through Mrs. Eddy's clear spiritual insight. That, however, remains for another time. Elizabeth Earl Jones (a practitioner of Mrs. Eddy's day) recounts, "One of the

Christian Science helpers in our beloved Leader's‡ home told something of how Mrs. Eddy worked for the world. Every evening from 8 to 9, Mrs. Eddy withdrew to work for the world. This member of her household told that when the hour was up, and she rejoined her household,—she was so loving,—so tender,—so Christlike,—that it almost made one's heart hurt. It touched the tenderest fibers of one's heart."[3] Mrs. Eddy writes about Jesus holding "uncomplaining guard over a world," in *Science and Health*. What Mrs. Eddy accomplished for the benefit of mankind when she "worked for the world," is something again that is beyond the scope of this work, but could easily comprise another volume or two.

The purpose of this book is to reveal the Christ-like character of the greatest woman who ever lived. The examples of Mrs. Eddy's healing work show the efficacy of her writings and illustrate how to make the teachings, the Christ, Truth, of the Bible, practical in our human experience.

The compiler is among the many millions that owe a forever debt of gratitude to our dear Master and to this inspired woman's work, having received benefit on numerous occasions. How can we repay this debt? By our simple obedience to her admonition, "to be more Christlike, to possess the Christ-spirit, to follow the Christ-example and to heal the sick as well as the sinning."[4] It is the hope of the compiler that the perusal of this volume by interested readers will kindle a desire in the reader for a greater understanding of the divine healing principle involved in Mrs. Eddy's lifework and a true appreciation of what this remarkable woman did for all mankind.

David L. Keyston   Christmas, 1994

CONTENTS

ILLUSTRATIONS

THE HEALER

THE HEALING WORK OF
MARY BAKER EDDY

INTRODUCTION

Mary Baker Eddy understood the importance of bringing the authority of Jesus into her healing work.

Annie Louise Robertson relates in *We Knew Mary Baker Eddy,*

> She was the most consistent follower of the teachings of Christ Jesus the world has ever known. She reflected the immortal courage that dared to face the whole world and tell it that it was wrong. When Mrs. Eddy talked about the Cause (of Christian Science), which she invariably did, it was easy to realize that we were living in a time like that of the early Christians.

Yet, now the world asks—Who is Mary Baker Eddy?

No other woman in history has accomplished so much or has even come close to what she has done, and yet she is virtually unknown. Why has the world not known her? Why has this woman, who has accomplished greater healing work and more of it than any other woman in history become such an obscure figure?

> At one time when [Mrs. Eddy] was talking with me of the importance of more and better healing work in our movement, she asked if I had been careful to keep a record of my own cases of healing for future reference. I said it had never occurred to me to take any particular note of them. To this Mrs. Eddy replied with earnestness, as near as I can recall her words, 'You should, dear, be faithful to keep an exact record of your demonstrations . . . .' Then she added, sadly, 'I regret to say that in the rush of a crowded life it is easy to forget even important experiences, and I am sorry that this has been true of much of my best healing work.' *We Knew MBE*, First Series, p. 68-9

This book shows the selfless love Mary Baker Eddy naturally expressed in every aspect of her life as a child of God. She showed others how to demonstrate man's God-given ability to heal through a proper understanding of their relationship to their Father-Mother God. The following scripture mirrors her comments to so many of her students.

I can of mine own self do nothing: ...the Father that dwelleth in me,
he doeth the works. John 5:30, 14:10

There was rarely a time that healings of one kind or another did not take place when in Mrs. Eddy's presence. Many were those who publicly testified of their healings through her preaching and sermons.

Along these lines, Mrs. Eddy herself alludes to what St. Paul so beautifully elucidates in I Corinthians 13, when she says:

> I walk the earth in the atmosphere of Love which holds me in spiritual gravitation. The Love that I reflect repels every error of mortal mind, for Love is the only law and Love is all activity. Love fills all channels and expels all error. Love purifies, inspires, protects, and satisfies. Love contains, Love maintains, Love sustains, Love does liberate, unbind, unseal and deliver; naught can hinder Love. Love does supply with perfect freedom, Love does furnish, provide, adorn with great liberty. Love does glow, warm, shine, light with its rays of glory. Love does illumine, irradiate, beam with resplendent brilliancy. Love is the only and all of spiritual attainment in spiritual growth. Without it healing is not done and cannot be, either morally or physically. Every advance step will show you this until victory is won and you possess no other conscious-ness but <u>Love</u> divine.[5]

Mrs. Eddy's spirituality was reflected in her physical appearance. She has been described by news reporters as well as her students and under varying circumstances. In 1896, William Elmer Crofut, at the time a young reporter for the *Syracuse Post* noted for his interviews of national and international personages, was given the opportunity of an interview with Mrs. Eddy.

> I knew then and I know now that I was in the presence of an extraordinary person. It was as though here was one who had fasted—had been in long periods of prayer and solitary communion with her God and her Christ and that something of the great spiritual life eternal had settled upon her .... I have always felt that this was my greatest interview. Her presence has always been with me. Her name is surely enrolled among the greatest religious leaders of all time.6

Mrs. Eddy about 1898

One could not be in Mrs. Eddy's presence for long without feeling the wonderful spiritual animus that was expressed through her tender loving consideration. Julia Johnston shares a memory of Mary Baker Eddy related by her mother:

> ...Mrs. Eddy was an impressive figure. Slender, graceful, and erect, filled with the majesty of divine anointing, she seemed always to be imparting wisdom freshly drawn from the wells of salvation. Looking beyond the finite to the infinite her countenance seemed alight with spiritual radiance. In her movements there was animation, but never agitation. There seemed to be in her consciousness a fountain of Life everspringing forth in peaceful, persistent strength. One could not look at her without being aware of her holy calling. Speaking of her first glimpse of Mrs. Eddy, my mother Mrs. Annie Rodgers Michael, involuntarily uttered the words, "The moment I saw her I knew that I was in the presence of one inspired of God."[7]

Another aspect of Mrs. Eddy's presence is imaged forth in a description by Clara Shannon, another of her students.

> I was very much impressed by listening to our Leader's audible communion with God (as we call prayer). I heard her address God as "Precious Mother Love, darling Mother, show me Thy way." There seemed to be such a perfect communion with divine Love as a child has with its mother. When referring to God, she nearly always called God Love, and would say, "Love will show me."

Her spiritual poise was reflected in her appearance, manner and speech. Irving Tomlinson recorded,

> That she never lost her great gift of eloquence in after years I am able to testify, for it was my privilege on February 26, 1898, to hear Mrs. Eddy deliver a remarkably inspiring address in Christian Science Hall, Concord, New Hampshire." He goes on to say, "At that date Mrs. Eddy was in her seventy-seventh year, yet except for her white hair there was no trace of age in her appearance, manner, gesture or voice. The *Concord Evening Monitor* of February 27, 1898, in its account said, 'Mrs. Eddy appeared at her best, as sprightly and energetic as a young woman.'[8]

Arthur Brisbane, a well respected reporter in Mrs. Eddy's day, provides a glimpse of what it was like to meet Mrs. Eddy.

> Mrs. Eddy is eighty-six years old. Her thick hair, snow-white, curls about her forehead and temples. She is of medium height and very slender. She probably weighs less than one hundred pounds. But her figure is straight as she rises and walks forward. The grasp of her thin hand is firm; the hand does not tremble. It is hopeless to try to describe a face made very beautiful by age, deep thought, and many years' exercise of great power. The light blue eyes are strong and concentrated in expression. And the sight, as was soon proved, is that of a woman one-half Mrs. Eddy's age. Mrs. Eddy's face is almost entirely free from wrinkles—the skin is very clear, many a young woman would be proud to have it. The forehead is high and full, and the whole expression of the face combines benevolence with great strength of will. Mrs. Eddy has accumulated power in this world. She possesses it, she exercises it, and she knows it. But it is a gentle power, and it is possessed by a gentle, diffident, and modest woman. [9]

Rev. Severin E. Simonsen described his encounter with Mary Baker Eddy in 1902 in a wonderful word-picture that brings forth the Christly character of this woman.

I was most singularly impressed with the purity and beauty of her countenance, and her almost transparent face, so radiant with peace, joy, and love. But to me the most striking attraction was her wonderful eyes, the like of which I have never seen in all my experience of contact with people; they expressed volumes. It is beyond my power to describe how they responded to, and in various ways portrayed the sacred subject she would at the moment be discussing. You realized that she reflected the Christ mind so fully that she discerned without effort your mental state; but it did not disturb you. The sense that came to you was her desire not to injure, but to help and save—the same as our Master did when he discerned the thoughts of the people. Hence your heart filled with gratitude for such a helping hand.

There was almost a supernatural keenness to discern your innermost thoughts, but only for the purpose of helping, counseling and guiding you into a higher understanding of your heavenly Father. Yea, to bring out a more perfect confidence in God as your ever present help, and in your ability to do whatsoever God had for you to do.

Her talk with us and the instructions she gave were beautifully illuminating, deeply comprehensive, and wonderfully helpful—never to be forgotten....

Before it was my great privilege to be invited to visit her in her own home and listen to her, I used to wonder how it was that her faithful followers were so eager to carry out her every wish and command. But after I met her personally, and came in contact with this great heart of love, it all became clear to me. I realized then that she manifested such Christ-love, such unselfed love for God and all mankind, and it was so apparent that she was divinely directed in all her efforts, that she required of her followers only that which was for the glory of God, their own unfoldment in Truth and Love, and the good of mankind.

It has been my privilege to meet and to listen to many of the foremost religious leaders of my time, both in this country and abroad; and I can truthfully say that in all my experience I have never met or listened to any one who, to my mind, reflected and manifested so fully the spirit and love of Christ as did Mrs. Eddy. ...

I know of no words adequate to express fully my gratitude to God for this noble and wonderful woman, who was good enough, pure enough, unselfish enough, and intelligent enough to receive this revelation of divine Science, and to record it in such a language as to make plain to the benighted understanding of mankind the way of God's full salvation through Christ.[10]

Many have confirmed the fact that various incidents of healings have been published at one time or another, but scores of Mrs. Eddy's healings have never been published and many, many more never even recorded.

Paul Smillie illustrates the significance of Mrs. Eddy's healing work from a practical human standpoint in his biography, *Mary Baker Eddy, The Prophetic and Historical Perspective*, on p. 5. He makes so clear the key ingredient of Christ Jesus' healing ministry in what Mrs. Eddy expressed in her daily life.

> The Word must be made flesh to be appreciated humanly. The absolute perfection must be manifest in our relative human experience to have practical meaning and application. In the first series of *We Knew Mary Baker Eddy* , p. 80, we read: 'Mrs. Eddy presented two aspects to her pupils which were so perfectly blended that one gained, in her presence, the feeling of her perfect harmony with Life. One aspect was her clear and unfailing spiritual sense; her unswerving reliance on God; her consciousness of His ever-presence, and of His nearness, as a friend is near. The other aspect was her great humanity; her uncommon, common sense, as shown in her practical application of Jesus' teachings to all the little things of everyday living.' Mrs. Eddy lived the human and divine coincidence. She always proved the absolute and in doing so brought it forth in the relative. Mrs. Eddy always made the Word flesh. Christian Science was not a dreamy-like proposition for Mary Baker Eddy. It was practical and regenerative.

Mary Baker Eddy realized the importance of good healing work. Clara Choate, one of Mrs. Eddy's students, remembers in her reminiscence nearly a century ago:

> As near as I can quote from memory she said this: "Healing is what the world needs. Christ taught this healing. Our religious advancement or righteous living, one and the same, can be better gained by *good healing* than in any other way...." She then explained how the students might be led, or swayed into thinking of *less* important ways of the work, but healing is *the* work needed first and last. ..."All the emoluments in the world, all the admiration that can ever be excited is not nor can be *surpassed* by the gratitude of a sick person healed, or, by the

dejected, painful, suffering one relieved and restored." Mrs. Eddy never belittled this part of the work. She always impressed upon me that soul-healing would inevitably come with the demonstration of *bodily healing*. "I join the work of Christ when I heal the sick." As she said this she rose and laying her hand gently upon my shoulder, with tears in her deep glorious eyes, "Then are we the true soldiers of the Christ and His followers."[11]

This volume reveals the magnitude of Mary Baker Eddy's healing work and brings to light the motherly, loving character of this remarkable woman. It is hoped that by Mrs. Eddy's example all can see how to express more of the Christ character in their daily lives. It is even hoped that her example will turn more readers to the consecrated study of the Bible and of *Science and Health with Key to the Scriptures* in an effort to share more of the Christ-spirit with their fellow man in wanting to follow Mrs. Eddy's example as her life emulated that of the Master Christian's healing work. It is to these individuals this book is dedicated.

NOTE

Some instances of healing and other demonstrations are exact quotes and are properly referenced while there is minor editing to others. Almost all examples provided can be quoted from at least two, or in some cases up to fifteen different sources. Each instance is numbered. A referenced bibliography is at the end of this book in Appendix Two. Any book referenced is the first edition of that book, unless stated otherwise. The number following each instance will be indicated preceding the appropriate title in the bibliography.

Some illustrations appearing herein are from the private collection of the compiler with several photographs having never before been published.

Throughout this book the letters "C. S." may have been substituted for Christian Science, for sake of brevity.

Any time one is dealing with a large number of examples of anything it is possible that there may be two different versions of the same example that were treated as two separate instances. The compiler apologizes in advance if such is the case with any recollection here. However, such discrepancies, if any, would be extremely minimal.

If you have an authentic account of healing performed by Mary Baker Eddy that is not presented here and you would like to share it, it will be included in subsequent editions of this book. Please forward a copy with any other pertinent information to the address below. Thank you.

"Healings"
Cross & Crown Publications
2100 Third Ave., No. 1901
Seattle, WA 98121

. . . *and a little child shall lead them.* Isaiah 11:6

CHILDHOOD YEARS

1821-1839

Therefore will he give them up, until the time that she which travaileth hath brought forth: then the remnant of his brethren shall return unto the children of Israel. Micah 5:3

"During the time of Mrs. Eddy's mother's period of maternity, she told her neighbor Mrs. Gault that she heard a voice saying, 'That which is to be born of you will be born of God,' and I am so worried and pray over it that I might be delivered from such thoughts of profanity." 1

Mrs. Baker was a devout Christian, a congregationalist, but as the passage above illustrates, she was held in bondage to the belief that man is a miserable sinner and incapable of that inspiration that regenerated so many and elevated thought as in Christ Jesus' day.

"Some years ago [Mrs. Eddy] explained to me why she struggled in coming out from the belief of life, substance, and intelligence in matter, and revealing life, substance and intelligence as wholly spiritual. The reason was prenatal. One day, about four and a half months before her birth, her mother, Mrs. Baker, went into the attic to get some wool in order to spin yarn for knitting. This wool, after it had been shorn from the sheep's backs and cleansed, was stored in a room in the attic until needed. Collecting her wool together, suddenly she was overwhelmed by the thought that she was filled with the Holy Ghost and had dominion over the whole earth. At that moment she felt the quickening of the babe, and then she thought, 'What a sin I am guilty of,—the sin of presumption—in thinking that I could be filled with the Holy Ghost! That I could

1

have dominion!' Indeed she was very troubled."

"A dear old friend came to see her, and finding her so sorrowful, asked her what was the trouble. Mrs. Baker told her that she had been guilty of the sin of presumption, because of her conviction that she was filled with the Holy Ghost and had dominion over the whole earth. Her friend told her that this was the kind of man which God created, of which we read in the first chapter of Genesis; that this man was made in God's image and likeness and was given dominion. She stayed and comforted Mrs. Baker." 2

> And it came to pass, that, when Elisabeth heard the salutation of Mary, the babe leaped in her womb; and Elisabeth was filled with the Holy Ghost: Luke 1:41

> And God said, Let us make man in our image, after our likeness: and let them have dominion. . . Gen. 1:26

"When she was only a few years old, she used to sleep in a trundle bed. . . . Sometimes her mother would go out into the evening after putting the baby to bed, and her father would sit in the parlor reading. Mary would call out, 'Father, I know what you are doing; you are reading the newspaper.' To this he would reply, 'Hush, child, go to sleep.' Then she would say, 'I'll read it to you,' and she would tell him what he was reading although she could not pronounce the long words." 3

Mrs. Eddy confirms this ability to read thought in the first edition of *Retrospection and Introspection.* Also in *Christian Science History* by Judge Septimus J. Hanna, we read, "I can discern in the human mind, thoughts, motives and purpose; and neither mental arguments nor psychic power can affect this spiritual insight. It is as impossible to prevent this native perception as to open the door of a room and then prevent a man who is not blind from looking into the room and seeing all it contains. This mind-reading is first sight; it is the gift of God. And this phenomenon appeared in my childhood; it is associated with my earliest memories, and has increased with years. It has enabled me to heal in a marvelous manner, to be just in judgement, to learn the divine mind,—and it

2

cannot be abused; no evil can be done by reason of it. If the human mind communicates with me in sleep, when I awake, this communication is as palpable as words audibly spoken." 4

> And the scribes and Pharisees watched him, whether he would heal on the sabbath day; that they might find an accusation against him. But _he knew their thoughts,_ and said to the man which had the withered hand, Rise up, and stand forth in the midst. And he arose and stood forth. (emphasis added) Luke 6:7, 8.

When Mrs. Eddy was a small child (probably age 3), she often intervened in quarrels that took place between her brothers. Even though the boys might resort to their fists in the settlement of their arguments, young Mary never neglected the role of peacemaker. Irrespective of how difficult the dispute seemed she never failed to bring about an amicable reconciliation. When the gulf between her brothers seemed wide she would go from one with a message for the other, and this was repeated back and forth until the brothers asked one another for forgiveness. 5

> Thou lovest righteousness, and hatest wickedness: therefore God, thy God, hath anointed thee with the oil of gladness above thy fellows.
> Psalms 45:7

"Again, when Mrs. Eddy was a little girl, her brother George climbed a tree for some apples. He lost his balance and fell to the ground on a broken bottle. The glass made a very deep gash in his thigh. His father picked him up, took him into the house, and sent for a surgeon to put in some stitches. It was a long, deep gash and the boy was screaming in agony. Mr. Baker at once picked up little Mary and took her backwards into the room so that she could not see her brother. The father put her hand on the wound, and the pain ceased. He held it there while the doctor put in the stitches; (anesthetics had not been heard of at that time.) The doctor thought there must be something very wonderful and very strange about her." 6

Just think, her father must have seen many instances of his little Mary's unusual prowess to think the child capable of healing George—unfortunately he did not acknowledge her special spiritual nature—he was quite harsh with little Mary as she grew up.

When she was just a tot little Mary would go out in the cold nights to sing the pigs to sleep.

"[Her mother] did not at first consent to Mary's request, but as Mary kept insisting, Abigail gave in, learning not to interfere with what Mary wished to do. The tot would put warm clothes on, put a shawl over her head, sit down near the pig pen and sing to the little pigs until they ceased squealing and went off to sleep. She did not just sing but prayed too, and the effect of her prayers was always felt. Mary was sometimes given the responsibility of caring for the lambs which were sick. Her father would say, 'Here is another invalid for Mary.' It was never very long before the little one would return to the flock." 7

"An incident illustrating Mary Baker's unusual development as a child is shown in the following: The family had a dog in the house named 'Ben' and when they were assembled in the sitting room the dog was made to understand that he must always lie under the table. Sometimes he would disregard this injunction and come out and sit before the fire with the family. Mrs. Eddy says she found out that by mentally addressing the dog he would obey her without her speaking a word aloud. When she saw that Ben was in for trouble, because of his presence in the room, she would mentally say, 'Ben, go under the table and lie down,' and immediately the dog would rise and walk under the table and lie down. This she said occurred many, many times and was one of the incidents of her childhood which she always kept to herself." 8

"From the time Mrs. Eddy was a small child she always wanted to go and visit children—any of her little friends who were ill or had had accidents. She said they always seemed to forget their pain and to get well when she could be with them. The same thing occurred when any one of them were hurt at play; she was always able to help them." (related by Julia Bartlett in an interview she had in later years with Mrs. Eddy) 9

4

Is it any wonder that this precious spiritually minded little child would go out to the shed where she would pray seven times *each day*? She wanted to follow David's example. Imagine such a desire to serve God, that this little one would mark with chalk on the wall of the shed every time she prayed just so she might not miss her obligation to God. This was a characteristic that was to mark every aspect of her earthly life in service to God and in her work of establishing her church.

Even her Bible was well worn from use having studied regularly, memorizing whole chapters and Psalms.

The Baker farm—Bow, New Hampshire

"Once when Mary was very small, her elder brother was chopping wood. The axe slipped and he suffered a severe wound in the leg. When the wound refused to heal and the family had begun to despair of the brother's recovery, Mark Baker, their father, carried the little girl into her brother's room and had her gently touch the wound. From that very moment the wound began to heal and in a short time the leg was wholly restored. But as a result Mary suffered for days from a high fever." 10

5

That it might be fulfilled which was spoken by Esaias the prophet, saying, Himself took our infirmities, and bare our sicknesses. Matt. 8:17

"Her father thought that her health was impaired from too much reading and studying, and he would hide her books, but she was always able to find them. This ability which she has said was with her from her earliest years, was considered by her father to be a manifestation of the devil; he considered it uncanny." This was unsettling to Mark Baker because it contradicted the theological beliefs of the day, beliefs that held the healing of Christ Jesus to be for a time long past, impossible in their present day. It did not help that the theology of the day held that women were "God-ordained inferiors," and everything Mary represented to her Father contradicted this, she was superior in every sense.

"At play Mrs. Eddy was always able to find the things which the children would hide. Some of the children did not like her because she was always able to win in the games in which things were hidden. In that day a very popular game was 'Hide the Thimble,' and one time the children gave her what they considered to be a great test by hiding the thimble in the ashes of the kitchen stove. To their great astonishment Mrs. Eddy went directly to it and found it among the ashes." 11

This special child was ordained of God in a most extraordinary manner.

"When about eight years old she frequently heard a voice calling *Mary* three times, and supposing it was her mother ran to her and asked her what she wanted, but always to be told she had not called her, until one time when her little cousin was with her, she too heard the voice and asked her why she did not go to her mother who had called her. Then she went to her and told her she did call because her cousin had heard her. Her mother, who had been much perplexed before, read to her that night the story of little Samuel [see I Samuel 3:4-11], and told her she must reply as he did, 'Speak, Lord; for thy servant heareth.' She was afraid and did not answer when it came again, and wept and prayed God to forgive

6

her. The next time was after her mother had put her in her little bed for the night. The voice called, 'Mary,' and she replied, 'Speak, Lord; for thy servant heareth,' and it was as if she was gently lifted up."

Most remarkable was that when she responded to the voice her body was lifted to a height of about a foot then gently laid back on the bed; this was repeated three times. 12

Adam H. Dickey later recorded that Mrs. Eddy told him the following regarding this incident:

> . . . As a child she was afraid to tell the circumstances to anybody but she pondered it deeply in her thought of it many years afterward when she was demonstrating the nothingness of matter. 13

"At another time there was an occurrence that illustrated this special little girl's spiritual perspicacity. After a church service one Sunday Mrs. Baker took her little Mary with her to visit the pastor's wife, who was quite ill. It was believed that she was suffering from a tumor. The pastor and his wife had been married for fifteen years, yet they had not been able to have children, which had been a great disappointment, as she loved children dearly. When the Bakers came to visit they read the Bible and sang hymns to the Pastor's wife, with little Mary joining in the songs. After they left the house little Mary exclaimed, 'Mother, I saw a dear little baby all cuddled up close and warm inside.' However, Mrs. Baker told her little Mary that there were no babies there. But Mary was insistent, saying, 'But Mother, I saw a dear little baby all cuddled up inside.' Later on this revelation was a wonder to many of their friends as this woman did indeed give birth to a baby boy." 14

> Now Abraham and Sarah were old and well stricken in age; and it ceased to be with Sarah after the manner of women. Therefore Sarah laughed within herself, saying, After I am waxed old shall I have pleasure, my lord being old also? And the Lord said unto Abraham, Wherefore did Sarah laugh, saying, Shall I of a surety bear a child, which am old? Is any thing too hard for the Lord? At the time appointed I will return unto thee, according to the time of life, and Sarah shall have a son. Gen. 18:11-14

When Mary was eight or ten years old, her elderly grand-mother was suffering from the delusion that there was a great big black dog underneath her bed, and she could not sleep until Mary would come and drive the animal out. "So every night, 'Mary, come in and drive the dog out,' was the request from her. Mary would come in and go through the motions of driving out the dog. Finally, she resolved to pretend no longer in supporting a falsehood, and went and reasoned with her grandmother so earnestly and successfully, by *showing* her that there was *no* dog under the bed, that she was healed of the claim!" 15

Mary could not reconcile the idea of a loving and merciful God with her father's theology (Calvinism) along with its inherent sentence of predestination. So, when Mary was ready to join the church of her parents this conflict disturbed Mary greatly, climaxing in her being confined to bed with a fever. When the doctor was unable to relieve her suffering, her mother admonished her to turn to God, to lean on God's ministering love. This wonderful motherly intuition turning Mary to prayer, enabled her to feel God's ever-present love, and to rise joyfully, wholly above the decree of her father's relentless theology. She was completely free of the fever, and dressed herself. 16

When Mary was attending the Sanbornton Academy (she was fifteen at the time), there was an incident that was related for years by the residents of that town. One day a lunatic escaped from an asylum at Concord, invading the schoolyard, brandishing a club. The terrified children ran into the schoolhouse—that is, all except Mary. She advanced towards the man. The lunatic wielded the club above his head, but Mary walked straight up to him and took his free hand. To the children watching the schoolyard scene from the windows it looked as though Mary was to be struck down. At that moment the man dropped the club down to his side and Mary led him to the gate. He reappeared the next Sunday at church, and stood beside Mary during the hymn singing. After the service he allowed the authorities to take him into custody without resistance. 17

And when he was come out of the ship, immediately there met him
out of the tombs a man with an unclean spirit, Who had his dwelling

among the tombs; and no man could bind him, no, not with chains:
Because that he had been often bound with fetters and chains, and the
chains had been plucked asunder by him, and the fetters broken in
pieces: neither could any man tame him. . . . And they come to Jesus,
and see him that was possessed with the devil, and had the legion,
sitting, and clothed, and in his right mind. . . . Mark 5:2-4, 15

In the following year, Mary continued her education with the Rev. Enoch Corser. Even at this early age his perception ably confirmed what many others had seen of this young girl. "I never before had a pupil with such a depth and independence of thought. She has some great future, mark that. She is an intellectual and spiritual genius." 18

spake as one having authority. . . see Matt. 7:29

EARLY YEARS

1840-1865

"On her wedding day (her marriage to George Glover), in 1843, our Leader, after leaving home, stopped at Concord for the night to visit her old home at Bow (New Hampshire) on the next day. The young bride and groom were journeying to the South by a sailing ship, and before leaving home, her mother had given her a letter addressed to herself with the injunction that she read it with her husband when they were half-way through the sea voyage. Before this time, however, a severe storm arose and the captain said that he did not think there was any hope of saving the ship. It was a sailing ship, and therefore more at the mercy of the wind and waves than the liners of today. So she and her husband kneeled down in their cabin, praying to God to save them. She said, 'I want to read my mother's letter. I know we are not half-way across yet, but this may be the opportunity." She read the letter which contained such good advice. It was treasured and was helpful to them then; she saw all its meaning and its love, and this helped her very much. They continued in their prayer to God. In a short time the captain came below to say, 'The wind has suddenly subsided, and we are safe.' Coming on deck they found a peaceful sea, and the journey was continued in calm and peace, without further misadventure." 19

The captain of the ship was grateful to the Glovers for their prayers and the situation showed the efficacy of their sincere appeal to God, resulting in the immediate abatement of the storm and their consequent safe passage to harbor.

> And there arose a great storm of wind, and the waves beat into the ship, so that it was now full. And he was in the hinder part of the ship, asleep on a pillow: and they awake him, and say unto him, Master, carest thou not that we perish? And he arose, and rebuked the wind, and said unto the sea, Peace, be still. And the wind ceased, and there was a great calm. Mark 4:37-39

10

The very next year while they were on a business trip to Wilmington, North Carolina, Mary Glover's husband contracted yellow fever, and nine days later expired (on June 27, 1844), the doctor attending to Mr. Glover stating that but for Mrs. Glover's prayers he would have died many days sooner. This example took place 22 years before she discovered the Science of the Christ, or the divine principle back of Christ Jesus' healing work. 20

Mrs. Eddy's motherly, loving disposition was always lifting the thoughts of others, lessening suffering, and bringing regeneration. She could not help doing this. Her mothering nature was felt by all, and especially by the young children, resulting in immediate healing.

> *Verily I say unto you, Except ye be converted, and become as little children, ye shall not enter into the kingdom of heaven. Whosoever therefore shall humble himself as this little child, the same is greatest in the kingdom of heaven. And whoso shall receive one such little child in my name receiveth me. But whoso shall offend one of these little ones which believe in me, it were better for him that a millstone were hanged about his neck, and that he were drowned in the depth of the sea.* Matt. 18:3-6

"When Mrs. Eddy was a very young woman she started a primary school, and among her pupils was a very bad boy who had caused his parents and playmates continual trouble and apprehension. Mrs. Eddy dealt patiently with him, but seemingly to no avail at first. Finally, one day she required him to remain after school until the other children had gone home; then she began to talk with this boy, not upbraiding him, but telling him about the Love of God for him, and also praying for him. When the boy reached home that night, his whole nature had undergone an utter transformation through this transmuting touch of divine Love, as expressed to him by his teacher. His parents were astonished and spoke to her later about it, saying that the hateful disposition which he had formerly shown had been entirely dispelled, and he was now gentle and loving and obedient. The boy had also manifested great interest in the Bible, and to love to read it, while his reverence and affection for his teacher were unbounded." 21

Mrs. Eddy relates, "In the fifties, Mrs. Smith of Rumney, N. H., came to me with her infant, whose eyes were diseased, a mass of inflammation, neither pupil or iris discernible." She thought of the words of Jesus, "Suffer the little children to come unto me and forbid them not." "Who," she wondered, "has forbidden this little one, who is leading it into the way of blindness?"

"I gave the infant no drugs,—held her in my arms a few moments while lifting my thoughts to God, then returned the babe to her mother healed. In grateful memory thereof Mrs. Smith named her babe 'Mary.' and embroidered a petticoat for me. I have carefully preserved that garment to this day." This leaning on God brought instantaneous healing and joy to both the mother and Mrs. Eddy. 22

The beginning of the Civil War found many a young man off to fight. Living near Mrs. Eddy's home was a kindly woman who had befriended her, who had an only son who was going to join the forces of the North. Although he had been a disobedient and wild boy Mrs. Eddy knew the need this young man had and wished to give to him a copy of the Bible. With but a dollar in her purse she purchased the Bible and inscribed his name in it and a Scriptural quote she wished him to repeat each morning and night. Just before he was to leave the next day Mrs. Eddy asked his mother to bring him to her room. She told him that that book would save him. She wanted him to promise that he would read a portion every day. The young man was very impressed with all that she said. One day, after the end of the war, there came a knock on her door. The young soldier had returned. "You do not remember me," he said. "I am the soldier to whom you gave a Testament when I left to join my regiment. I have come to thank you for the blessed book, which has always been a help to me, and which saved my life." Thereupon he gently took from the pocket of his uniform a well-worn Bible and gave it to her. He showed her where the book had stopped a bullet from piercing him. 23

12

He that dwelleth in the secret place of the most High shall abide under the shadow of the Almighty. I will say of the Lord, He is my refuge and my fortress: my God; in him will I trust. Surely he shall deliver thee from the snare of the fowler, and from the noisome pestilence. He shall cover thee with his feathers, and under his wings shalt thou trust: his truth shall be thy shield and buckler. Thou shalt not be afraid for the terror by night; nor for the arrow that flieth by day; Nor for the pestilence that walketh in darkness; nor for the destruction that wasteth at noonday. Psalms 91:1-6

"During the years she spent in bed (as an invalid), she got up a petition for the abolition of slavery which she sent to President Lincoln, signed by thousands of people. Her husband, a surgeon dentist, Dr. Patterson, was sent with two senators to pay the soldiers of the North. On arrival near the boundary, he was enticed into conversation by Southerners in disguise, who induced their enemies to cross the boundary about three feet. They then suddenly pronounced them prisoners and took them to Libby prison. The senators never were heard from again, but Dr. Patterson escaped in a marvelous manner, returning home some weeks later. This was the result of his wife's prayers for his protection. During this time our Leader had been removed to her husband's brother's house and her bed was placed near the window. One day she saw approaching what appeared to be a tramp in tattered clothing. He knocked at the door and told his brother that he was starving, after weeks of exposure in finding his way home. His brother did not recognize him and sent him away. Our Leader, however, called out that it was Dr. Patterson and told them to take him in and give him food. After this, he lectured in many places, telling of his many experiences and wearing part of the same clothing in which he had returned home." 24

And when he had apprehended him, he put him in prison, and delivered him to four quaternions of soldiers to keep him; intending after Easter to bring him forth to the people. Peter therefore was kept in prison: but prayer was made without ceasing of the church unto God for him. And when Herod would have brought him forth, the same night Peter was sleeping between two soldiers, bound with two chains: and the keepers before the door kept the prison. And, behold, the angel of the Lord came upon him, and a light shined in the prison: and he smote Peter on the side, and raised him up, saying, Arise up quickly. And his chains fell off from his hands. And the angel said unto him, Gird thyself, and bind on thy sandals. And so he did. And he saith unto him, Cast thy garment about thee, and follow me. And he went out, and followed him; and wist not that it was true which was done by the angel; but thought he saw a vision. When they were past the first and the second ward, they came unto the iron gate that leadeth unto the city; which opened to them of his own accord: and they went out, and passed on through one street; and forthwith the angel departed from him. And when Peter was come to himself, he said, Now I know of a surety, that the Lord hath sent his angel, and hath delivered me out of the hand of Herod. . . Acts 12:4-11

During the time that Mrs. Eddy was studying the methods of Dr. Phineas P. Quimby, in Portland, Maine, in 1862, she helped an invalid that was in a terrible state. "In the absence of Dr. Quimby . . . a man was brought to the hotel where I was staying, who was in a pitiable condition. He had sometime previous met with an accident and he was well-nigh broken to pieces. His knees and ankles were out of place and he was suffering untold agonies. The proprietor of the hotel came to me and besought me to do something for the poor sufferer. At first I thought I could not. Then I said, 'God can do it.' I went to his bedside and lifted my thought silently to God. At the conclusion of my prayer I said, 'Now you can arise and open the door for me.' The man arose, and with the iron clamps he wore rattling as he walked, and went and opened the door." 25

Another incident of healing that occurred when Mrs. Eddy [who was at the time married to Daniel Patterson], was visiting Quimby in Portland, Maine, took place in the hotel near the train station of that city. Apparently a woman was taking her dying husband to his family home in Canada, when a doctor on the train advised the woman against further travel with her husband in such a dire condition. They stopped at the hotel where Mrs. Eddy was staying. Soon after she had heard of the woman's husband passing on there in the hotel, she went to the room of the grieving wife in the attempt to comfort her. "She said, 'Let us go and waken him.' They went, and she stood beside him for a few minutes and told his wife that he was waking, and that she must be close by so that he could see her when he opened his eyes which he shortly did. He said to his wife, 'Oh, Martha, it was so strange, to be at home and you not there,' and he spoke about meeting his parents and others of the family who had died before." Martha had witnessed the true power of the Christ to resurrect her husband just as the Christ had done nineteen centuries before.

This was to be one of the first of many, many times that Mrs. Eddy raised one from the dead. When Mrs. Eddy left the hotel three days later the woman's husband was living. During this time Mrs. Eddy cured another man who had been severely injured and had broken limbs. Before leaving Portland, she healed a number of Dr. Quimby's patients as well. 26

> And when he was come in, he saith unto them, Why make ye this ado, and weep? the damsel is not dead, but sleepeth. And they laughed him to scorn. But when he had put them all out, he taketh the father and the mother of the damsel, and them that were with him, and entereth in where the damsel was lying. And he took the damsel by the hand, and said unto her, Talitha cumi; which is, being interpreted, Damsel, I say unto thee, arise. And straightway the damsel arose, and walked. . . Mark 5:39-42

On March 31, 1864, while on a trip to see Phineas Quimby, Mrs. Eddy was able to help Mrs. Mary Ann Jarvis, another of Dr. Quimby's patients. "A woman, whom I cured of consumption [tuberculosis], always breathed with great difficulty when the wind was from the east. I sat silently by her side a few moments. Her breath came gently. The inspirations were deep and natural. I then requested her to look at the weather-vane. She looked and saw that it pointed due east. The wind had not changed, but her thought of it had and so her difficulty in breathing had gone. The wind had not produced the difficulty. My metaphysical treatment changed the action of her belief on the lungs, and she never suffered again from east winds, but was restored to health." This incident has appeared in many editions of *Science and Health with Key to the Scriptures*. 27

Although Mrs. Eddy was yet to make her discovery of the science of Jesus' healing ministry, her reflection of God's everpresent love was a blessing to many. "Mrs. Sarah Crosby, of Albion, Maine, sent for my [Mrs. Eddy's] aid because of an injury to her eye. She was hundreds of miles away, but after receiving her first letter, as soon as the mail could bring it, I received another from her, of which the following is an extract:—'Since the accident to my eye, it has been so exceedingly sensitive to the light, I have shaded it, unable to do any writing or sewing of any note. The Sunday I mailed you a letter I suffered a great deal with it; Monday it was painful until towards night, when it felt better; Tuesday it was *well*, and I have not worn my shade over it since a week ago Monday, and I have read, sewed, and written, and still all is well. Now you may form your own conclusions. I told a friend the other day you had cured my eye, or perhaps my fear of my eye, and it is so; though I am sure, for the life of me, I cannot understand a word of what you write me about the possibility of a spirit like mine having power over a hundred and seventy pounds of live flesh and blood to keep it in perfect trim.'" 28

One of Mrs. Eddy's students, Clara Sainsbury Shannon, asked her why she wrote *Science and Health*. "She told me that one day she was called to a lady who was dying of consumption, and that there were three or four doctors there—fine men who had expended all their medical knowledge in trying to save this lady from death." Mrs. Eddy said, "When they found that there was no hope for her recovery, they decided to test 'that woman,' as they had heard of someone who had been cured by her. The husband of this lady sent for her, and when she entered the room the patient was propped up with many pillows and could not speak. Our Leader saw that what she needed was an arousal and quickly pulled all the pillows away from behind her. As she fell backwards, the patient said, 'Oh, you have killed me.'" "Mrs. Eddy told her that she could get up and that she would help her to dress. She was instantaneously healed and well. Mrs. Eddy asked the doctors to leave the room while she helped her to put on her clothing, after which they rejoined the doctors and her husband in the sitting room."

Miss Shannon continues, "One of the doctors, an old experienced physician, witnessed this, and he said, 'How did you do it? What did you do?' She said, 'I can't tell you—it was God,' and he said, 'Why don't you write a book, publish it, and give it to the world?' When she returned home, she opened her Bible, and her eyes fell on the words, 'Thus speaketh the Lord God of Israel, saying, Write thee all the words that I have spoken unto thee in a book'! (Jer. 30:2), which showed her God's direction." 29

"Though they stumble and fall, yet they rise again the stronger. . . ." Mary Baker Eddy, 1890

MARY BAKER EDDY'S HEALING

The first week of February, 1866.

In early 1866, Mrs. Patterson, as Mrs. Eddy was then known, was living in Swampscott, Massachussets at 23 Paradise Road.

On the first evening of February, 1866, Mary Patterson was on her way to a meeting at the Good Templar's Lodge in Lynn. The conditions of that evening were severe. The temperature was below zero, and there was snow and ice on all the streets and walkways. Perhaps the account of Saturday, February 3, 1866, appearing in *The Lynn Reporter*, is the most widely known description of what followed.

> Mrs. Mary M. Patterson, of Swampscott, fell upon the ice near the corner of Market and Oxford Streets, on Thursday evening [February 1st], and was severely injured. She was taken up in an insensible condition and carried to the residence of S. M. Bubier, Esq., nearby, where she was kindly cared for during the night. She was removed to her home in Swampscott yesterday morning, though in a very critical condition. 30

Mrs. Eddy describes the particulars of this momentous event and discovery during an interview years afterward.

> . . . I slipped upon the pavement, fell across the curbstone, and that induced an injury that they considered as fatal as if my head had been severed. The papers I have clippings from advertised me as fatally injured, and the doctors said they could do nothing for me, but chloroformed me and took me home on a mattress. When I got home the dear ones around me said, "If you can't live, tell us something, do tell us something

18

as you always do of your views," and I said to them, "Why, I can't conceive in this vestibule that there is death."

I was then in a position that I do not like to name, because I want to dismiss it from my mind, but it was called spinal dislocation. I said, "It does not seem death to me; life seems continuous, and my Father's face dearer than ever before," and as I talked they did not know what to make of it. Finally I said to them, "Won't you leave the room a little while? I am getting oppressed." The clergyman was just about to come and see me, and he entered, and then he talked with me a little, and he said, "You seem near heaven. Do you realize that you cannot recover?" I said, "They tell me so, but I cannot realize it," and he said to me, "I must see you again; I am engaged now, but I will call in a little time. I want to see you again living if I can."

He stepped out, and was gone perhaps a half hour. I requested the others to leave the room and they did. Then I rose from my bed perfectly sound; never knew health before, as I was always an invalid. I went downstairs and met mother*. (*—Mrs. Baker had died in November of 1849.)

The clergyman returned. He was so startled he did not know whether to conclude it was I in the body or out! He said, "What does this mean?" I said, "I do not know." The doctor was sent for, who had given me up and was not coming again. He said, "How was this done?" I said, "I cannot tell you in any wise whatever, except it seemed to me all a thing or state of my mental consciousness. It didn't seem to belong to the body, or material condition. When I awakened to this sense of change I was there, that is all I know."

It came to me in a bit of Scripture, (Matt. xi:2). . . and I immediately rose from my bed; and before that my feet were dead. . . . He said, "It is impossible that that could have been. It must have been the medicine." I said, "Your medicine is every bit in the drawer, go and look." There it was in my drawer, and I had not taken one bit of it. When I had showed him that, he said, "This is impossible, " and immediately I felt I was back again, and I staggered. He caught me and set me in a chair, saying, "There, I will go out. If you have done that much, you can again." My limbs crippled under me just like that. This is veritable. There are people living in Swampscott now who can tell. When I found myself back again I felt more discouraged than ever. As I sat there it all seemed to come to me again with such a light and such a presence, and I felt, "It is all the mind. These are spiritual stages of consciousness," and rose right up again.

Then I felt I never could be conquered again, and as they came rushing in I said, "Do not talk with me much at present; wait a little, and I will tell you all I can," and they would keep me up till twelve o'clock talking, and I stood it and at that time

I had a big task of material duties —my husband happened to be gone [Dr. Patterson]—and I seemed in such a bother I did not know what to do, until at last I got away a little while, and then I began to steady down, and say, "I *can* tell this, and the world can know what it means," and from that time I have demonstrated it.   31

This experience was the catalyst for Mrs. Eddy's discovery of the science of Mind healing. She recounts in *Retrospection and Introspection* the subsequents steps to this experience and prior to the publishing of the first edition of her textbook, *Science and Health with Key to the Scriptures.*   See Appendix for pages 24-39 of *Retrospection and Introspection.*

Following Mrs. Eddy's fall and three days later her subsequent rise from her deathbed, a most fascinating report appeared in *The Lynn Reporter*, of February 7, 1866.

> "THE DEAD ALIVE.—The people of Norwich, Conn., are much exercised about an occurrence which took place in that city a few nights since. On Sunday night the resurrectionists dug up the body of a young lady who had been buried that afternoon, and succeeded beyond their anticipations. She had been buried while in a cataleptic fit, and upon being exposed to the night air animation was restored. The resurrectionists fled and she walked home. Her parents refused to admit her, believing her to be a ghost. She then went to the house of a young man to whom she was engaged. He took her in, and on Monday morning they were married. This reads like romance, but is said to be the literal truth."   32

Another report was related by Elizabeth Earl Jones, one of the early workers in the cause of C. S.

> . . . I spent most of the winter of 1909-10, in Boston, as I was taking time off for quiet study and work after a very strenuous year in the State Publication Committee work (I was Committee for North Carolina) — I felt the need and great desire for a time for quiet and uninterrupted study. Knowing that I had a free time (so to speak) one of the members of our C. S. Board of Directors in Boston, asked me if I would look over a bundle of

old newspapers from Lynn, Mass. for the month of February 1866, — and see if there were any items of interest that could be attributed to this greatest event in history, excepting the life of Jesus. I found one item of great interest, under date of February 12th, 1866, (I think it was.) It was the account of a "miracle" that had happened in Lynn on, or close to that date. A girl 12 years of age who had been an invalid all her life, had died, and was lying in her coffin with the lid open, so that the family and friends could see her before the coffin was finally closed, and taken to the burying ground. She had been dead 2 or 3 days, when she suddenly opened her eyes, sat up, and was perfectly well. Of course, there was no funeral. The doctor could not account for it, — so they all said it was the work of God and a miracle.   33

Jesus, when he had cried again with a loud voice, yielded up the ghost. And, behold, the veil of the temple was rent in twain from the top to the bottom; and the earth did quake, and the rocks rent; And the graves were opened; and many bodies of the saints which slept arose, And came out of the graves after his resurrection, and went into the holy city, and appeared unto many. Matt. 27:50-53

Mrs. Eddy states in the third edition of *Science and Health*, 'There were results connected with our recovery at the time we have named that rendered it still more remarkable, which we have not given to the public.' One of these 'results' was mentioned in a letter to a student of hers, Caroline W. Frame, in later years.

'The first experience of mine in entering upon the discovery of C. S. was the entire stoppage of the periods that are believed to be concurrent with the moon. Hence that saying of the Revelator of the spiritual idea, 'The moon was under her feet.' (see Rev. 12:1) Often it seems to be discouraging to hear my female students talk of this period as if it was part of their life, normal and scientific.   34

And a certain woman, which had an issue of blood twelve years, And had suffered many things of many physicians, and had spent all that she had, and was nothing bettered, but rather grew worse, When she had heard of Jesus, came in the press behind, and touched his garment. For she said, If I may touch but his clothes, I shall be whole. And straightway the fountain of her blood was dried up; and she felt in her body that she was healed of that plague. And Jesus, immediately knowing in himself that virtue had gone out of him, turned him about in the press, and said, Who touched my clothes? And his disciples said unto him, Thou seest the multitude thronging thee, and sayest thou, Who touched me? And he looked round about to see her that had done this thing. But the woman fearing and trembling, knowing what was done in her, came and fell down before him, and told him all the truth. And he said unto her, Daughter, thy faith hath made thee whole; go in peace, and be whole of thy plague. Mark 5:25-35

There were two fascinating occurrences that took place in February, 1866 as well, events of nature that were most unusual, even prophetic in their significance.

On February 26 a memorable example of the Aurora Borealis took place. It's phenomenal description is recounted in the *Christian Science Journal.* (Vol. IX, No. 37, p. 675) See Appendix for a reproduction of this account.

Doris Grekel, in the second volume of her magnificent biographical work on Mrs. Eddy provides illumination on the significance of these events.

"The Arctic Aurora of February 26 is not the only sign that appeared in the heavens in 1866 to herald the end of the world,—i.e., the end of the world of matter and the beginning of the understanding that 'man is not material, he is spiritual.' The fact that the moon (matter) was under the feet of the Woman of the Apocalypse was signified in a manner that had never before occurred in the history of the world. [The Granite Monthly recorded,] 'February, 1866, had no full moon. This remarkable feat of nature had never happened before [when a full moon *had been forecast*].'" 35

and they were healed every one. . . Acts 5:16

ENLIGHTENMENT AND PROGRESS
1866-1891

Dorr Phillips, son of Thomas and Hannah Phillips, was the first healing through Mrs. Patterson's demonstration of Mind Science. The lad had a bone felon on the end of one of his fingers that kept him awake at night and away from school during the day. Mrs. Patterson had not been to the Phillips' house for several days, and when she did so and found the boy in agony walking the floor, she gently and sympathetically questioned him. "Dorr, will you let me heal that felon?" "Yes, indeed, Mrs. Patterson, if you can do it," replied the lad. "Will you promise not to do anything for it or let any one else, if I undertake to cure it?" "Yes, I promise, and I will keep my word," said Dorr. He had heard his father and their friend discuss divine healing many times, and had a boy's healthy curiosity to see what would happen if all this talk was actually tried on a wicked, tormenting, festering felon that was making him fairly roar with rage one minute and cry like a girl the next. That night the boy stopped at his sister Susie's house. "How is your finger?" she asked solicitously. "Nothing the matter with my finger; it hasn't hurt all day. Mrs. Patterson is treating it." "What is she doing to it? Let me look at it." "No, you'll spoil the cure. I promised not to look at it or think about it, nor let any one else touch it or talk about it. And I won't." The brother and sister looked at each other with half smiles. They were struggling with skepticism. "Honest, Dorr, doesn't it hurt?" "No." "Tell me what she did." "I don't know what she did, don't know anything about this business, but I'm going to play fair and keep my word." The boy actually forgot the felon and when his attention was called to the finger it was found to be well. This strange result made an impression on the family. No one quite knew what to say, and they were scarcely ready to accept the healing of a sore finger as a

23

miracle. "But it is not a miracle," said Mary Baker. "Nor would it be if it had been a broken wrist or a withered arm. It is natural, divinely natural. All life rightly understood is so." 36

Mrs. Eddy (Patterson) with a child-1861

"Mother told me how she happened to have that little baby in her arms. She went into a photographer's studio to ask about the price of photographs, and when she entered his reception room, she found a lady there holding a baby which she was trying to pacify. The child was screaming, which made it impossible for him to be photographed, and our Leader noticed that every little while the baby looked at her, and then screamed again, so she said to his mother, 'Won't you let me hold your baby for a little while? Perhaps I can quiet him.' And the baby put his arms up to meet hers. As soon as she took him, he put his thumb in his mouth as you will see, and there is a picture of contentment. Then the
24

photographer, unknown to Mrs. Eddy, took a photograph of her and the child, and afterwards sent her a copy, asking her to accept it and said that it was such a beautiful picture, he could not help taking it." Mrs. Eddy's natural motherlove was always perceived by the little children.   37

Suffer the little children to come unto me, and forbid them not: for of such is the kingdom of God. Mark 10:14

One summer day in 1866, Mrs. Patterson was on the beach in Lynn when she saw a sad sight that needed healing. Mrs. James Norton of Lynn had taken her seven-year-old son George to Lynn Beach and left him there while she hitched the horse and went for water. The child had club feet and had never walked. When the mother returned, she was stunned to see her boy walking hand in hand with a strange woman. Mrs. Norton and the stranger, Mrs. Patterson, looked into each other's eyes; then both wept and joined in thanks to God. The child was completely and permanently healed and lived a happy, useful life. (see also the account by Clifford Smith in, *Christian Science: Its Legal Status*, p.83.) 38

Most of Mrs. Eddy's practice for particular persons occurred during the twenty years, 1867-1886, that followed her discovery of C. S.. . . . She never made practice for particular persons her chief occupation. Always she devoted her thought chiefly to her own obligations as Discoverer, Founder, and Leader. From 1883, she gave notice in The Christian *Science Journal* that she would not take patients. Yet, she was the instrument for many healings after that.

In the historical files of The Mother Church there is a letter to Mrs. Eddy dated December 9, 1904, from a lady who described herself as "one of the lepers who has come at last to give thanks for his healing." Presumably, she alluded to the ten lepers whom the Master healed, as related in Luke 17:11-19, of whom one returned to give thanks. She continued: "You healed me many years ago of a loathsome disease with just a word. The trouble has never returned. Words fail to express my gratitude for that healing." She also inclosed a check, which Mrs. Eddy returned with an appreciative letter. 39

At the Oliver home lived a rich young man from Boston who had come to Lynn to learn the shoe business. He was intense and active, eager to show his father his business sagacity. But severe application to business and excitement over his new responsibilities threw him into a fever. He was brought home from the factory and put to bed, where he promptly lapsed into delirium. The Olivers saw that he was very ill, and sent for his parents. Before they arrived Mrs. Patterson came to the house and found Susan Oliver in distress over the serious situation.

"If he should die before they come, what would I do?" she asked excitedly. "Perhaps I should call our physician. But they might not like it. He is their only child. Think of his prospects, his father's fortune—and for him to be stricken in this way!"

"He is not going to die, Susie," said Mary Baker. "Let me go in and see him."

"You may go in, if you think it best; but he won't recognize you," said Mrs. Oliver.

Mary Baker went into the sick chamber and sat down at the side of the bed. The young man was tossing from side to side, throwing his arms about wildly and moaning. She took his hand, held it firmly, and spoke clearly to him, calling him by a familiar name.

"Bobbie," she said, "look at me. You know me, don't you?"

The young man ceased his monotonous moaning, his tossing on the pillows, and his [spasmodic fits]. He lay quiet and gazed steadfastly at the newcomer.

"Of course you know me, Bobbie," she persisted gently. "Tell me my name."

"Why, yes," he said with perfect sanity, "it's Mrs. Patterson." In a few minutes he said, "I believe I will go to sleep."

He did go to sleep and waked rational, and did not again have delirium.   40

Several instances of Mrs. Eddy's healing ability appeared in many editions of her book *Science and Health*:

> I take pleasure in giving to the public one instance, out of the many, of Mrs. Glover-Eddy's skill in metaphysical healing. At the birth of my

youngest child, now eight years old, I thought my approaching confinement would be premature by several weeks, and sent her a message to that effect. Without seeing me, she returned answer that the proper time had come, and that she would be with me immediately. [Just imagine—she knew when the baby was to be born before the mother knew!] Slight labor-pains had commenced before she arrived. She stopped them at once, and requested me to call an accoucheur, but to keep him below stairs until after the birth. When the doctor arrived, and while he remained in a lower room, Mrs. Eddy came to my bedside. I asked her how I should lie. She answered, "It makes no difference how you lie," and added, "Now let the child be born." Immediately the birth took place, and without a pain. The doctor was then called into the room to receive the child, and he saw that I had no pain whatever. My sister, Dorcas B. Rawson, of Lynn, was present when my babe was born, and will testify to the facts as I have stated them. I confess my own astonishment. I did not expect so much, even from Mrs. Eddy, especially as I had suffered before very severely in childbirth. The physician covered me with extra bedclothes, charged me to be very careful about taking cold and to keep quiet, and then went away. I think he was alarmed at my having no labor-pains, but before he went out I had an ague coming on. When the door closed behind him, Mrs. Eddy threw off the extra coverings and said, "It is nothing but the fear produced by the doctor that causes these chills." They left me at once. She told me to sit up when I chose, and to eat whatever I wanted. My babe was born about two o'clock in the morning, and on the following evening I sat up several hours. I ate whatever the family did. I had a boiled dinner of meat and vegetables the second day. I made no difference in my diet, except to drink gruel between meals, and never experienced the least inconvenience from this course. I dressed myself the second day, and the third day felt unwilling to lie down. In one week I was about the house and was well, running up and down stairs and attending to domestic duties. For several years I had been troubled with *prolapsus uteri*, which disappeared entirely after Mrs. Eddy's wonderful demonstration of Christian Science at the birth of my babe. 41

Lynn, Mass., 1874   Miranda R. Rice

Mrs. Patterson's first student was Hiram Crafts, a shoe maker in the town of Lynn. While Mrs. Patterson was staying with the Crafts in nearby Stoughton (Mass.) she agreed to teach him her system of mental healing in exchange for room and board. During her stay with the Crafts, she met the Wentworths, and on one of their visits they brought their daughter, Celia. Celia had been suffering from consumption, and Mrs. Patterson's tender ministrations healed the girl, creating quite an impression on the mother. 42

In *Retrospection and Introspection*, Mrs. Eddy recalls yet another healing she performed when she was asked to speak at the Lyceum Club, at Westerly, Rhode Island.

> On my arrival my hostess told me that her next-door neighbor was dying. I asked permission to see her. It was granted, and with my hostess I went to the invalid's house.
>
> The physicians had given up the case and retired. I had stood by her side about fifteen minutes when the sick woman rose from her bed, dressed herself, and was well. Afterwards they showed me the clothes already prepared for her burial; and told me that her physicians had said the diseased condition was caused by an injury received from a surgical operation at the birth of her last babe, and that it was impossible for her to be delivered of another child. It is sufficient to add her babe was safely born, and weighed twelve pounds. The mother afterwards wrote to me, "I never before suffered so little in childbirth."
>
> This scientific demonstration so stirred the doctors and clergy that they had my notices for a second lecture pulled down, and refused me a hearing in their halls and churches. This circumstance is cited simply to show the opposition which Christian Science encountered a quarter-century ago, as contrasted with its present welcome into the sickroom.
>
> Many were the desperate cases I instantly healed, "without money and without price," and in most instances without even an acknowledgment of the benefit.   43

"Mrs. Eddy's healing of a woman of dumbness in Lynn, about the year 1867, was related to me many years later by her son. She had been treated by many physicians without relief, when a friend proposed that she see Mrs. Eddy. People seldom turned to Christian Science in those days until all other hope was exhausted, for Mrs. Eddy was considered a strange woman. So desperate was his mother's condition, however, that she asked for treatment from one of Mrs. Eddy's students. The student found difficulty in handling the case. Each day when the woman, who was then a girl, returned from a visit to the practitioner, the first words of her mother were, 'Fannie, can you speak?' Fannie would sadly shake her head in the negative. At last it was decided to call on Mrs. Eddy for help."

"On the day of her return from her visit to Mrs. Eddy, the

daughter was again greeted with the old question, 'Fannie, can you speak?' Instantly the answer came back, 'Yes, I can,' and she continued, 'When Mrs. Eddy saw after my treatment that I still could not speak, she suddenly said with authority, 'In the name of God, speak!' Instantly I spoke my first word, saying 'Oh!' After that experience the patient found herself fully healed." 44

The religious thought of the day was filled with such resistance to her healing works that she was maligned, burned in effigy and attempts at incarceration were made. Claims of witchcraft or that her "works by her faith," were of the devil, were not infrequent from the clergy of the day. At one time it is reported that when she was visiting Worcester, Mass., the superintendent of a mental institution called on Mrs. Eddy with the intent of locking her up for her radical statements and stand for what Jesus taught and practiced. However, once he met Mrs. Eddy and talked with her, he was apologetic, saying that he had learned a lot that would assist him in the treatment of his patients. 45

> *. . . when the Pharisees heard it, they said, This fellow doth not cast out devils, but by Beelzebub the prince of the devils. And Jesus knew their thoughts, and said unto them, Every kingdom divided against itself is brought to desolation; and every city or house divided against itself shall not stand: And if Satan cast out Satan, he is divided against himself; how shall then his kingdom stand? And if I by Beelzebub cast out devils, by whom do your children cast them out? therefore they shall be your judges. But if I cast out devils by the Spirit of God, then the kingdom of God is come unto you.* Matt. 12:24-28

Just six or seven months later Mrs. Patterson was traveling to Tilton, New Hampshire, where she had been when a teen. She was visiting her brother, George Baker and her sisters, Abigail Tilton and Martha Pilsbury. Abigail had an unreasoned hatred of Christian Science, but when all material avenues failed she implored her sister to come and aid her daughter. George's wife related that when Mary arrived there was a definite feeling of divine presence in the house. Within fifteen minutes Mrs. Patterson healed her niece, Ellen Pilsbury, who was critically ill with enteritis in its severest form following typhoid fever, and who had been given up by three physicians. Previously, she had been so ill that for two weeks one could barely step lightly enough while in her room so as not to jar the room and cause her great pain. Ellen was soon up and walking back and forth across the room at her aunt's bidding, and even stamped her foot on the floor to show that no vestige of the previous discomfort remained. The next day she was dressed and joined the family for dinner; and on the fourth day made a hundred mile journey in the cars. Abigail however, was later heard to say her sister's loving ministrations "were the work of the devil." Although, she was the recipient of Mrs. Patterson's loving care, Ellen later turned on her, repudiating her healing and expressing an inordinate amount of hostility towards her. She was responsible for convincing her mother not to call for Mrs. Eddy, even when her mother was at death's door.   46

About 1867, Mrs. Eddy was working with a student in the healing work in Lynn. One authentic witness of her healing work was a Mrs. Mosher. She describes the experience of a life-long friend in an excerpt from the May 11, 1914 issue of *The Christian Science Monitor*:

There are authentic witnesses, however, of the healing work of Mrs. Eddy in those days (the 1860's to 1870's). One of them was a Mrs. Mosher, a life-long friend of one of the Christian Scientist's now at work in Lynn. When the latter was healed in Christian Science, Mrs. Mosher, returning from the West, sought out her friend expressly to tell her this story, and said she could make an affidavit that this is what she saw. She had not told it to her friend sooner because she was ashamed of having tried the new kind of healing.

Several years before this she went to the office where Mrs. Eddy and a student were at work, and was treated by the student. She saw there a girl afflicted with dumbness whom the student had not been able to heal. At last he asked Mrs. Eddy to help.

Mrs. Mosher was present when Mrs. Eddy walked up to the dumb girl and said: "God did not send this upon you. You can speak. In the name of Jesus Christ of Nazareth, I command you to speak!" The girl shrank back, and cried out, "I can't and I won't" and fled out of the room. But she was able to speak ever after.

The Scientist who tells this had already heard a different

version of the case from others, (see p.54 of *Twelve Years with Mary Baker Eddy* by Irving C. Tomlinson) who said that Mrs. Eddy threatened the girl in some way. Possibly such was the impression made on the girl, under stress of the mighty, redeeming word of spiritual authority. Mrs. Mosher, not knowing that her friend had heard the story, volunteered this account of the occurrence. She herself had received little benefit from treatment by this student, [believed to be either Richard Kennedy or Daniel Spofford, both of which viciously turned against Mrs. Eddy later on] .... This student was one of those who afterwards withdrew from the work. He persisted in using methods which Mrs. Eddy did not approve, and could not perceive either her power of spiritual understanding nor her right to correct their mistaken notions. The world was slow to accept her restatement of the radical position of Jesus, and the purely spiritual means of healing, looking to God for help, not to matter not to the human intelligence, when he said: "These signs shall follow them that believe." 47

One time Mrs. Patterson was leaving her house to call on a patient when a woman leading her blind daughter met her on the steps of her home. They wanted Mrs. Patterson to go back into the house with them to treat the girl. Mrs. Patterson told them that God was just as well able to heal such a case as He had ever been, and spoke to them about God. The girl's eyeballs were white, but while Mrs. Patterson was speaking to them she saw the eyes begin to clear up a little on the right side. She watched and saw the free part gradually enlarge until the eyes were completely cleared and the girl could see perfectly. 48

> ... *blind Bartimaeus, the son of Timaeus, sat by the highway side begging. And when he heard that it was Jesus of Nazareth, he began to cry out, and say, Jesus, thou Son of David, have mercy on me. And many charged him that he should hold his peace: but he cried the more a great deal, Thou Son of David, have mercy on me. And Jesus stood still, and commanded him to be called. And they call the blind man, saying unto him, Be of good comfort, rise; he calleth thee. And he, casting away his garment, rose, and came to Jesus. And Jesus answered and said unto him, What wilt thou that I should do unto thee? The blind man said unto him, Lord, that I might receive my sight. And Jesus said unto him, Go thy way; thy faith hath made thee whole. And immediately he received his sight, and followed Jesus in the way.* Mark 10:46-52

In the first edition of *Science and Health with Key to the Scriptures* by Mrs. Eddy, there appear several healings performed by this loving one. One such is the healing of James Ingham, of East Stoughton, Mass., in 1867.

> I was suffering from pulmonary difficulties, pains in the chest, a hard and unremitting cough, hectic fever, and all those fearful symptoms that made my case alarming. When I first saw Mrs. Glover, I was reduced to such a state of debility as to be unable to walk any distance, or to sit up but a portion of the day; to walk up stairs gave me great suffering for breath. I had no appetite, and seemed surely going down the victim of consumption. I had not received her attention but a short time, when my bad symptoms disappeared, and I regained health. During this time, I rode out in storms to visit her, and found the damp weather had no effect on me. From my personal experience I am led to believe the science by which she not only heals the sick, but explains the way to keep well, is deserving the earnest attention of the community; her cures are not the result of medicine, mediumship, or mesmerism, but the application of a Principle that she understands. 49

Mrs. Eddy once went into a house where she saw a woman weeping in the hallway. The woman said, "My daughter is dying of consumption [tuberculosis]. The doctor has just left and he told me he could not do any more for her." Mrs. Eddy asked if she might go up and heal the daughter. The mother consented, and Mrs. Eddy went upstairs to the bedroom. The father, who was very antagonistic to Mrs. Eddy, was standing by the bed; but Mrs. Eddy felt that, having the mother's permission to help the girl, it was right for her to go ahead, so she said to the sick girl, "Get up and come for a walk." The girl got up and Mrs. Eddy helped her dress and they went off for a walk together. The father followed them, secretly as he thought, dodging behind trees and watching around corners, expecting every moment to see his daughter drop dead. Mrs. Eddy knew that he was following, but that did not interfere with her healing work, for when they returned from the walk the daughter was completely healed. 50

> *And they brought young children to him, that he should touch*
> *them: and his disciples rebuked those that brought them. But when*

In 1868, at Lynn, Mrs. Eddy healed by one treatment a lunatic who had escaped from an asylum. As he wandered insanely, he entered the house where she had a room. His clothes were in tatters; his appearance was frightful. The mother and daughter who occupied most of the house were badly frightened. The daughter fled; the mother called for Mrs. Eddy to come. When she responded, the man raised a chair as if to strike her, but she felt a great compassion for him, and faced him without fear. Immediately he dropped the chair, approached her and, pointing upward, exclaimed: "Are you from there?" Then he fell on his knees at her feet, his head pressed hard into his hands and began to sob. Reaching out her hand as if she were giving him a benediction, she touched his head. When he asked what she was doing, she told him she was anointing his head with oil (alluding to Psalms 23:5), and told him to go in peace. Thereupon he left the house, evidently restored to sanity. Long afterward (in 1884), this man called on Mrs. Eddy at her home in Boston to express his gratitude. He told her that he had returned to the asylum, had been discharged as cured, and had traced his healing to her. He told her, further, that he had gone to live in the West, had married, had become the father of children, and had never been insane after she anointed him as if with oil. She meant by her answer to his question, as she once said when relating this case, the anointing of Truth. 51

The Winslows were friends of Mrs. Patterson's and Abbie Winslow had been confined to her invalid chair for sixteen years. It was Mrs. Patterson's desire to heal her.

"If you make Abbie walk," said Charles Winslow, "I will not only believe your theory, but I will reward you liberally. I think I would give a thousand dollars (equivalent to about $15,000 today) to see her able to walk."

"The demonstration of the principle is enough reward," said

Mrs. Patterson. "I know she can walk. You go to business and leave us alone together."

"But I want to see you perform your cure, Mary," said Charles Winslow, half mirthfully. "Indeed, I won't interfere."

"You want to see me perform a cure," cried Mary Baker, with a flash of her clear eyes. "But I am not going to do anything. Why don't you understand that God will do the work if Mrs. Winslow will let Him? Leave off making light of what is a serious matter. Your wife will walk."

And Mrs. Winslow did walk, walked along the ocean beach with Mary and around her own garden in the beautiful autumn of that year. She who had not taken a step for sixteen years arose and walked, not once but many times. Though a wonderful thing had been accomplished, the woman's pride kept her from acknowledging a cure. The method seemed so ridiculously inadequate. To accept it was like convicting her of never having been ill. So she returned to her former beliefs. 52

An interesting contrast to this is the healing of Naaman, the Syrian, as recounted in the Preface of this book. Naaman humbled himself, was meek in his acceptance of God's blessing, and *kept* his healing.

[Mrs. Webster] did witness many healings as did the others in her house, until Mrs. Glover was the talk of the small town. One such healing was that of Mrs. Mary M. Gale of Manchester who was a friend of the Websters. Mrs. Gale was critically ill with pneumonia on May 30 when she sent Mrs. Glover a telegram asking her to come to her. Mary went immediately to Manchester and healed Mrs. Gale. While there she saw a copy of *A Dictionary of the Bible* by William Smith which had recently been published and which interested her very much. 53

One of Mrs. Eddy's early healings in Lynn was of a friend, Mrs. Abigail Winslow. She wrote of this experience:

> When I went there Mrs. Winslow was very lame and sick, had not walked upstairs naturally for years and given up trying to go out at all. I stopped two days and when I came away she

walked to the Depot with me almost a mile. They were one and all urgent for me to stay, but I am not of their opinion. I don't want society.   54

In the summer of 1868, an acquaintance of Mrs. Patterson's who was a friend of the poet, John Greenleaf Whittier took her to visit the well known author. In Mrs. Patterson's words, "About 1868, the author of *Science and Health* healed Mr. Whittier with one visit, at his home in Amesbury, of incipient pulmonary consumption." This healing was brought to life in one of Whittiers' poems—

The Healer

He stood of old, the holy Christ,
    Amid the suffering throng,
With whom his lightest touch sufficed
    To make the weakest strong.
That healing gift God gives to them
    Who use it in His name;
The power that filled the garment's hem
    Is evermore the same.

So shalt thou be with power endued
    Like him who went about
The Syrian hillsides doing good
    And casting demons out.
The Great Physician liveth yet
    Thy friend and guide to be;
The Healer by Gennesaret
    Shall walk the rounds with thee.   55

About this time (late 1868) Mrs. Eddy stopped using the name of Mrs. Patterson and was known as Mrs. Mary Baker Glover, using the name of her first husband. (She began using the name of Eddy upon her marriage to Asa Gilbert Eddy, January 1, 1877.)

"About the year 1869, I was wired to attend the patient of a distinguished M.D., the late Dr. Davis of Manchester, N. H. The patient was pronounced dying of pneumonia, and was breathing at intervals in agony. Her physician, who stood by her bedside, declared that she could not live. On seeing her immediately restored by me without material aid, he asked earnestly if I had a work describing my system of healing. When answered in the negative, he urged me immediately to write a book which should explain to the world my curative system of metaphysics." 56

> ... *when Jesus was come into Peter's house, he saw his wife's mother laid, and sick of a fever. And he touched her hand, and the fever left her: and she arose, and ministered unto them.*   Matt. 8:14,15

"The article of Professor T——, [published in Zion's Herald], December third, came not to my notice until January ninth. In it the Professor offered me, as President of the Metaphysical College in Boston, or one of my students, the liberal sum of one thousand dollars if either would reset certain dislocations without the use of hands, and two thousand dollars if either would give sight to one born blind.

"Will the gentleman accept my thanks due to his generosity; for, if I should accept his bid on Christianity, he would lose his money.

"Why?

"Because I performed more difficult tasks fifteen years ago. At present, I am in another department of Christian work, 'where there shall no signs be given them,' for they shall be instructed in the Principle of Christian Science that furnishes its own proof.

"But, to reward his liberality, I offer him three thousand dollars if he will heal one single case of opium-eating where the patient is very low and taking morphine powder in its most concentrated form, at the rate of one ounce in two weeks,—having taken it twenty years; and he is to cure that habit in three days, leaving the patient well. I cured precisely such a case in 1869.

"Also, Mr. C. M. H——, of Boston, formerly partner of George T. Brown, pharmacist, No. 5 Beacon St., will tell you that he was my student in December, 1884; and that before leaving the class he took a patient thoroughly addicted to the use of opium—if she went without it twenty-four hours she would have delirium—and in forty-eight hours cured her perfectly of this habit, with no bad results, but with decided improvement in health." 57

> *And these signs shall follow them that believe; In my name shall they cast out devils; they shall speak with new tongues; They shall take up serpents; and if they drink any deadly thing, it shall not hurt them; they shall lay hands on the sick, and they shall recover.*   Mark 16:17,18

"... *McClure's* April [1907] issue came out with pages of 'history' of Mrs. Eddy's early years of teaching Christian Science as told by Mary Crafts and others of that ilk. One of the many falsehoods in this issue of *McClure's* was Mary Crafts' assertion that Mrs. Eddy did not heal. On March 12 the Leader said to her household students:

"I was just thinking how I am abused (Glover-case lawsuit and newspaper articles) and I could feel the tears starting to come, when suddenly I thought of two cases of healing I had, and then joy took the place of sorrow. One of them was one of the worst cripples I ever saw. I was walking along the street in Lynn—I walked because I hadn't a cent to ride—and saw this cripple, with one knee drawn up to his chin; his chin resting on his knee. The other limb was drawn up the other way, up his back. I came up to him and read a piece of paper pinned on his shoulder: 'help this poor cripple.' I had no money to give him so I whispered in his ear, 'God loves you.' And he got up perfectly straight and well. He ran into the house of Mrs. Lucy Allen, who saw the healing from her window, and asked, 'Who is that woman?' pointing to Mrs. Glover [afterward Mrs. Eddy]. Mrs. Allen replied, 'It is Mrs. Glover.' 'No it isn't, it's an angel,' he said, Then he told what had been done for him.

When she finished she said: 'The papers are writing up my history; the history of my ancestry; writing lies. My history is a holy one.' ... " 58

> ... *a certain man lame from his mother's womb was carried, whom they laid daily at the gate of the temple which is called Beautiful, to ask alms of them that entered into the temple; Who seeing Peter and John about to go into the temple asked an alms. And Peter, fastening his eyes upon him with John, said, Look on us. And he gave heed unto them, expecting to receive something of them. Then Peter said, Silver and gold have I none; but such as I have give I thee: In the name of Jesus Christ of Nazareth rise up and walk. And he took him by the right hand, and lifted him up: and immediately his feet and ancle bones received strength. And he leaping up stood, and walked, and entered with them into the temple, walking, and leaping, and praising God. And all the people saw him walking and praising God. ....*Acts 3:2-9

There is a similar account that has appeared in the records of healings preserved by Arthur Fosbury with sufficient details as to lead one to believe it might be a separate account.

Mrs. Eddy told some of her students that the discovery and founding of C. S. was along these lines: "She said she had prayed, struggled and suffered up the steep pathway that led to her discovery of Christian Science; but when she reached the summit of the high mountain all was glorious, beautiful, heavenly, joyous spiritual reality. Her healing was instantaneous, and she healed others spontaneously. But, she said, she had to come down and demonstrate in Science every step back to the mountain top. She said: 'Jesus never had to come down because of his virgin birth.'"[12] On another occasion Mrs. Eddy said to a student, regarding the first healing work she did after her discovery of C. S.:

> I saw the love of God encircling the universe and man, filling all space, and that divine Love so permeated my own consciousness with Christlike compassion that I loved everything I saw. This realization of divine Love called into expression 'the beauty of holiness, the perfection of being,' which healed and regenerated and saved all who turned to me for help. [13]

At first after Mrs. Eddy discovered C. S., most of the people who had any knowledge of it regarded it more as a cure without medicine than a religion. The healings that she wrought, however, proved its moral and spiritual value. Many of the persons whom she healed manifested not only a change in bodily health but also a change in conduct, an improved condition of thought.

An instance was furnished by a farmer named John Scott in 1870. He had a bad case of enteritis. He had no bowel movement for two weeks, he suffered terribly, and a medical consultation gave him no promise of recovery. Mrs. Eddy healed him in less than an hour. His bowels began to act normally, he said he felt perfectly well, and he resumed work the next day. Later, his wife reported to Mrs. Eddy that Mr. Scott had also become a different man. After giving details, such as his changed attitude toward their children, she said, "Oh, how I thank you for restoring my husband to health, but more than all else I am grateful for what you have done for him morally and spiritually." [59]

> *Jesus answered them, Verily, verily, I say unto you, Whosoever committeth sin is the servant of sin. And the servant abideth not in*

Mrs. Linscott (one of Mrs. Eddy's students) relates, "From early girlhood I had an infirmity in the limbs that prevented me walking up stairs easily. One day at the College, I was going up to my room on the third floor, groaning and complaining, and as I reached the landing on the second floor said aloud, 'I know I'll never get up to the next floor.' Just as I said it, the door opened, and Mrs. Glover came out and heard me. She gave a sweep of her hand, and commanded, '*Run up those stairs!* run up those stairs!' I started running, and have been running up stairs ever since." 60

Mrs. Eddy told her household of a patient who had passed on with consumption, whom she had raised from the dead. She said such a flood of realization of the continuity of Life poured into her consciousness that she was able to say with full confidence, "Arise," and the young woman did arise, healed.   61

> *And he took the damsel by the hand, and said unto her, Talitha cumi; which is, being interpreted, Damsel, I say unto thee, arise. And straightway the damsel arose, and walked; for she was of the age of twelve years. And they were astonished with a great astonishment.*
> Mark 5:41,42

Mrs. Eddy was called to treat a young girl in Lynn, who the doctors said, had only a little piece of lung left, and was dying. There were Spiritualists around and Mrs. Eddy could not reach her thought at first, so she said to her: "Get up out of that bed," and pulled the pillow from under the girl's head, Then she called to those in the other room to bring her clothes. The girl got up and she was well; she never even coughed again. But the mother was offended at Mrs. Eddy and would not speak to her afterwards because she said Mrs. Eddy had spoken disrespectfully to her dying daughter. 62

Another of Mrs. Eddy's students told me that one time a mother brought her dead baby to Mrs. Eddy and placed it on her lap. Our Leader asked her to come back in an hour, and began to treat the child. She realized that "infinite Love was infinite Life, and infinite Life was infinite Love and was everpresent," and kept on realizing this more clearly.

After a while she felt something moving on her lap (she had forgotten the baby). She looked down, and saw the child smiling at her, and kicking its feet.   63

> . . . *when the child was grown, it fell on a day, that he went out to his father to the reapers. And he said unto his father, My head, my head. And he said to a lad, Carry him to his mother. And when he had taken him, and brought him to his mother, he sat on her knees till noon, and then died. And she went up, and laid him on the bed of the man of God, and shut the door upon him, and went out. . . . And when Elisha was come into the house, behold, the child was dead, and laid upon his bed. He went in therefore, and shut the door upon them twain, and prayed unto the Lord. And he went up, and lay upon the child, and put his mouth upon his mouth, and his eyes upon his eyes, and his hands upon his hands: and he stretched himself upon the child; and the flesh of the child waxed warm. Then he returned, and walked in the house to and fro; and went up, and stretched himself upon him: and the child sneezed seven times, and the child opened his eyes. And he called Gehazi, and said, Call this Shunammite, So he called her. And when she was come in unto him, he said, Take up thy son. Then she went in, and fell at his feet, and bowed herself to the ground, and took up her son, and went out.* II Kings 4:18-21, 32-37

Mrs. Eddy was called to treat a child; and when she arrived and saw the child and its mother, she paid no attention to the [disease] (a serious disfigurement) which the child was showing, but turned to the mother and said: "You fell before this child was born." The mother answered: "No, Mrs. Eddy, I never fell when I was carrying the child." But Mrs. Eddy declared: "There is no effect from prenatal shock or fear," and the child was immediately healed of a condition very remote seemingly from any effect from a fall. The the mother said: "Yes, I do remember that a few days before this child was born, I fell down two steps, but I had forgotten."   64

> The relations of God and man, divine Principle and idea, are indestructible in Science; and Science knows no lapse from nor return to harmony, but holds the divine order or spiritual law, in which God and all that He creates are perfect and eternal, to

have remained unchanged in its eternal history.   *Science and Health*, 471:31

One of Mrs. Eddy's early recollections regarding the healing work was interesting: "We are all learning together, and I must tell you of some of the funny things I used to do when I first saw that I had this wonderful power. My family and the friends around me saw what was done and knew that if they sent for me they would be well, but I could not make them acknowledge it. I could not make them admit what had done the healing work.

One day I said, "Oh, I <u>must</u> make them acknowledge it; I must make them see that God does this." Sometimes as soon as they sent for me they would be healed, before I could get there, and then they would not <u>know</u> that it was God who had done it. So one day when I was called to see a child, I was so anxious to have the power of Truth acknowledged that I said to myself, "He <u>must</u> not get well until I get there." Of course that was not right, for I knew I must leave it all to God, but pride had come in and I lost my humility, and the patient was not healed.

Then I saw my rebuke, and when I reached home I threw myself on the floor, put my head in my hands, and prayed that I might not be for one moment touched with the thought that I was anything or did anything; I realized that this was God's work and I reflected Him. Then the child was healed. 65

> . . . *not my will, but thine, be done.*   Luke 22:42

Another version of this account is as follows from Doris Grekel's wonderful biography of Mrs. Eddy.

"Her healings were so immediate that often God was not acknowledged as the healer. She told them on one of those early occasions she had asked that the patient not be healed until she got there that God might get the glory and Christian Science be acknowledged; but when she got there she couldn't do a thing. 'I couldn't do a thing. I went home and put my face upon the carpet, and there I stayed, until I found Jacob's ladder, from the bottom to the top. Then I saw that God in His own time and way, would take unto Himself the glory, and it was not for me to say.' The patient

41

was healed; and there was not a dry eye in the hall when she finished her story." (see Gen. 32:24-30) 66

About the year 1870, before Mr. Charles Slade's door in Chelsea, Mass., there stopped an emaciated, pale-faced cripple, strapped to crutches. His elbows were stiff, and the lower limbs so contracted, his feet touched not the ground. Mrs. Eddy was there, and gave him some scrip.

A few weeks thereafter, sitting in her carriage, Mrs. Slade noticed a smart-looking man, having that same face, vending some wares on the grounds where General Butler held parade. They drove to where he stood. Their gaze met, and simultaneously they exclaimed: "Are you that man?" and "Where is that woman?" Then followed the explanation, he narrating that after leaving her house, he hobbled to the next door and was given permission to enter and lie down. In about an hour he revived, and found his arms and limbs loosed—he could stand erect and walk naturally. All pain, stiffness and contraction were gone, and he added: "I am now a well man, and am that man!"

Mrs. Slade then answered his question as to "that woman," and afterwards narrated to Mrs. Eddy these circumstances connected with his recovery, but not until she had inquired of her, if she thought that terrible-looking cripple, whom they both saw, was healed? To which Mrs. Eddy quickly answered, "I do believe that he was restored to health." Later, on being asked by her students as to how she healed him, Mrs. Eddy simply said: "When I looked on that man, my heart gushed with unspeakable pity and prayer." 67

> ...lift up the hands which hang down, and the feeble knees; And make straight paths for your feet, lest that which is lame be turned out of the way; but let it rather be healed. Heb. 12:12,13

The following is from a lady in Lynn: "My little son, one year and a half old, was a great sufferer from disease of the bowels, until he was reduced to almost a skeleton, and growing worse constantly; could take nothing but gruel, or some very simple nutriment. At that time the physicians had given him up, saying they could do no more for him, but you came in one morning, took him up from the cradle in your arms, kissed him, laid him down again and went out. In less than an hour he called for his playthings, got up and appeared quite well. All his symptoms changed at once. For months previously nothing but blood and mucous had passed his bowels, but that very day the evacuation was natural, and he has not suffered since from his complaint, and it is more than two years since he was cured. Immediately after you saw him, he ate all he wanted, and one thing was a quantity of cabbage just before going to bed, from which he never suffered in the least." 68

> Jesus loved little children because of their freedom from wrong and their receptiveness of right. While age is halting between two opinions or battling with false beliefs, youth makes easy and rapid strides towards Truth.   *Science and Health 236:28*

Mr. R. O. Badgely, of Cincinnati, Ohio, wrote: "My painful and swelled foot was restored at once on your receipt of my letter, and that very day I put on my boot and walked several miles." He had previously written me: "A stick of timber fell from a building on my foot, crushing the bones. Cannot you help me? I am sitting in great pain, with my foot in a bath." 69

> *Strengthen ye the weak hands, and confirm the feeble knees. Say to them that are of a fearful heart, Be strong, fear not: behold, your God will come with vengeance, even God with a recompence; he will come and save you. . . . Then shall the lame man leap as an hart. . . .* Isa. 35:3,4,6

A lady at Louisiana wrote:—"Your wonderful science is proved to me. I was a helpless sufferer six long years, confined to my bed, unable to sit up one hour in the twenty-four. All I know of my cure is this: the day you received my letter I felt a change pass over me, I sat up the whole afternoon, went to the table with my family at supper, and have been growing better every day since. I call myself well. Jenny R. Coffin" 70

The following is a case of heart disease described in a letter from a lady at New York.

"Please find inclosed a check for five hundred dollars (equivalent to about $7500 today) in reward for your services, that can never be repaid. The day you received my husband's letter I became conscious, for the first time for forty-eight hours; my servant brought my wrapper and I rose from bed and sat up. The attack of the heart had lasted two days, and no one thinks I could have survived but for the mysterious help I received from you. The enlargement of my left side is all gone, and the M. D.'s pronounce me entirely rid of heart disease. I have been afflicted with it from infancy, until it became organic enlargement of the heart and dropsy of the chest. I was only waiting, and almost longing to die; but you have healed me; and yet how wonderful to think of it, when we have never seen each other! We return to Europe next week. I feel perfectly well. L. M. Armstrong"   71

> *And the people, when they knew it, followed him: and he received them, and spake unto them of the kingdom of God, and healed them that had need of healing.*   Luke 9:11

A most interesting demonstration of the overcoming of material laws took place in the latter 1870's. Mrs. Eddy was always one to maintain the utmost in personal cleanliness. It was normal at this time for people to bathe once a week; Mrs. Eddy however, bathed daily. After her discovery of the Science of Mind healing she saw cleanliness to be mental not physical, and proved this in the following excerpt from the diary of her long-time secretary Calvin Frye, January 25, 1890.

> From daily baths she entirely stopped bathing and *never bathed for seven years*. One of her students who roomed with her, one night said upon retiring, "Oh, Mrs. Glover, how sweet you smell," to which she replied, "Why, I use no cologne." "No, I don't mean that," was the reply, "but how sweet and clean your person is." Mrs. Glover said, "Well, now I will tell you. I have not bathed for seven years." "Oh, don't tell any one that," was the reply, "for if you do, people will think you the dirtiest person that ever lived."   72

"I (Mrs. Eddy) was called to visit Mr. Clark in Lynn, confined to his bed six months with hip-disease, caused by a fall upon a spike when a boy. On entering the house I met his physician, who said he was dying. He had just probed the ulcer on the hip, and said the bone was carious for several inches. He even showed me the probe, which had on it the evidence of this condition of the bone. The doctor went out. Mr. Clark lay with his eyes fixed and sightless. The dew of death was upon his brow. I went to his bedside. In a few moments his face changed; its death-pallor gave place to a natural hue. The eyelids closed gently and the breathing became natural; he was asleep. In about ten minutes he opened his eyes and said, 'I feel like a new man. My suffering is all gone.' It was between three and four o'clock in the afternoon when this took place.

"I told him to rise, dress himself, and take supper with his family. He did so. The next day I saw him in the yard. Since then I have not seen him, but am informed that he went to work in two weeks, and that pieces of wood were discharged from the sore as it healed. These pieces had remained ever since the injury in boyhood.

"Since his recovery I have been informed that his physician claims to have cured him, and that his mother has been threatened with incarceration in an insane asylum for saying; 'It was none other than God and that woman who healed him.' I cannot attest the truth of this report, but what I saw and did for that man, and what his physician said of the case, occurred just as I have narrated." 73

> In healing the sick and sinning, Jesus elaborated the fact that the healing effect followed the understanding of the divine Principle and of the Christ-spirit which governed the corporeal Jesus. For this Principle there is no dynasty, no ecclesiastical monopoly. Its only crowned head is immortal sovereignty. Its only priest is the spiritualized man. The Bible declares that all believers are made "kings and priests unto God." The outsiders did not then, and do not now, understand this ruling of the Christ; therefore they cannot demonstrate God's healing power. Neither can this manifestation of Christ be comprehended, until its divine Principle is scientifically understood.
>
> *Science and Health 141:13*

Daniel Spofford was one of Mrs. Eddy's earliest students. He had the opportunity to treat the grand-daughter of the woman with whom he boarded on one occasion. Ethel West fell down the stairwell at school and was gravely injured. The child was brought home still unconscious. Spofford offered to heal her, and the child's grandmother was relieved to see her respond so quickly to his treatment. Ethel then thought it would be "smart" to go back to school. However, the surprise at her appearance was so great that she was taken home again, unconscious. But, this time Spofford was unable to heal her (he had not handled the claim of "reversal"), and he immediately called Mrs. Eddy to help the child. As soon as Mrs. Eddy knew of the child's need, Ethel was instantaneously healed, completely and permanently. 74

> ... there sat in a window a certain young man named Eutychus, being fallen into a deep sleep: and as Paul was long preaching, he sunk down with sleep, and fell down from the third loft, and was taken up dead. And Paul went down, and fell on him, and embracing him said, Trouble not yourselves; for his life is in him. When he therefore was come up again, and had broken bread, and eaten, and talked a long while, even till break of day, so he departed. And they brought the young man alive, and were not a little comforted.   Acts 20:9-12

When Mrs. Eddy was living in Lynn, one day someone was sent to her from a distance in the city and asked her to come to visit a lady who was dying with consumption, and she said she would.

She took a cab at the door-way and went to this person, and on the way when near her destination, saw a hunchback in the street and the carriage passed very close to him; as it passed him, one wheel went down into a rut and splashed him all over with water. He immediately became angry, but she leaned out of the carriage and said to him, "Little man, God loves you," and went on her way a few hundred feet. The young fellow watched her.

She went into the house, stayed about a half hour, healed her patient, and as she came out, there was a tall young man standing at the curbstone, and he went up to her and said, "Are you the lady that told me God loved me?" She looked at him closely, and he said, "Look at me, how I have straightened up," and expressed gratitude. 75

> The blind receive their sight, and the lame walk, the lepers are cleansed, and the deaf hear, the dead are raised up, and the poor have the gospel preached to them. And blessed is he, whosoever shall not be offended in me. Matt. 11:5,6

Mrs. Eddy met casually a woman who had a son afflicted with epileptic fits. The son was not present when Mrs. Eddy met the mother, and Mrs. Hulin thought Mrs. Eddy did not know of the case at all. But Mrs. Eddy turned to the mother and said: "You never had a tyrannical father whom you were afraid of," and the son was instantaneously healed of the epilepsy when Mrs. Eddy uncovered and destroyed the latent fear in the mother's thought of her father, which had made her nervous when it was born, developing into epilepsy. 76

> . . . there came to him a certain man, kneeling down to him, and saying, Lord, have mercy on my son: for he is lunatick, and sore vexed: for ofttimes he falleth into the fire, and oft into the water. And I brought him to thy disciples, and they could not cure him. Then Jesus answered and said, O faithless and perverse generation, how long shall I be with you? how long shall I suffer you? bring him hither to me. And Jesus rebuked the devil; and he departed out of him: and the child was cured from that very hour. Then came the disciples to Jesus apart, and said, Why could not we cast him out? And Jesus said unto them, Because of your unbelief: for verily I say unto you, If ye have faith as a grain of mustard seed, ye shall say unto this mountain, Remove hence to yonder place; and it shall remove; and nothing shall be impossible unto you. Howbeit this kind goeth not out but by prayer and fasting.   Matt. 17:14-21

Mrs. Eddy passed a drunken man in Lynn and turned to the one with her and said, "If that is the man I see, that is the man I am and I refuse it because it is not the man I wish to be." The man was healed. 77

This is true of all erroneous conditions. If one holds in thought, or accepts, that someone expresses certain character traits that are not Christ-like we are not viewing our fellow man as our dear Master did. How can we expect then to effect a healing if we acknowledge them less than the "image and likeness" of our Father? We must refuse to acknowledge or see what the devil is trying to say to us about our fellow man.

In one of Mrs. Eddy's classes a clergyman who was very elderly had a partial belief of blindness, and asked our Leader if it could be cured. She answered, "Yes, if you only touch the hem of *His* garment." The man was healed during class. 78

And the blind and the lame came to him in the temple; and he healed them.   Matt. 21:14

. . . In the early period of her work in Christian Science, in the house where our Leader was boarding, there was a little boy, only a few years old, and it was during the winter. He was in her room one day, and while she was talking to him, he looked out of the window and saw the snow in the trees in their garden amongst which were some apple trees. The little boy later asked his mother, "If Mrs. Eddy should say a blossom would come out, wouldn't it?" His mother said, "No, not at this time of the year." Some days later Mrs. Eddy said to the boy, "I will tell you something if you will not tell anyone." He asked if he could tell his mama. Mrs. Eddy said, "No, not anyone." He said, "Well, I will not." Then Mrs. Eddy said, "You see that apple tree?" He said, "Yes." She said, "Now watch that tree every day and you will see a blossom come on it." He did so and in three days there was a blossom and she had him pick it.   79

And when he saw a fig tree in the way, he came to it, and found nothing thereon, but leaves only, and said unto it, Let no fruit grow on thee henceforward for ever. And presently the fig tree withered away. And when the disciples saw it, they marvelled, saying, How soon is the fig tree withered away! Jesus answered and said unto them, Verily I say unto you, If ye have faith, and doubt not, ye shall not only do this which is done to the fig tree, but also if ye shall say unto this mountain, Be thou removed, and be thou cast into the sea; it shall be done. And all things, whatsoever ye shall ask in prayer, believing, ye shall receive.   Matt. 21:19-22

One of Mrs. Eddy's students related the following testimony which appeared in editions of *Science and Health*.

I cheerfully give my testimonial to the wonderful efficacy of the Science Mrs. Glover teaches, in its application to my case. I was the melancholy victim of sciata in the hip for many long years; at times I could neither lie, sit or stand without great suffering. When I first saw Mrs. Glover she told me she could cure me; but I must say it seemed impossible, after suffering so long and trying so many things, that I could be healed without medicine or application of any sort. Yet, such was the case. After she had conversed with me I improved until my hip disease left me, and I am completely rid of it.

Stoughton, Mass., 1873   Alanson C. Wentworth

I was also cured of an inveterate habit of smoking and chewing tobacco.   A. C. Wentworth   80

In the early days it was hard for Mrs. Eddy to find patients to treat; and one day she went out on the street to see if she could find someone to heal. She saw the doctor's gig tied in front of a house, and when he had come out and driven away, Mrs. Eddy crossed the street and rang the doorbell of the house out of which the doctor had come. A tear-stained woman opened the door, and Mrs. Eddy asked if anyone were sick in this house. The lady said that her daughter had just died. Mrs. Eddy asked if she could go in and see the daughter. The woman at first demurred, but finally let her go in where the body lay. In a little while the mother heard voices, and looking into the room, she saw her daughter sitting up in bed, and talking to Mrs. Eddy.

Mrs. Eddy said that "A wordless flood of life" filled her consciousness, and the girl was raised from the dead. Mrs. Eddy asked the mother to bring her daughter's clothes, and the amazed mother asked why. Our Leader answered that she wanted to take the girl out for a walk. The mother said: "You don't know what you are asking, my daughter has been ill with consumption for months, and she could not go out." Mrs. Eddy reassured the mother, and told her that no harm could come to her daughter through anything Mrs. Eddy should do, and finally the mother brought the girl's clothes. Mrs. Eddy then took the girl out and walked her up and down for about half an hour, the mother and father following behind to see what was done. The girl's color came back, and she was not only alive, but healed of the disease!

When they got back to the house, the mother took off her diamond ring and gave it to Mrs. Eddy, and this ring our Leader always wore. 81

And, behold, there came a man named Jairus, and he was a ruler of the synagogue: and he fell down at Jesus' feet, and besought him that he would come into his house: For he had one only daughter, about

twelve years of age, and she lay a dying. But as he went the people thronged him. . . . While he yet spake, there cometh one from the ruler of the synagogue's house, saying to him, Thy daughter is dead; trouble not the Master. But when Jesus heard it, he answered him, saying, Fear not: believe only, and she shall be made whole. And when he came into the house, he suffered no man to go in, save Peter, and James, and John, and the father and the mother of the maiden. And all wept, and bewailed her: but he said, Weep not; she is not dead, but sleepeth. And they laughed him to scorn, knowing that she was dead. And he put them all out, and took her by the hand, and called, saying, Maid, arise. And her spirit came again, and she arose straightway: and he commanded to give her meat. And her parents were astonished: but he charged them that they should tell no man what was done.
Luke 8:41-56

Mrs. Eddy relates a healing that took place when she was living in Lynn, Massachusetts. "The four and a half year old boy of one of my students was taken seriously ill with what was called brain fever. He had been a little tyrant. The mother cared for the child without avail, and at length came running to my home with the baby in her arms."

"When she came in, she placed him on the bed saying, 'I am afraid I have come too late. I think he is gone.' And to all appearances the sick child had ceased to live. I told her to leave me and not to return for an hour."

"After her departure I went to God in fervent prayer and very soon the boy sat up in bed. I told him to jump down and come to me. He came and I took him in my arms and was *silently* declaring that he was not sick, when I saw the little fellow double up his fist and strike at me saying, 'I *is* tick, I *is* tick.' Although he struggled and fought in my arms, love prevailed, and he was soon at play with some spools that I had made into a cart with a darning needle. I still continued treating him and again he came to me and struck me with his fist, saying, 'I *is* tick, I *is* tick.' Then I said, 'You are not sick and you are a good boy.' Then he fell at my feet limp and lifeless, and I took him in my arms and my thought went out to my heavenly Father. The boy soon returned to consciousness and was ready to play again.

"When I saw his mother coming, I told him to go to the door to meet her. When she opened the door and found her child healed, she was so overcome that she nearly swooned and I had for a time another patient. What astonished her so much, even more than the fact that he was alive, was that he was walking, because he had never done so before; he had been paralyzed from birth. On the way home her little boy talked of God and said how good God is." 82

"A case of convulsions, produced by indigestion, came under my observation. In her belief the woman had chronic liver-complaint, and was then suffering from complication of symptoms connected with this belief. I cured her in a few minutes. One instant she spoke despairingly of herself. The next minute she said, 'My food is all digested, and I should like something more to eat.'" 83

A lady brought her daughter to Mrs. Eddy one day and asked her to leave her with her as she could not speak. After doing all she could to help the girl, with apparently little effect, it occurred to her to test her in another way, and she said to her, "Well, I suppose the reason you do not talk is because you cannot talk!" At once the girl answered, "I can talk and I do talk, and I will talk! as much as I like and you can't stop me." So Mrs. Eddy was able to send her home to her parents cured of the devil of dumbness. 84

> As they went out, behold, they brought to him a dumb man possessed with a devil. And when the devil was cast out, the dumb spake: and the multitudes marvelled, saying, It was never so seen in Israel. Matt. 9:32,33

Miss Lucretia Brown was a middle-aged spinster from Ipswich who had been a semi-invalid since a severe injury received in girlhood. She had been marvelously healed by Mrs. Eddy when she began the studying of Christian Science in 1877. 85

[Abigail Thompson relates] My mother used to speak of an experience that Mrs. Eddy once told her, of walking along the street and coming upon a cripple piling wood. As she passed him, she touched him on the shoulder and said, "God loves you," and instantly the man was healed. 86

51

A man brought his wife to Mrs. Eddy for treatment for dumbness. Mrs. Eddy looking at her, detected the devil of stubbornness. She said, severely, "It is well madam, that you have not been talking these years," and the woman opened her mouth and began to defend herself! 87

Later, when Mrs. Eddy lived in Boston, she healed another deformed or crippled man. His arms seemed useless; his legs appeared to have withered. He had to be cared for, even fed. The niece of this man reported the testimony in the *Christian Science Sentinel* of July 18, 1908. This is a rare occurrence when Mrs. Eddy took two treatments to effect a healing.

Leominster, Mass., July 2, 1908

Dear Leader:—I had an uncle by marriage who was a helpless cripple and who was deformed. All his limbs were withered, and on very pleasant mornings a special policeman would wheel him out on Boston Common in his wheel chair. One morning a number of years ago, he sat there in his wheel chair as you were passing through the Common, and you stopped and spoke to him, telling him that man is God's perfect child, and a few other words. Later, after you had left him, he declared you had helped him. The next morning he looked and looked for you in the same place, and morning after morning continued to do so, until one day you came. Again you repeated to him what you had said before, and this time he was healed and made perfect,—every whit whole; and after that he was able to go into business for himself and provide his own living. No doubt you will remember the whole circumstance. His bones had hardened so that when sitting or lying down his knees were drawn up and rigid, his brother having to carry him up and down stairs, and feed him and care for him all the time; but after he was healed through your spoken word, he was able to be as active as other men and earned his own living; and whereas before he could not even brush a fly from his face, he regained the use of his hands and became an ordinary penman.

It was you dear Leader, who spoke to him of the healing Christ and set him free, when you met him so long ago on Boston Common, and many times I have desired to tell you about it, and to express to you my gratitude for the many benefits I also have received from Christian Science. Words can never express it.

With deepest love, in which my husband joins me,

Your loving student,

Mrs. Charlotte F. Lyon 88

And there sat a certain man at Lystra, impotent in his feet, being a cripple from his mother's womb, who never had walked: The same heard Paul speak: who stedfastly beholding him, and perceiving that he had faith to be healed, Said with a loud voice, Stand upright on thy feet. And he leaped and walked.   Acts 14:8-10

A child was brought to her with a cataract on each eye, blind. Mrs. Eddy began to talk to her of God, Truth and Love, when the child, animated by error, stamped her foot and said, "I hate you. I hate you. I could sit up all night to hate you!" Mrs. Eddy replied, "My darling, I love you. I love you, why I could sit up all night to love you!" and at once the cataracts fell out and the child saw. 89

Truth casts out all evils and materialistic methods with the actual spiritual law,—the law which gives sight to the blind, hearing to the deaf, voice to the dumb, feet to the lame.
Science and Health 183:26-29

"Three students to whom Mrs. Eddy told the following story recounted it to me (A. L. Fosbury). One time Mrs. Eddy was called to see a sick child. A girl of about fifteen opened the door for her and she had to pass through a room, in which the father was in bed with consumption, to get to the room where the child and its mother were. The child was so thin that its bones were sticking out.

"The mother went out of the room, and Mrs. Eddy healed the baby in about fifteen minutes, so that "It's cheeks stuck out like rosy apples (to quote our Leader's own words).

"When the mother came to the door, the child called out lustily, 'Mama! Mama!' The woman exclaimed: 'Have I gone mad!'

"Then Mrs. Eddy went into the other room with her and saw the father sitting on the side of the bed, healed of his consumption; and learned that the girl of fifteen who opened the door for her had been healed of deafness. These three healings were all made in the space of about fifteen minutes.

"Later I was told that Mrs. Eddy turned away from the sick child and looking out of the window said, "This is not right; it is not Love, and God is Love,' and that when she looked around at the child it was healed." 90

Love is impartial and universal in its adaptation and bestowals. It is the open fount which cries, "Ho, every one that thirsteth, come ye to the waters." *Science & Health 13:2*

all they that had any sick with divers diseases brought them unto him; and he laid his hands on every one of them, and healed them.
Luke 40:4

"My mother often related the following experience [which occurred] in the Lynn household. I was sick, and my mother called a medical doctor. The physician gave my father a prescription to fill at a drugstore. While he was gone Mrs. Glover came in. She stopped at the door and listened to my mother's fears about me. Mrs Glover said, 'Put away the medicine. Flora is all right.' When my Father returned with the medicine, I was playing on the floor, perfectly well. . . . I have been well all my life.'" 91

"I was told that one of the early students went to our Leader for advice. The student told Mrs. Eddy that she had a claim (of sickness), and also other difficulties which she had prayed over, faithfully, and had solicited help of other practitioners, and yet her needs had not been met. She asked our Leader to advise her what to do.

"Mrs. Eddy, (so I was told) advised her to read *Science and Health* through in one month. The lady did so, and was healed and her difficulties were all worked out harmoniously." 92

In early 1876, a dinner guest of Mrs. Glover's (Mrs. Eddy's married name at the time) was the recipient of a healing and was later to be the instrument in bringing together Mrs. Glover with her future husband. Mrs. Godfrey of Chelsea, Mass., was summoned to Mrs. Glover's house at the request of her nephew, William Nash. Mr. Nash's wife and baby were both ill and he wished his aunt to come to help him. Mrs. Godfrey, along with her young daughter were at dinner with Mrs. Glover, (Mrs. Glover had meals with her tenants), when she noticed the bandaged finger of the genial woman. Upon inquiry Mrs. Godfrey explained that she had run a needle deep into her finger, and that the doctors told her that should she not amputate the finger she would lose her entire arm.

54

She refused to consider such actions.

The next morning Mrs. Godfrey ran into the adjoining room, exclaiming to her nephew, "William, look at my hand!" The finger, appearing almost normal, elicited a remark from William that it was the result of Mrs. Glover's work. Mrs. Godfrey turned to Mrs. Glover as her only physician. 93

Shortly afterwards, on a Sunday in March of 1876, Mrs. Godfrey invited Asa Eddy to come visit and have dinner at home and it was at this gathering that Mrs. Glover came to meet her future husband. Mrs. Glover was to heal Mr. Eddy of a complaint, and after his second visit he was so well improved that he enrolled to take her class of instruction in healing. 94

The first encouragement Mrs. Eddy received after issuing the first edition of *Science and Health* was from A. Bronson Alcott, the writer, who called to see her and said, "I have faith in you." His comment on *Science and Health* was that it, "has the seal of inspiration, gives the facts of immortality, and reaffirms the Christian revelations!" She afterwards healed him from a severe form of rheumatism which had confined him to his chair. 95

> *For verily I say unto you, That many prophets and righteous men have desired to see those things which ye see, and have not seen them; and to hear those things which ye hear, and have not heard them.*
> Matt. 13:17

"A carpenter came to our house, for some reason, who had his arm in a sling. Father asked him what the trouble was and he said that he had strained the ligaments and paralysis had set in. The arm was partly withered and all the physicians said that it would continue to wither. He said that he had been to the best physicians and hospitals there were. Father told him about Mrs. Eddy and asked him if he went to her to come and tell him the result. About a week later the carpenter came to the house to tell Father that he was completely healed.

"I might add that when this man came to see Mrs. Eddy she was too busy to come down to talk with him and just opened a window in her parlor room on the second floor and called down to him.

Father never told me any details of this experience other than those I have related, but as far as I know this was the only conversation Mrs. Eddy had with the man and he came away healed." 96

The Nashes. . . , while being tenants of Mrs. Glover's, did not show an interest in Christian Science. They in fact had their own doctor and nurse. They did however have the highest regard for Mrs. Glover and even had their little girl named Flora Glover Nash. On one occasion Mrs. Nash asked Mrs. Glover's opinion about the condition of her daughter, which seemed worse than usual. She didn't take control of the situation or interfere in any way but only spoke quietly, soothing the troubled thought of the mother and shortly everything was all right. 97

> *His work is honourable and glorious: and his righteousness endureth for ever. He hath made his wonderful works to be remembered: the Lord is gracious and full of compassion. . . . He hath shewed his people the power of his works, that he may give them the heritage of the heathen. The works of his hands are verity and judgment; all his commandments are sure.* Ps. 111:3,4,6,7

"It was only a few months after our stay with my cousins, early the following winter, that I [Mary Godfrey] had an attack of membranous croup. I had suffered with this all during childhood, and Father and Mother both used to become very fearful that they would lose me during one of these attacks. But this time Mother was so sure that Mrs. Glover [as Mrs. Eddy was known at the time] could heal me that she wrapped me up in a blanket and started off to Lynn in a heavy snowstorm, my Aunt Nancy accompanying us to the station.

"Aunt Nancy kept telling Mother that she was crazy to take me on such a journey on a day like that and I would surely die. But Mother went right on and finally got me to Lynn. When she reached Mrs. Glover's house, she went straight to the back door so that she could get in more quickly. Mrs. Glover came to the door at once and, as calmly as if nothing was the matter, said that if I would run upstairs and play I would be all right. I do not remember much about it, except that I did as she told me, for I had been taught to be obedient. I ran upstairs to the Nashes' [boarders of Mrs. Eddy's] apartment and immediately I was all right. That was the end of the awful condition."

They stayed at the house that night and in the morning Mr. Godfrey came over to be with them. Mrs. Glover saw him then and told him that it was his fault that his daughter had had those problems. The little girl was very upset at hearing Mrs. Glover say this to her father as she thought her father was a wonderful man. Of course, she did not then understand what Mrs. Glover meant and possibly her father did not either. Mrs. Eddy was alluding that the fear of the parent thought about the child is frequently the cause of the physical problem in the child. 98

According to the reminiscence of Alice Swasey Wool another example of Mrs. Eddy's healing work was accomplished in the following manner:

"In about the year 1876 or 1877, when Mrs. Eddy was living on Broad Street, Lynn, I was living in Beverly, and was very ill with pain in the abdomen, and the doctor had not been able to relieve me. Someone proposed that I go to Lynn to see the 'medium' who healed without medicine. So I went to Lynn to see her.

"Mrs. Eddy opened the door herself and invited me in. I told her what seemed to be the matter, and she talked with me a few minutes and then said, 'Now we won't talk any more.' She closed her eyes and sat with her hands in her lap for about ten minutes. Then she said, 'You will not have that trouble any more,' and I said, 'Aren't you going to rub me, or do anything?' and she said, 'You are healed,' and I was." 99

Mrs. Ellen Linscott told me this: She lived with Mrs. Eddy at the College [Massachusetts Metaphysical College] on Columbus Avenue and one day a woman called to see [then] Mrs. Glover. On that day Mrs. Glover had directed she was not to be disturbed. The woman expressed her regret, saying she was in town only for the day, and wished to see and thank Mrs. Glover for healing her of cancer in the throat. Afterwards when Mrs. Glover was told of it, she said (about this): 'Oh, I am so sorry not to have seen her. Sometime ago she came and showed me her throat with an awful cancer eating into the jugular vein. The sight was so awful, I turned away and knew in the most positive way that God knew nothing of such a thing. That was all the treatment I gave her,' and she quoted the incident in *Unity of Good*. [see reference in epigram at front of this book]. Mrs. Linscott said (in 1903) 'not long ago I had a letter from Mrs. Eddy asking me to find out about this woman, and the incident that happened fifteen or more years ago.' 100

"Mrs. Eddy was called to a case of fever where two physicians were present; they said the man could not live; he had refused to eat anything for a week. As she went to his door he was saying, 'This tastes good and that tastes good,' and he did not have any food in the room. Mrs. Eddy said, 'With that consciousness he can live without eating.' The physicians laughed at it. 'Well he can eat,' she said, and instantly he was in his right mind, recognized someone in the room and called for something to eat. They brought him a bountiful supply, and he ate it all, dressed himself, and went out in the yard, entirely well." 101

> *[The Lord] satisfieth thy mouth with good things; so that thy youth is renewed like the eagle's.* Psalms 103:5

> *The Lord will not suffer the soul of the righteous to famish* Prov. 10:3

In January of 1877, there appeared an article in the *Ipswich Chronicle*, titled, *Metaphysical Science* by Mrs. Eddy. It read, in part:
". . . The tree is known by its fruit and the fruits of this knowledge are sin, sickness and death; but the fruits of our opposite discovery and higher perception of spiritual things are health and immortality, in which the material fades out of all calculations of being. This is the only true statement of Christian Science by which we have caused a man with a decayed bone to stand almost instantly on that limb and to be healed; the most terrible distortions of limbs and the most hopeless chronic diseases have yielded at once to our spiritual position; the example placed before us by our blessed Master reiterated this truth that enables us to handle serpents unharmed.
". . . We have discovered dormant disease in this mind three

months before it was reproduced on the body or to mortal consciousness; also have destroyed disease in this unconscious source and told the patient he was healed three weeks before the body would indicate this fact and never in a single instance were we mistaken." 102

"Eleven-year-old Grace [Choate], her mother, and her infant sister were among the tenants at 8 Broad Street. . . . Mrs. Glover . . . greatly loved the baby and 'would come downstairs and hold her in her arms. She seemed hungry for children and the affection children expressed.' This love of children is a constant theme throughout her life.

"The little girl had often noticed the sign at 8 Broad Street which read,

Mary B. Glover's
Christian Scientists' Home

and she had heard that Mrs. Glover was a doctor. Childlike she reasoned: 'If I must have a doctor I will go to the lady on Broad Street. The sign shows she is a Christian, and a Christian—even if she is a doctor—wouldn't hurt a little girl.' So off she took herself to a room with the crimson carpet and the gilt cornices where a pleasant-faced lady chatted with her a minute or two, closed her eyes for a few more minutes, then took her hand and said, 'If you are not better tommorrow, come see me again.' Nothing was said about Christian Science either by Mrs. Glover or by Asa Eddy, who met the child at the door, but the pain was gone and the child ran all the way home. 'I was filled with wonder,' she wrote later, 'at the loving kindness of the people who were so good to a little girl.'" 103

Jesus called them unto him, and said, Suffer little children to come unto me, and forbid them not: for of such is the kingdom of God. Verily I say unto you, Whosoever shall not receive the kingdom of God as a little child shall in no wise enter therein. Luke 18:16,17

Mrs. Eddy was known to help even those that did their best to harm her. One such account is her healing of a student George

Barry, of tuberculosis. He later attempted to bring suit against her for alleged damages. 104

> *Ye have heard that it hath been said, Thou shalt love thy neighbour, and hate thine enemy. But I say unto you, Love your enemies, bless them that curse you, do good to them that hate you, and pray for them which despitefully use you, and persecute you; That ye may be the children of your Father which is in heaven. . .* Matt. 5:43-45

Another instance where Mrs. Eddy had to rise above the attacks of former students was recounted in the Choate reminiscences. The following makes reference to a fabricated suit against her husband for murder.

"Something of what the episode cost her is suggested in an incident recorded by Clara Choate. Mrs. Eddy had just returned to Lynn from all day in the courtroom in Boston. Obviously ill, she left Mrs. Choate and Miranda Rice in the sitting room, but a little while later passed through the room again, her face pale, blood on her lips, and shakily bearing in her hands a basin with blood in it. The two women ran forward to her, but she motioned them back saying, 'God can heal me, God can heal me,' and went into the next room.   Later she came out again with what Mrs. Choate characteristically described as a 'sweet fearless smile' and an 'awe-inspiring' countenance. 'I knew God would heal me,' she told them, 'and he has. . . . Now dear [to Mrs. Choate], go home—be happy for all is well and *we can trust God*.'" 105

> *The people that walked in darkness have seen a great light: they that dwell in the land of the shadow of death, upon them hath the light shined.* Isa. 9:2

"Twice during my childhood I was instantly healed through the tender ministrations of our precious Leader from what the physicians would have regarded as hopeless physical conditions. From babyhood I had been an extremely delicate child, with three generations of serious lung trouble as a background on my father's side. On one occasion, previous to going East with my mother, I developed a severe cold which left me with a deep, hollow-sounding cough. As soon as Mrs. Eddy heard the cough she quickly detected the seriousness of the condition and gave me one treatment, which was all I needed to eradicate completely every vestige of the lung difficulty. The rasping cough ceased at once, and not only did this distressing condition yield, but the whole mortal law which lay back of the trouble was broken, and through the years that followed I have rejoiced in complete freedom from any return of this so-called family inheritance." 106

Confirmations of Mrs. Eddy's grand love for all was exemplified in the healings manifested during her preaching. One account of this appears in *Retrospection and Introspection*.

"Our last vestry meeting was made memorable by eloquent addresses from persons who feelingly testified to having been healed through my preaching. Among other diseases cured they specified cancers. The cases described had been treated and given over by the physicians of the popular schools of medicine, but I had not heard of these cases till the persons who divulged their secret joy were healed. A prominent churchman agreeably informed the congregation that many others present had been healed under my preaching, but were too timid to testify in public.

"One memorable Sunday afternoon, a soprano,—clear, strong, sympathetic,—floating up from the pews, caught my ear. When the meeting was over, two ladies pushing their way through the crowd reached the platform. With tears of joy flooding her eyes— for she was a mother—one of them said, 'Did you hear my daughter sing? Why, she has not sung before since she left the choir and was in consumption! When she entered this church one hour ago she could not speak a loud word, and now, oh, thank God, she is healed!'

"It was not an uncommon occurrence in my own church for the sick to be healed by my sermon. Many pale cripples went into the church leaning on crutches who went out carrying them on their shoulders. 'And these signs shall follow them that believe.'" 107

Our Master taught no mere theory, doctrine, or belief. It was the divine Principle of all real being which he taught and practised. His proof of Christianity was no form or system of religion and worship, but Christian Science, working out the harmony of Life and Love. Jesus sent a message to John the Baptist, which was intended to prove beyond a question that

61

the Christ had come: "Go your way, and tell John what things ye have seen and heard; how that the blind see, the lame walk, the lepers are cleansed, the deaf hear, the dead are raised, to the poor the gospel is preached." In other words: Tell John what the demonstration of divine power is, and he will at once perceive that God is the power in the Messianic work.

Science and Health 26:28

"One of Boston's early practitioners told me that a number of years ago he went to Lynn with several people who had come to the Annual Meeting. He was pointing out to one Westerner a very old house, when an elderly gentleman passing offered to show them a much older house. This man, a Mr. Green, in the course of conversation, asked if they had come on to the Annual Meeting, and being answered in the affirmative, told them the following story:

"Years before in Lynn, Mrs. Eddy called at his house looking for a room. His wife said they could not let her have a room because they had a sick daughter in the house who was dying of consumption. Mrs. Eddy went upstairs to the daughter, and he and his wife could remember nothing that happened after that till they saw Mrs. Eddy and their daughter walk in the front door. He and his wife were in a kind of daze and had not seen them go out. It was a cold raw day, but the daughter was completely healed when she returned from the walk.

"They rented a room to Mrs. Eddy, but a neighbor woman told his wife some tales against our Leader and said she was a dangerous woman, so Mrs. Green would not let Mrs. Eddy come. (Imagine, after saving the child's life, they would not so much as rent her a room!) Mrs. Eddy left him *Science and Health*, which he put in his bookcase. Some time after this Mr. Green was suffering from nervous prostration, and it occurred to him to read the book our Leader left. He read, and woke up well the next morning. Later, he had a running sore on his arm which had to be dressed daily. One day he decided to try and heal it by reading the book. He read and was healed. His wife got an attack of asthma which went on for some time, to the disturbance of the whole household. He decided to read her well without saying anything to her about it. He read the book again and she was completely healed. But his wife and one of his daughters, not the one who was healed, remained opposed to Christian Science." (It is possible that this healing is the same as recounted in *Historical Papers* by Judge Clifford P. Smith, although the healing there was of brain fever, even though the date was similar and the name of the young girl was Josephine Green, daughter of Mr. and Mrs. C. E. L. Green) 108

> *... if I cast out devils by the Spirit of God, then the kingdom of God is come unto you.*   Matt. 12:28

In a reminiscence related by Calvin A. Frye, C.S.D., Mrs. Eddy's secretary for 28 continuous years, one can see the power she commanded when she relied totally on God.

"During my first preaching in Boston I (Mrs. Eddy) had this experience. K (Richard Kennedy—one of her first students who later turned on her in a relentless barrage of attacks) — influenced young men to go to church where I preached, Dr. Williams' church, corner of Shawmut Ave. and Madison St. (Baptist Tabernacle), and disturb the service. As soon as service had well begun they, having taken seats in front, would get up one at a time and go out of church just to disturb the meeting. Finally, Dr. William's seeing their intention placed himself inside the door, and when they began to go out he rose and locked the door, and ordered them to their seats threatening them with arrest for disturbing the services.

"After that stopped, one day as I was preaching a stone came through the glass crashing through the glass and fell at my side; upon which a venerable gentleman arose and implored me not to attempt to go on with the service. I replied that I feared no harm and called upon them to stand still and see the salvation of God. Then of a sudden a heavy thunderbolt burst which shook the house and members of the audience say that they saw the lightning playing all around me. At the same time my voice was heard above it all saying, 'He uttered His voice, the earth melted.' [Psalms 46:6] During this time there were no clouds to be seen in the sky. We were never more troubled with any attempts to thus disturb the meetings." 109

> *The days will come, when ye shall desire to see one of the days of the Son of man, and ye shall not see it. And they shall say to you, See here; or, see there: go not after them, nor follow them. For as the lightning, that lighteneth out of the one part under heaven, shineth unto the other part under heaven; so shall also the Son of man be in his day. But first must he suffer many things, and be rejected of this generation.* Luke 17:21-25

Clara E. Choate, in her reminiscences relates what it was like to take part in the meetings of the early Christian Scientists at this time, and how Mrs. Eddy's provoking of thought brought about wonderful progress and healing and above all, caused her students to think.

"... The power of this truth thus uttered by her was not lost upon the students and was more or less felt by all present. One said she had come with a headache, another with a fear of spine, another with throat and cough, and so each one thinking of their troubles suddenly found the *air* changed, and their conditions also changed to their immediate consciousness of relief from evil." 110

> *Thou wilt keep him in perfect peace, whose mind is stayed on thee: because he trusteth in thee.*   Isa. 26:3

"At another time, in Lynn, Mrs. Choate was suffering from what she believed to be diphtheria. The symptoms were such as are commonly shown by a bad case of that disease. She was a Christian Scientist, and two other Christian Scientists besides herself had failed to heal her. Then Mrs. Eddy, on being called to save Mrs. Choate's life, healed her by one treatment. As Mrs. Choate afterward wrote, 'Our beloved Leader, Mrs. Eddy, came to my bedside and healed me of a terrible attack of diphtheria instantly.'" 111

An article entitled *Mind Cure* that appeared in the June 14, 1879 edition of the *Peabody Reporter* issued forth another testimony of the power of Spirit, God as reflected by this great lady.

"... It was offered in evidence that a young woman, who had been afflicted with softening of the brain from her earliest childhood until she was twenty-six years old, had been wholly cured by the exercise of Mrs. Eddy's mind-cure, so that now she was able to fill the position of a school teacher." 112

Mrs. Eddy told a student in her home [Miss Lane] the following regarding the *doctrines of men* and in so doing related perhaps the only instance where she did not effect a healing of someone.

> . . . [Ralph] Waldo Emerson was a man fitting a niche in history well, and we all in Mass. love him; but he was as far from accepting Christian Science as a man can be who is a strict moralist. Bronson Alcott is far in advance of him. I saw Emerson some months before his demise; went for the purpose of *healing* him. Let no one but my husband, Dr. Eddy, who went with me, know it. As soon as I got into the deep recesses of his thoughts I saw his case was hopeless. I can work only by God's graces and by His rules. So when I said, in reply to his remark, 'I am old and my brains are wearing out from hard labor'—and then chattered like a babe—'But you believe in the powers of God above all causation, do you not?' He answered 'Yes,' and this followed in substance: 'but it would be profane for me to believe a man does not wear out. I don't believe God can or wants to prevent this result of old age.' Now Miss L., what would this be for an item of history—that Normal Class Students from the only College or School in our land teaching the supremacy of Mind over all error should relapse into studying the ethics of one who died in that belief? Can you find in any work as good a system of hygiene? Do you understand all that work? If you do not, then it is your bounden duty to do it; and, if you wish to graduate at my College, under the seal of the State of Mass., you must know this great textbook sufficiently to be examined in it throughout, before you can receive a diploma and graduate at the only chartered mind-healing College *on earth.*   113

> *A prophet is not without honour, save in his own country, and in his own house. And he did not many mighty works there because of their unbelief.*   Matt. 13:57,58

Mrs. Eddy had a son by the name of George Glover (from her first marriage to her husband of the same name), who on occasion would visit her, as he lived far from Boston. George's daughter, going by the name of Mrs. Billings in 1934, had an interesting healing to relate.

"During the fall and winter of 1879 and 1880, when we lived at Deadwood, South Dakota, and I was three years old, my father went to visit his mother in Boston. At that time my eyes were what is termed crossed, and during his visit he told grandmother about them. According to my father, grandmother said, 'You must be mistaken, George; her eyes are all right.'

"When he returned to our home in Deadwood, and during a conversation with my mother at my bedside while I was asleep, they awakened me and discovered that my eyes had become straightened. Mother has a picture of me taken before this incident, showing my eyes crossed. This healing was often told me by my father and mother, and is at this time verified by my mother, who is with me." 114

> Christian Science separates error from truth, and breathes through the sacred pages the spiritual sense of life, substance, and intelligence. In this Science, we discover man in the image and likeness of God. We see that man has never lost his spiritual estate and his eternal harmony. *Science and Health* 548:2-8

In 1880 the Eddys moved to a house on Shawmut Avenue in Boston, along with the Choates, early interested students of Christian Science. George Choate would be away much of the time in establishing his healing practice in Portland, Maine. However, he would ask Mrs. Eddy questions regarding certain cases he had. On one occasion he asked Mrs. Eddy about a case that he had had trouble healing. Mrs. Eddy addressed the case mentally (in metaphysical healing distance is no impediment to the infinite ability of God to heal), and told George that the belief that needed to be addressed was due to a fall that the patient had several years previous. The unerring accuracy of Mrs. Eddy's spiritual assessment was immediately confirmed in a letter written to her upon George's return to Portland.

> April 2, 1880
> Last Saturday, when I was at home, and you examined my patient [mentally], she had the most wonderful chemical, or something of the kind, that I ever heard of. She was sitting talking with some ladies, and felt a little faint, her head ached, and she said she would go to bed, when she felt a crash, just as when she was thrown from a carriage, and knew nothing for four hours. Great black and blue spots, just where she was bruised years ago when she fell, appeared, and she acted and talked like a person under the influence of morphine. After the discoloration was gone, the cuticle came off in scales, and she is better than ever now, and walks without a cane. Has been out to ride to-day. What can it be? What does it mean?
> G. D. Choate

Of course, Mrs. Eddy's realization of man's present perfection, and her mental detection and correction of the belief harbored by the patient brought about immediate healing results.   115

> Christian Science brings to the body the sunlight of Truth, which invigorates and purifies. Christian Science acts as an alterative, neutralizing error with Truth. It changes the secretions, expels humors, dissolves tumors, relaxes rigid muscles, restores carious bones to soundness. The effect of this Science is to stir the human mind to a change of base, on which it may yield to the harmony of the divine Mind. *Science and Health* 162:4

Mrs. Eddy's ability to discern thought spiritually was made evident on many, many occasions. She was able to read thought as easily as we might read a newspaper; however, her motive in so doing was always to bless the recipient.

Miss [Julia] Bartlett and Dr. Eddy went through Mrs. Eddy's first class at 569 Columbus Avenue (afterwards Mrs. Eddy moved to 571 and Miss Bartlett went to stay with her there). This was before the charter for the [Massachusetts Metaphysical] College was obtained. There were several others in the class but Miss Bartlett and Dr. Eddy were the two who had previous class instruction from Mrs. Eddy. Mrs. Eddy told them she had to answer their questions first before she came to the others. They had not asked any questions but Mrs. Eddy felt their thought. In this class or another Miss Bartlett had some phase of Science which she was studying in her mind. Mrs. Eddy started in asking questions of each member of the class in turn—different questions. When she came to Miss Bartlett she asked her a question on the subject she had been studying over. Miss Bartlett then saw that she had been sounding each one separately on the query in his own mind as she went through the class with her questions.   116

> All we correctly know of Spirit comes from God, divine Principle, and is learned through Christ and Christian Science. If this Science has been thoroughly learned and properly digested, we can know the truth more accurately than the astronomer can read the stars or calculate an eclipse. This

Mind-reading is the opposite of clairvoyance. It is the illumination of the spiritual understanding which demonstrates the capacity of Soul, not of material sense. This Soul-sense comes to the human mind when the latter yields to the divine Mind.

Such intuitions reveal whatever constitutes and perpetuates harmony, enabling one to do good, but not evil. You will reach the perfect Science of healing when you are able to read the human mind after this manner and discern the error you would destroy. The Samaritan woman said: "Come, see a man, which told me all things that ever I did: is not this the Christ?"

Science and Health 84:28-14

The period that saw Mrs. Eddy in Lynn was probably the most prolific period of her healing career. One constantly heard of her success in curing the incurable and always the healing was instantaneous.

In mid-1880 Mrs. Eddy healed a young man named Hanover P. Smith. For nineteen years, since his birth, Hanover's mother had exhausted every medical means possible to cure her son of being deaf and dumb. In the institution where he was the doctors pronounced him incurable. Finally, his mother took him to Mrs. Eddy, who healed him quickly. Afterward, he became an active member of the Church of Christ, Scientist. For many years after his healing he attended services and gave testimonies in the Mother Church. 117

> *When Jesus saw that the people came running together, he rebuked the foul spirit, saying unto him, Thou dumb and deaf spirit, I charge thee, come out of him, and enter no more into him. And the spirit cried, and rent him sore, and came out of him: and he was as one dead; insomuch that many said, He is dead. But Jesus took him by the hand, and lifted him up; and he arose. And when he was come into the house, his disciples asked him privately, Why could not we cast him out? And he said unto them, This kind can come forth by nothing, but by prayer and fasting.* Mark 9:25-29

Another reminiscence of Julia Bartlett's was of the first Christian Science service, which she attended in the parlor of Mrs. Eddy's home. "There were about twenty people present. Mrs. Eddy preached the sermon which healed a young woman sitting near me of an old chronic trouble which physicians were unable to heal.

Her husband, who was present with her, went to Mrs. Eddy the next day to thank her for what had been done for his wife." 118

"I was once called to visit a sick man to whom the regular physicians had given three doses of Croton oil, and then had left him to die. Upon my arrival I found him barely alive, and in terrible agony. In one hour he was well, and the next day he attended to his business. I removed the stoppage, healed him of enteritis, and neutralized the bad effects of the poisonous oil. His physicians had failed even to move his bowels,—though the wonder was, with the means used in their effort to accomplish this result, that they had not quite killed him. According to their diagnosis, the exciting cause of the inflammation and stoppage was—eating smoked herring. The man is living yet; and I will send his address to any one who may wish to apply to him for information about his case." 119

"In front of Mrs. Eddy's home a good many years ago, out on the highway a man was one day run over by a very heavily laden wagon from which he had fallen, the wheels passing across his body. The teamster was thought dead and the body was brought into her home and laid on the floor."

"Mrs. Eddy was upstairs at the time, and they besought her to come down. My remembrance is that she hesitated at first, but finally came down and, looking away from the body, began to declare the truth, and had such a wonderful sense of mental uplift that she became entirely oblivious to her surroundings. After spending some moments in this spiritual contemplation of Truth, she suddenly came to herself and found that the man had risen. Passing his hand over his eyes in a somewhat dazed way, he said: 'Why I thought I was hurt, but I am all right.'" 120

Experiments have favored the fact that Mind governs the body, not in one instance, but in every instance. The indestructible faculties of Spirit exist without the conditions of matter and also without the false beliefs of a so-called material existence. Working out the rules of Science in practice, the author has restored health in cases of both acute and chronic disease in their severest forms. Secretions have been changed, the structure has been renewed, shortened limbs have been elongated, ankylosed joints have been made supple, and carious bones have been restored to healthy conditions.   *Science and Health 162:12-22*

There were many instances of healings recounted in her classes, in addition to healings of students that took place in class. Julia Bartlett remembers an interesting moment in class, which commenced September 30, 1880.

"When the class was through, my friend [Mrs. Ellen Clark] who first told me of Christian Science and who was also in the class, and I lingered a little and were sitting beside our dear teacher while she was talking to us of mortal mind's hatred of Truth and the evil to be overcome. She mentioned an incident of a person coming to her door armed against her, but he was not able to perform his evil work. . . . We were seeing a little of what it meant for her to stand where she did—a representative of Truth before a world of error—the cost of it and the glory of it, but we said in a playful, childlike way that amused and comforted her, 'They shall not touch you; *we* will help you.' My greatest joy today is that I may have been the means of lightening her burdens somewhat in the years that followed. . . ." 121

> *I have declared thy faithfulness and thy salvation: I have not concealed thy lovingkindness and thy truth from the great congregation. Withhold not thou thy tender mercies from me, O Lord: let thy lovingkindness and thy truth continually preserve me. For innumerable evils have compassed me about . . . Be pleased, O Lord, to deliver me: O Lord, make haste to help me. Let them be ashamed and confounded together that seek after my soul to destroy it; let them be driven backward and put to shame that wish me evil . . . . Psalms 40:10-14*

The thirteen-year-old daughter of a Boston family had a growth on her neck which was so large that she could not turn her head without turning her entire body. Mrs. Eddy was asked to help. The growth disappeared, leaving no trace excepting for a scar where the doctor had lanced it previously. 122

Student's Account of a Victory over Death by Mrs. Eddy:

"Mrs. Eddy became aware of a baby who lived across the street, and one morning she noticed the doctor's carriage leaving the home of the child. Mrs. Eddy went over to the house, spoke with the mother and asked to see the child. The mother said the child had passed on while the doctor was there. Mrs. Eddy went and sat beside the child, realizing the truth of being as no one else has since the time of Jesus, and the child was healed. Instead of gratitude being expressed by the mother, she took the child and showed much resentment towards Mrs. Eddy. The child remained well." 123

If we are ungrateful for Life, Truth, and Love, and yet return thanks to God for all blessings, we are insincere and incur the sharp censure our Master pronounces on hypocrites. In such a case, the only acceptable prayer is to put the finger on the lips and remember our blessings. While the heart is far from divine Truth and Love, we cannot conceal the ingratitude of barren lives. *Science and Health* 3:27

Jesus endured the shame, that he might pour his dear-bought bounty into barren lives. What was his earthly reward? He was forsaken by all save John, the beloved disciple, and a few women who bowed in silent woe beneath the shadow of his cross. The earthly price of spirituality in a material age and the great moral distance between Christianity and sensualism preclude Christian Science from finding favor with the worldly-minded. *S & H* 36:10

"In line with this lesson [on mesmerism] a student records that she once told Mrs. Eddy she had healed a boy run into by a train. Mrs. Eddy asked how she had treated the case, and the response was: 'I just knew that I could not be mesmerized.' Her teacher applauded the recognition that 'I' is all that is involved, adding: 'That is all you ever have to do.'" 124

When speaking of God's children, not the children of men, Jesus said, "The kingdom of God is within you;" that is, Truth and Love reign in the real man, showing that man in God's image is unfallen and eternal. Jesus beheld in Science the perfect man, who appeared to him where sinning mortal man appears to mortals. In this perfect man the Saviour saw God's own likeness, and this correct view of man healed the sick. Thus Jesus taught that the kingdom of God is intact, universal, and that man is pure and holy.   *Science and Health* 477:28-5

"Mrs. Eddy's correspondence with her students as well as their later reminiscences provide scores of examples of her ability to sense currents of thought and troublesome situations of which she had no explicit knowledge. Although she repudiated clairvoyance in the usual psychic meaning of the word, she did believe that spiritual intuition should forewarn one of special needs that required one's attention. Susie M. Lang, who was in her class of May, 1882, tells of receiving a message from her later that summer saying, 'If you cannot come to me I shall go to you.' On turning up, Miss Lang was amazed to discover that Mrs. Eddy had sensed her sharp need in a situation of which she (Mrs. Eddy) had no knowledge and had reached out at once to help her." 125

And the Spirit of the Lord fell upon me, and said unto me, Speak; Thus saith the Lord; Thus have ye said, O house of Israel: for I know the things that come into your mind, every one of them. Ezek. 11:5

"In one of Mrs. Eddy's classes there was a woman who had a strong sense of resentment and condemnation toward her husband, who was very immoral. Mrs. Eddy said to her that Jesus healed the Magdalen by condemning the sin but not the woman. The lady answered, 'Yes, but I have not the consciousness that Jesus had.' Our Leader instantly rebuked this by saying that she could claim the Christ-consciousness, for otherwise she could not heal a single case of sin or sickness. The students consciousness was so illuminated that her state of mind completely changed toward her husband, and when she returned home she found her husband healed." 126

And the scribes and Pharisees brought unto him a woman taken in adultery; and when they had set her in the midst, They say unto him, Master, this woman was taken in adultery, in the very act. Now Moses in the law commanded us, that such should be stoned: but what sayest thou? This they said, tempting him, that they might have to accuse him. But Jesus stooped down, and with his finger wrote on the ground, as though he heard them not. So when they continued asking him, he lifted up himself, and said unto them, He that is without sin among you, let him first cast a stone at her. And again he stooped down, and wrote on the ground. And they which heard it, being convicted by their own conscience, went out one by one, beginning at the eldest, even unto the last: and Jesus was left alone, and the woman standing in the midst. When Jesus had lifted up himself, and saw none but the woman, he said unto her, Woman, where are those thine accusers? hath no man condemned thee? She said, No man, Lord. And Jesus said unto her, Neither do I condemn thee: go, and sin no more. John 8:3-11

Mrs. Eddy always had a friendly attitude towards the clergy and would frequently have ministers in her classes. One instance was recited by Irving C. Tomlinson in the first edition of his biography, *Twelve Years With Mary Baker Eddy* .

"While I was stopping in Washington, D. C., with my husband, Asa G. Eddy, we attended the church formerly frequented by President Garfield. The clergyman was introduced to us and begged the privilege of paying us a call . . . . He early took the opportunity of visiting us and spent the afternoon in listening to our explanation of the Bible and Christian Science. He asked the privilege of remaining to the six o'clock dinner, explaining that he enjoyed the sociability of the occasion though he could not partake of the repast, saying that for years he had been troubled with a stomach difficulty which the physicians declared had developed into cancer of the stomach. He avoided all hearty food and confined himself exclusively to a fluid diet.

"All this he told us just as we were preparing to go to the dining room. I said to him briefly that this was an excellent opportunity to put to a test our talk of the afternoon. He replied by saying that he hardly could consent to test the doctrine for the sake of killing himself. However, I voiced the truth and asserted his ability to eat in comfort. He went with us to the table, soon forgot himself and his false fears and partook heartily of the salad, meat and pastry. At the conclusion of the dinner he said, 'What have I done? Will I ever survive?' We assured him there was no danger. He felt no harm and never was troubled again." 127

And these signs shall follow them that believe; In my name shall they cast out devils; they shall speak with new tongues; They shall take up serpents; and if they drink any deadly thing, it shall not hurt them. . . . Mark 16:17, 18

> In our age Christianity is again demonstrating the power of divine Principle, as it did over nineteen hundred years ago, by healing the sick and triumphing over death. Jesus never taught that drugs, food, air, and exercise could make a man healthy, or that they could destroy human life; nor did he illustrate these errors by his practice. *Science and Health 232:16-22*

Mrs. Eddy relates in *Miscellaneous Writings* (112:12) a curious incident regarding a criminal's realization of the significance of his crime and his subsequent healing.

"The mental stages of crime, which seem to belong to the latter days, are strictly classified in metaphysics as some of the many features and forms of what is properly denominated, in extreme cases, moral idiocy. I visited in his cell the assassin [Charles J. Guiteau] of President Garfield, and found him in the mental state called moral idiocy. He had no sense of his crime; but regarded his act as one of simple justice, and himself as the victim. My few words touched him; he sank back in his chair, limp and pale; his flippancy had fled. The jailer thanked me, and said, 'Other visitors have brought to him bouquets, but you have brought what will do him good.'" 128

One time when Mr. Eddy passed on and he was raised by Mrs. Eddy, he met Mrs. Eddy's mother [who had passed on years previous] even though he had never known her. They met because as Mrs. Eddy said, 'They both loved me.' Then she wrote the poem, *'Meeting of My Departed Mother and Husband.'* 129

See Appendix for text of poem.

"During his last illness in 1882 our Leader raised her husband, Dr. Asa G. Eddy, from the dead two or three times. After our talk with Miss Bartlett, she wrote to me as follows:

> The day Dr. Eddy seemingly left us he seemed so much better that I went out with him on a little car ride which he enjoyed. Mrs. Eddy had her work for the Cause to attend to, and as both she and I had been up with him so many nights, two students insisted on our getting some

74

rest, and came to take care of Dr. Eddy for that night.

Thereupon we retired, as he was so comfortable. He sat in his chair, because more restful to him than the bed; and seemed very peaceful and comfortable, until finally he had been quiet so long they went up to him to see if he was asleep—and found he was gone, but they did not know when it happened, as there was no sign or anything unusual, and they supposed him sleeping." 130

Later on Mrs. Eddy wrote the following in regard to her husband's death.

"Circumstances debarred me from taking hold of my husband's case. He declared himself perfectly capable of carrying himself through, and I was so entirely absorbed in business that I permitted him to try, and when I awakened to the danger it was too late. I have cured worse cases before, but took hold of them in time. I don't think that Dr. Carpenter [Well known for his public demonstrations of hypnotism.] had anything to do with my husband's death, but I do believe that it was the rejected students—students who were turned away from our college [Massachusetts Metaphysical College] because of their unworthiness and immorality. Today I sent for one of the students [Arens] whom my husband had helped liberally and given money, not knowing how unworthy he was. I wished him to come that I might prove to him how, by metaphysics, I could show the cause of my husband's death. He was as pale as a ghost when he came to the door and refused to enter, or to believe that I knew what caused his death. Within half an hour after he left I felt the same attack that my husband felt—the same that caused his death. I instantly gave myself the same [metaphysical] treatment that I would use in the case of arsenical poison, and so I recovered, just the same as I could have caused my husband to recover had I taken the case in time." 131

"Only a few days ago I disposed of a tumor in 24 hours that the doctors had said must be removed by the knife. I changed the course of the mind to counteract the effect of the disease. This proves the myth of matter. Mesmerism will make an apple burn the hand so that the child will cry." 132

If sickness is real, it belongs to immortality; if true, it is a part of Truth. Would you attempt with drugs, or without, to destroy

75

a quality or condition of Truth? But if sickness and sin are illusions, the awakening from this mortal dream, or illusion, will bring us into health, holiness, and immortality. This awakening is the forever coming of Christ, the advanced appearing of Truth, which casts out error and heals the sick. This is the salvation which comes through God, the divine Principle, Love, as demonstrated by Jesus. *Science and Health* 230:1

The following recollections are from the experiences of Janet T. Coleman, one of the early workers in the Cause of Christian Science, who studied with Mrs. Eddy January 22, 1883.

"I never shall forget my first experience when my mother and myself called upon her. After talking with her for a while, I said I would like to study with you, and then the wondrous purity of the one before me came to my thought, and I added, if I am good enough. Such a look as came into her face, and she answered, that for my answer she would teach me. I never had been in such an atmosphere of thought in my life before. I felt my own shortcomings. It was unfolded to me a glimmer of the divine inspiration which encircled her, and this is what gave me the blessed privilege of becoming her student, which I have never regretted. I can truthfully say, that the light that shone into my thought has never left me, and I never doubted our Leader's inspiration or wisdom in guiding our Cause. Such wisdom is not of this world.

"I remember the day when I was first brought in contact with one who had been healed by the reading of *Science and Health with Key to the Scriptures* by Mary Baker Eddy. She had been an invalid in bed for about fifteen years, and a friend had gone to the College and bought *Science and Health* and read it to her just a few pages (think it was fifteen pages) and she rose up and walked; her eyes and other claims had been healed also. As I walked into Hawthorne Rooms this Sunday, I saw a beautiful young lady go towards our Leader and embrace her. She walked as though she was on air, she was so happy and she was telling of her healing by her friend reading to her from *Science and Health*. It was a happy time for us all. I knew that *Science and Health* could heal, but this was the first one that I had seen. Now I know it is the Christ in that book that heals all mankind." 133

76

> *. . . as many as received him, to them gave he power to become the sons of God, even to them that believe on his name: Which were born, not of blood, nor of the will of the flesh, nor of the will of man, but of God. And the Word was made flesh, and dwelt among us, (and we beheld his glory, the glory as of the only begotten of the Father,) full of grace and truth.*   John 1:12-14

Christian Science is dawning upon a material age. The great spiritual facts of being, like rays of light, shine in the darkness, though the darkness, comprehending them not, may deny their reality. The proof that the system stated in this book is Christianly scientific resides in the good this system accomplishes, for it cures on a divine demonstrable Principle which all may understand. *Science and Health 546:23*

The Scriptures are very sacred. Our aim must be to have them understood spiritually, for only by this understanding can truth be gained. The true theory of the universe, including man, is not in material history but in spiritual development. Inspired thought relinquishes a material, sensual, and mortal theory of the universe, and adopts the spiritual and immortal.

It is this spiritual perception of Scripture, which lifts humanity out of disease and death and inspires faith. "The Spirit and the bride say, Come! . . . and whosoever will, let him take the water of life freely." Christian Science separates error from truth, and breathes through the sacred pages the spiritual sense of life, substance, and intelligence. *Science and Health 547:23-5*

See also Revelation, Chapter 10

Many of those healed by Mary Baker Eddy went on to accomplish great things for the Cause of Christian Science, whether it was the opening of a branch church or helping with the establishment and growth of the periodicals of The Mother Church or the healing practice. One example appears in *Pulpit and Press*, by Mary Baker Eddy. The Baltimore, Maryland church was dedicated in January, 1895. Dr. Hammond was the pastor of the Baltimore church. (this was before the Bible and *Science and Health* were ordained the pastor of all churches of the Christian Science denomination)

"Dr. Hammond says he was converted to Christian Science by being cured by Mrs. Eddy of a physical ailment some twelve years ago, after several doctors had pronounced his case incurable." 134

"Mrs. Eddy said that a woman to whom she had been kind was stricken down with a disease, but that she did not know it until one day a man told her she was dead. 'Dead,' she said, 'DEAD?' He said, 'Well she was dying when I was there and I suppose she is dead by this time.' The next day she was around the house at her work, well, and remained so; said the family never knew what or who] healed the woman." 135

Mrs. Eddy was always showing the importance of spiritual understanding versus blind faith, in the healing process.

"Healing is demonstration; nothing else is. When I first heard them speak of demonstration I asked—who? I thought someone had been healed. I lectured one time where the Spiritualists tried to break up the meeting; they would jump up and contradict without being asked. A lady in the audience (with whom I boarded)—and the audience was large—was taken with one of her attacks of gallstones; fell on the floor in excruciating pain; I said to the Spiritualists present, 'Now is your time to prove what your God will do for you; heal this woman.' They jumped about and did what they could, but she grew worse and worse. I stepped down from the platform, stood beside her a moment and the pain left; she arose and sat in her chair and was *healed*. This went broadcast, and through the healing this Science was brought to notice. It is lost sight of and must be regained." 136

Elijah came unto all the people, and said, How long halt ye between two opinions? if the Lord be God, follow him: but if Baal, then follow him. And the people answered him not a word. Then said Elijah unto the people, I, even I only, remain a prophet of the Lord; but Baal's prophets are four hundred and fifty men. Let them therefore give us two bullocks; and let them choose one bullock for themselves, and cut it in pieces, and lay it on wood, and put no fire under: and I will dress the other bullock, and lay it on wood, and put no fire under: And call ye on the name of your gods, and I will call on the name of the Lord: and the God that answereth by fire, let him be God. And all the people answered and said, It is well spoken. And Elijah said unto the prophets of Baal, Choose you one bullock for yourselves, and dress it first; for ye are many; and call on the name of your gods, but put no fire under. And they took the bullock which was given them, and they dressed it, and called on the name of Baal from morning even until noon, saying, O Baal, hear us. But there was no voice, nor any that answered. And they leaped upon the altar which was made. And it came to pass at noon, that Elijah mocked them, and said, Cry aloud: for he is a god; either he is talking, or he is pursuing, or he is in a journey, or peradventure he sleepeth, and must be awaked. And they cried aloud, and cut themselves after their manner with knives and lancets, till the blood gushed out upon them. And it came to pass, when midday was past, and they prophesied until the time of the offering of the evening sacrifice, that there was neither voice, nor any to answer, nor any that regarded. And Elijah said unto all the people, Come near unto me. And all the people came near unto him. And he repaired the altar of the Lord that was broken down. And Elijah took twelve stones, according to the number of the tribes of the sons of Jacob, unto whom the word of the Lord came, saying, Israel shall be thy name: And with the stones he built an altar in the name of the Lord: and he made a trench about the altar, as great as would contain two measures of seed. And he put the wood in order, and cut the bullock in pieces, and laid him on the wood, and said, Fill four barrels with water, and pour it on the burnt sacrifice, and on the wood. And he said, Do it the second time. And they did it the second time. And he said, Do it the third time. And they did it the third time. And the water ran round about the altar; and he filled the trench also with water. And it came to pass at the time of the offering of the evening sacrifice, that Elijah the prophet came near, and said, Lord God of Abraham, Isaac, and of Israel, let it be known this day that thou art God in Israel, and that I am thy servant, and that I have done all these things at thy word. Hear me, O Lord, hear me, that this people may know that thou art the Lord God, and that thou hast turned their heart back again. Then the fire of the Lord fell, and consumed the burnt sacrifice, and the wood, and the stones, and the dust, and licked up the water that was in the trench. And when all the people saw it, they fell on their faces: and they said, The Lord, he is the God; the Lord, he is the God.

I Kings 18:21-39

Calvin Frye recorded this interesting demonstration by Mrs. Eddy that took place June 8, 1884.

"I was sad and sobbing at the thought of how imperfectly I was demonstrating this Science in my own life and struggling to find my way, when there came a voice saying, 'You don't need to struggle, but simply to waken and see you are there.' And immediately I could see those who had passed on in belief, and they were not dead, but were right here about us; but I had not gained their point so as to be conscious to them, but as it were

79

looked ahead to it; neither did I seem to be in an abnormal state of mind at the time I saw this and yet it seemed as real and tangible as anything ever was." 137

"During one of the periods from 1880 to 1885 when Mrs. Eddy preached in Hawthorne Hall, 2 Park Street, Boston, she healed Henry A. Littlefield of inflammatory rheumatism. He had been and was afterward a printer employed on Boston newspapers. In his eighty-sixth year, he related his healing as follows: 'I was born in 1846. I was attacked by inflammatory rheumatism in my early thirties in such a form that even the bed clothing was burdensome and painful. I had heard about Mrs. Eddy's meetings in Hawthorne Hall, and at the worst stage of the belief I was taken there on a stretcher. After the service, Mrs. Eddy came down from the platform and greeted personally the small group of about a dozen people who were there. When she came to me and shook my hand and spoke to me, I felt the healing and responded by telling her that I was healed. I walked out of the hall rejoicing, and that belief never made itself real to me again.'" 138

> *. . . when Jesus perceived in his spirit that they so reasoned within themselves, he said unto them [the scribes], Why reason ye these things in your hearts? Whether is it easier to say to the sick of the palsy, Thy sins be forgiven thee; or to say, Arise, and take up thy bed, and walk? But that ye may know that the Son of man hath power on earth to forgive sins, (he saith to the sick of the palsy,) I say unto thee, Arise, and take up thy bed, and go thy way into thine house. And immediately he arose, took up the bed, and went forth before them all; insomuch that they were all amazed, and glorified God, saying, We never saw it on this fashion.* Mark 2:8-12

"In many cases, pupils in Mrs. Eddy's classes were healed by her teaching. A typical instance was furnished by Eugene H. Greene, then of Portland, Maine, but afterward of Providence, Rhode Island, who was in her class of November, 1884. His widow, who was in the same class, has related his healing by Mrs. Eddy as follows: 'During this class, Mr. Greene was healed of a hernia he had for many years. Mrs. Eddy had previously healed him of tuberculosis.'" 139

"In November, 1884, when Mrs. Eddy lived in Boston, a lady called on her and said, 'I am blind; I have come only to say this, for I am told you take no patients because you have so much else to do.' In her reply, Mrs. Eddy spoke of goodness and health as more natural than badness and disease. She also spoke of one's duty to praise God and of one's need to leave evidences material for evidences spiritual. The lady said, 'I can see a little better,' and went her way. Within a week she sent a message to Mrs. Eddy saying that her sight was perfectly restored." 140

> And, behold, two blind men sitting by the way side, when they heard that Jesus passed by, cried out, saying, Have mercy on us, O Lord, thou Son of David. And the multitude rebuked them, because they should hold their peace: but they cried the more, saying, Have mercy on us, O Lord, thou Son of David. And Jesus stood still, and called them, and said, What will ye that I shall do unto you? They say unto him, Lord, that our eyes may be opened. So Jesus had compassion on them, and touched their eyes: and immediately their eyes received sight, and they followed him.
>
> Matt. 20:30-34

Julia Bartlett relates how perceptive Mrs. Eddy was in her ability to read thought.

"It was customary for a few of Mrs. Eddy's students in those days to remember her at Christmas time with a few gifts that would be useful or enjoyable to her. I had a picture of Jesus which was said to be copied from the portrait carved on an emerald by order of Tiberius Caesar. The face was such as I had never seen in ideal pictures of him, so I decided to have one painted from it for Mrs. Eddy for Christmas, 1884, but when the time came, it was not finished and was not to be mentioned. The other gifts were arranged in her reception room and she was asked in to see them. As she looked she seemed surprised and turned immediately to me and said, 'I thought it was a picture.' I replied, 'I do not see why you should think it was a picture.' 'Well,' she said, 'I did.' Then I told her there was one, but it was not done, and she said, 'I thought so.' She said every time she had seen me for some time, there was the most beautiful picture in my thought and it was a picture of Jesus and there seemed to be a history connected with it, and that it was so beautiful it almost filled her with awe." 141

And Jesus knew their thoughts. . . Matt. 12:25

Julia Bartlett recounted the following healing.

"A man who walked with crutches went to hear Mrs. Eddy preach in Hawthorne Hall. Two people, one on each side, helped him up the steps at the entrance. After the service, he left the hall carrying the crutches under one of his arms. Miss Bartlett saw this man enter and leave." (*Mind in Nature,* June, 1885, p. 62.) 142

[Irving C. Tomlinson relates,] "One day when I was taking dinner with Mrs. Eddy the doorbell rang and on learning that a lady had called to see her, she said she would not keep her waiting, so left the table and went to her. This lady proved to be a physician who had been to see her some time before and had now come to tell her that she had had a chronic trouble of long standing that drugs failed to heal, but that she had been entirely free from it from the day she first met Mrs. Eddy. She wished to give her something in return, so had brought a diamond ring which had been an heirloom in her family and which she prized most of anything she had. She had therefore chosen it as best showing her appreciation of what had been done for her. [Miss Julia Bartlett was with Mrs. Eddy when this lady called the second time.]" 143

In another case, when Mrs. Eddy lived on Columbus Avenue in Boston, she became fond of a neighbor's child, a little girl, who had never walked. Not seeing the child for several days, she called at her home to inquire about her. The child's mother, in great sorrow, replied that the child had been taken ill and had just died. Mrs. Eddy then asked to see the child and to be left alone with her. The mother assented reluctantly, saying that nothing could be done; it was too late. When left with the child, or with its lifeless body, Mrs. Eddy took it in her arms and began to pray. Becoming conscious only of infinite Life, Truth, and Love, she became oblivious of the material situation until the child recalled her to human surroundings by sitting up and asking for her mother.

82

Then, when the mother came in response to Mrs. Eddy's summons, the child ran to her, enabled to use her limbs as well as restored to life. 144

It is interesting that the child walked even though having *never learned* to walk before.

> Now Peter and John went up together into the temple at the hour of prayer, being the ninth hour. And a certain man <u>lame from his mother's womb</u> was carried, whom they laid daily at the gate of the temple which is called Beautiful, to ask alms of them that entered into the temple; Who seeing Peter and John about to go into the temple asked an alms. And Peter, fastening his eyes upon him with John, said, Look on us. And he gave heed unto them, expecting to receive something of them. Then Peter said, Silver and gold have I none; but such as I have give I thee: In the name of Jesus Christ of Nazareth rise up and walk. And he took him by the right hand, and lifted him up: and immediately his feet and ancle bones received strength. And <u>he leaping up stood, and walked,</u> and entered with them into the temple, <u>walking, and leaping,</u> and praising God.   Acts 3:1-8

"I applied for admission to the Metaphysical College . . . and at the close of the class, I came to New York at the request of my dear Teacher, Mrs. Eddy. This was early in October, 1885. I had been in this city over a year when Mrs. Eddy sent for me to come to Boston to spend Sunday with her. . . . She asked me no questions about my heart, although she told me nine years after that she had sent for me because of what one of her other students had said about me. One of them had called upon me in New York, and later told Mrs. Eddy that I was in a very bad condition physically, that my heart constantly made a creaking noise, such as a gate would make when swinging on a rusty hinge. When it was time for dinner I accompanied Mrs. Eddy to the dining-room, which was in the basement of the house. On returning to the parlor she ran up the stairs like a little girl. I was ashamed not to make at least an effort to do the same, but for twenty-four years I had never run upstairs. . . . This time I did go as fast as she did, but when I reached the top step I was in a sorry plight. How I looked I cannot tell. I only knew that I was seized with one of my old attacks, when it seemed as though an iron hand gripped my heart and was squeezing the very life out of it. She gave me one glance, and then, without asking me a question, she spoke aloud to the error. We are told that when

Jesus healed the sick, he spoke as one having authority.

"As I look back on that wonderful event, I do not remember that the thought came to me at the time that she was healing me. . . . A few months after, I was seized with another attack, but it lasted only a moment and went never to return. That was eighteen years ago. . . ." 145

> And they were all amazed, and spake among themselves, saying, What a word is this! for with authority and power he commandeth the unclean spirits, and they come out. And the fame of him went out into every place of the country round about.   Luke 4:36, 37

The second healing the compiler has ever heard of performed by Mrs. Eddy that was not instantaneous was a case where she restored the eyesight. In this case an engineer whose eye had been put out by a hot cinder was treated by Mrs. Eddy. She gave him a treatment and an eye was manifested, but it was smaller than the other and deficient. She is reported to have looked at it and said, "Is it possible that my understanding of God is as little as that?" Again she treated him and the eye was perfect. 146

> And he cometh to Bethsaida; and they bring a blind man unto him, and besought him to touch him. And he took the blind man by the hand, and led him out of the town; and when he had spit on his eyes, and put his hands upon him, he asked him if he saw ought. And he looked up, and said, I see men as trees, walking. After that he put his hands again upon his eyes, and made him look up: and he was restored, and saw every man clearly.   Mark 8:22-25

This instance of one of the Master's healings shows that two treatments were necessary as well.

Annie Louise Robertson tells in her memoirs of some of the healings that took place when Mrs. Eddy spoke in Tremont Temple.

"A friend who had persistently clung to an unreasonable dislike for Mrs. Eddy, told me that as Mrs. Eddy was coming down the aisle she [this friend] turned and looked into Mrs. Eddy's face, and her resistance melted away completely, her eyes filled with tears, and after that she was absolutely loyal to our Leader. There were many other similar experiences which I heard of at the time." 147

"One young man who frequently went to hear Phillips Brooks preach at Trinity Church on Sunday morning and Mrs. Eddy preach at Hawthorne Hall in the afternoon, suggests something of the difference in his reminiscences. Brooks, the great-hearted Episcopalian who regarded preaching as 'the bringing of truth through personality,' delivered an Easter sermon which the young man found eloquently 'uplifting.' But Mrs. Eddy, he wrote, seemed with less eloquence to carry him right to the sepulcher where Jesus stepped forth in spiritual triumph. Resurrection, as she presented it, was more than history or symbol; it was present fact.

"That was the way it looked also to those sick and crippled people who came to the services and walked out well and sound. In healing, Mrs. Eddy made clear, apostolic and scientific Christianity were one. Healing was both sacrament and validation." 148

> . . . when John had heard in the prison the works of Christ, he sent two of his disciples, And said unto him, Art thou he that should come, or do we look for another? Jesus answered and said unto them, Go and shew John again those things which ye do hear and see: The blind receive their sight, and the lame walk, the lepers are cleansed, and the deaf hear, the dead are raised up, and the poor have the gospel preached to them. And blessed is he, whosoever shall not be offended in me. Matt. 11:2-6

> Think not that I am come to destroy the law, or the prophets: I am not come to destroy, but to fulfil. Matt. 5:17

"When Joseph S. Eastaman, a simple sea captain of Spanish or Portuguese extraction, returned from a long voyage to Peru to find his bedridden wife in worse condition than ever, he came to Mrs. Eddy, of whom he had just heard, to ask her to take the poor woman's apparently hopeless case. To his utter astonishment, she asked him earnestly, 'Captain, why don't you heal your wife yourself?' In some bewilderment Eastaman enrolled in her next class, and by the end of the brief term his wife had recovered sufficiently to accompany him to the final session. 'That one lesson,' he wrote later, 'dispelled her every doubt as to whether Christian Science had any kinship with Mesmerism or Spiritualism—for which she had strong antipathies.'

"A somewhat similar healing had taken place when Dr. Silas

Sawyer of Milwaukee came to study with Mrs. Eddy a year earlier, bringing his invalid wife Jennie with him. While it seemed impossible at first that Mrs. Sawyer would be able to sit up through the daily classes, she not only succeeded in doing so but came out of the course healed. At the end, Mrs. Eddy asked her what she was going to do with what she had learned. As Mrs. Sawyer recounted it later, [I answered], 'I am filled with wonderful Truth. I do not know what I am to do with it.' Then she said in the most convincing way, 'You are going to heal with it.'" (Shortly after she returned home she did precisely that, healing a number of cases.) 149

> And into whatsoever city ye enter, and they receive you, eat such things as are set before you: And heal the sick that are therein, and say unto them, The kingdom of God is come nigh unto you.
> Luke 10:8,9

Lilian Whiting, a Boston reporter with the *Traveller*, wrote of her experience meeting Mrs. Eddy for an interview. "...I went, as I have already said, in a journalistic spirit. I had no belief or disbelief, and the idea of getting any personal benefit from the call, save matter for press use, never occurred to me. But I remembered afterward how extremely tired I was as I walked rather wearily and languidly up the steps to Mrs. Eddy's door. I came away, as a little child friend of mine expressively says, 'skipping.' I was at least a mile from the [Hotel] Vendome, and I walked home feeling as if I were treading on air. My sleep that night was the rest of elysium. If I had been caught up into paradise it could hardly have been a more wonderful renewal. All the next day this exalted state continued. I can hardly describe it; it was simply the most marvellous elasticity of mind and body. . . . In the evening I had callers, and I told of my visit to Mrs. Eddy and later. . . chanced to allude to the unusual, and indeed, utterly unprecedented buoyancy and energy I was feeling. 'Why that's the result of your going to Mrs. Eddy,' exclaimed a friend." 150

> How beautiful upon the mountains are the feet of him that bringeth good tidings, that publisheth peace; that bringeth good tidings of good, that publisheth salvation; that saith unto Zion, Thy God reigneth!
> Isa. 52:7

When Judge Hanna wrote Mrs. Eddy he had a pain, she replied, "That pain is not a pain and you know it." That was the end of it. It was animal magnetism (The term used by Mrs. Eddy for evil, or the claim of life, substance and intellignce in matter.). 151

"One day our Leader illustrated how it takes moral courage to do one's duty. She told of a gentleman who was in a street car in Boston and had his little daughter with him. The child wanted to sit on his knee and put her head on his shoulder and go to sleep, and he would not allow her to do that, insisting that she should stand and move about. His treatment of the child seemed so cruel that a Scientist who was sitting in the seat behind him spoke to him and asked what was the trouble. He explained that the child had unknowingly taken some poison and he was on the way to a physician to give her an antidote, and if he allowed her to lie down and go to sleep, she might never waken again. Our Leader wanted to show me how we needed such arousals if our eyes were not open to detect the error which must be overcome, or it would put us to sleep." 152

"In 1886, while Miss Mary H. Crosby (afterward Mrs. Mary H. Mahon) was a student at the New England Conservatory of Music in Boston, an illness from which she suffered resulted in the advice from her physician that the lining of her stomach was destroyed and that she should return to her home prepared to live only a short time. Hearing of Miss Crosby's distress, a lady connected with the Conservatory recommended that she call on Mrs. Eddy, who conducted the Massachusetts Metaphysical College in Boston, and was said to heal as Jesus did. Accordingly, Miss Crosby called on Mrs. Eddy, who listened to her story, but did not promise to treat her. In the evening of that day, however, the conditions of which she spoke to Mrs. Eddy disappeared, and Miss Crosby found herself entirely healed from them." 153

And, behold, a woman of Canaan came out of the same coasts, and cried unto him, saying, Have mercy on me, O Lord, thou Son of David; my daughter is grievously vexed with a devil. But he answered her not a word. And his disciples came and besought him, saying, Send her away; for she crieth after us. But he answered and said, I am not sent but unto the lost sheep of the house of Israel. Then came she and worshipped him, saying, Lord, help me. But he answered and said, It is not meet to take the children's bread, and to cast it to dogs. And she said, Truth, Lord: yet the dogs eat of the crumbs which fall from their masters' table. Then Jesus answered and said unto her, O woman, great is thy faith: be it unto thee even as thou wilt. And her daughter was made whole from that very hour. Matt. 15:22-28

"In 1886, Erwin L. Coleman of Omaha was in Boston as a pupil in a class that Mrs. Eddy was teaching. His wife, Janet T. Coleman, was in Omaha expecting the birth of a child. During a session of the class, he received a telegram that his wife was dying in childbirth. Mrs. Eddy saw him get it and leave the classroom. Following him, she inquired as to what he had heard, and he showed her the telegram. Then she assured him that his wife would not die, she would recover, he could return to the class. This he did; and as events proved, Mrs. Coleman was delivered quickly and safely. Afterward, she had a long and useful career as a practitioner and teacher of Christian Science." 154

... there was a certain nobleman, whose son was sick at Capernaum. When he heard that Jesus was come out of Judaea into Galilee, he went unto him, and besought him that he would come down, and heal his son: for he was at the point of death. Then said Jesus unto him, Except ye see signs and wonders, ye will not believe. The nobleman saith unto him, Sir, come down ere my child die. Jesus saith unto him, Go thy way; thy son liveth. And the man believed the word that Jesus had spoken unto him, and he went his way. And as he was now going down, his servants met him, and told him, saying, Thy son liveth. Then inquired he of them the hour when he began to amend. And they said unto him, Yesterday at the seventh hour the fever left him. So the father knew that it was at the same hour, in the which Jesus said unto him, Thy son liveth: and himself believed, and his whole house.

John 4:46-53

"Edward A. Kimball, a Christian Science lecturer and teacher had suffered many years with a condition that made him cross and irritable, and from which he gained only temporary relief through Christian Science. Finally it became so aggravated he wired Mrs. Eddy that he wanted to see her, and she wired back telling him to come. As he sat in the parlor waiting for her, he began to have misgivings, because he realized that under this claim he was so touchy that he was hardly fit to talk to anyone, even to his own family. He began to wonder how he was going to appear even civil before her. When he heard her step on the stair, he wanted to run out of the house. She entered the room, paused on the threshold, and holding out both her hands, she advanced to him and said, 'Doesn't it make one cross to be sick?' Then without a word from him, she changed the subject and began to talk about other things. She never referred to his reason for coming to Boston all the while he was there. His summary of this interview was, 'I had never been so loved in all my life.'" 155

"Mother* told me that when she was first at Chickering Hall, holding services and preaching, the caretaker one Sunday brought his daughter, who was ill with consumption, and who had a distressing cough. After the congregation left the building, she was sitting in one of the end seats, waiting for her father. As Mrs. Eddy went down the aisles to go out the front door, she saw the little girl and noticed how ill she looked. She stopped and spoke to the child and said to her, "Don't you know, dear, that you haven't any lungs to cough with or be consumed? You are God's child," and she talked the truth with her and told her that she was God's idea, and to know that she was well, and the child stopped coughing and was instantly healed. When her father came to take her home, he was amazed to find that she was well." 156

"It was Mrs. Eddy's habit to take a daily ride in her carriage. The horses were harnessed in the carriage house, and then the rig was driven around to the carriage entrance of the house where Mrs. Eddy was waiting.

"One day, the groom found that Major had injured his foot very badly on a nail. He sent the stable boy to tell Mrs. Eddy that Major was injured, and would not be able to walk.

"The boy returned with a message from Mrs. Eddy that Major was to be harnessed and the drive would take place as usual. As they were harnessing the horses Mrs. Eddy suddenly appeared on the scene. She walked up to the animal, put her hand on his neck and said, 'Major, you have been listening to stable talk. Now come on and mind your own business!' They went for the drive and Major was perfectly well." 157

Abigail Dyer Thompson was healed by Mrs. Eddy at two different times as a child. Her healings appeared in the *Christian Science Sentinel.*

"From her babyhood, Miss Thompson was a delicate child. She was believed to have inherited a tendency to lung trouble, and physicians expressed the opinion that she would not live to maturity. Once when this disorder was especially evident, her mother, one of Mrs. Eddy's students took Miss Thompson to call on Mrs. Eddy in Boston. As soon as Mrs. Eddy heard the child cough she gave Miss Thompson one treatment, which erased every vestige of the dreaded disease and completely freed her from the believed liability to it.

"A year or so later, when Miss Thompson was again in Boston with her mother, she was stricken suddenly by an acute and severe malady of a different kind. For two weeks, first one practitioner and then another failed to furnish relief. Finally, at five o'clock one morning, when Miss Thompson had seemed to endure as much pain as she could possibly stand, her mother went to Mrs. Eddy's home to beseech her help. Mrs. Eddy heard the talking in her hall; and, as she afterward told Mrs. Thompson: 'I said to myself, it is time for me to step in on this case and save that child. Then, hurrying back to my room I dropped into a chair and immediately reached out to God for the healing.' Miss Thompson responded to Mrs. Eddy's mental work instantly. She was much better before her mother returned, and in a few days she traveled fifteen hundred miles to their home in perfect freedom." 158

> The author has healed hopeless organic disease, and raised the dying to life and health through the understanding of God as the only Life. It is a sin to believe that aught can overpower omnipotent and eternal Life, and this Life must be brought to light by the understanding that there is no death, as well as by other graces of Spirit. We must begin, however, with the more simple demonstrations of control, and the sooner we begin the better. *Science and Health 428:30-6*

> *And when he was come into the house, his disciples asked him*

90

"... a letter of December 13, 1886, from Mrs. E.C. Heywoood thanking her for the good she had done Mrs. Heywood's teen-age daughter: 'The eve she called to see you at the College, she said, the minute you came into the room it seemed as though an electric shock went all over her and she seemed lifted beyond the earth. Since then she has appeared like another child and since coming to Worcester people will ask what she has done to herself and she says, 'I've seen Mrs. Eddy.' Mrs. Heywood went on to say that the girl had had a slight impediment in her speech which entirely disappeared that night." 159

*And his mouth was opened immediately, and his tongue loosed,
and he spake, and praised God.* Luke 1:64

"... Mrs. Eddy's correspondence is laced with healings, direct and indirect, recounted by her students. Mrs. A.M. Harvey wrote her on May 31, 1886, after returning to Cincinnati from Primary class with Mrs. Eddy, that she found her patients all healed: 'I was so delighted to see them so happy, it is wonderful (they said) that you could make us so strong and well and us here in Cin.'" 160

Mrs. Eddy brought up the definition of God in class, given in *Science and Health* (p. 587:5), and that through the understanding of this she had healed a man of blindness whose eyeballs had been destroyed and the eyes were restored completely. Someone in the class asked, "If Mind is all that sees, why was it necessary for the eyeballs to be restored?" Mrs. Eddy replied, "Ah, I anticipated that you would ask that question. The effect of Christian Science treatment is this: Science restores that standard of perfection which mortal mind calls for. If the eyeballs had not been restored no one would have believed him when he said he could see."

Every healing performed by the Master confirms this Christianly scientific axiom. 161

Another instance of healing that took place in the late 1800's was recorded in the first edition of Irving C. Tomlinson's book, *Twelve Years with Mary Baker Eddy*.

"I was called by a brokenhearted mother to attend her young son who was afflicted with anklyosed joints. The bones of the knees appeared to be solidified and the verdict of the doctors was, 'a hopeless case—the boy will never be able to walk again.' I treated the little fellow and told his mother that she need have no further fear, for her son would be able to walk and run with other children. Three days after, the boy was playing in the yard with his companions. An acquaintance who saw him romping with his friends asked him what business he had to be out there and told him to go into the house, and stay there. The response from the little fellow was: 'You are not my doctor. Mrs Eddy is my doctor, and I can play if I want to.' Sometime later his mother brought him to me to thank me for his wonderful healing. As he walked across the floor, I noticed that he toed in with one foot, and spoke to him of it. He said, 'My momma said I should tell you about that. I have always walked that way.' I told him to walk in the right way, just like the other little boys. He did so at once, being healed instantaneously, and ever after walked naturally." 162

Truth casts out error now as surely as it did nineteen centuries ago.   *Science and Health 495:2-3*

The following is related by a Mrs. Allen to Irving C. Tomlinson and appears as a testimony in the December, 1905 issue of *Christian Science Journal*.

"Two years ago I had a man [name of Carter] come up to my house to repair some window-shades in the parlor. When he had finished his work I asked him to come to my study. I left him in my room for a time, and when I returned he said, 'I see that you are a Christian Scientist,' because he saw my literature in the room. Then he said, 'I was healed by the Discoverer and Founder of Christian Science, Mrs. Mary Baker Eddy.' I said, 'I want you to tell me all about it.' Then he gave me these facts: 'About eighteen years ago, while living in Boston, I fell from the third story of a building on which I was working, to the pavement. My leg was broken in three places. I was taken to a hospital, where they tried to help me. They said that the leg was so bad that it would have to be amputated. I said, 'No, I would rather die.' They permitted it to heal as best it might, and as a result I had to wear an iron shoe eight or nine inches high.

"I was called to Mrs. Eddy's home on Commonwealth Avenue, in Boston, to do some light work. Mrs. Eddy came into the room where I was busy, and observing my condition, kindly remarked, 'I suppose you expect to get out of this some time.' I answered, 'No; all that can be done for me has been done, and I can now manage to get around with a cane.' Mrs. Eddy said, 'Sit down and I will treat you.' When she finished the treatment she said, 'You go home and take off that iron shoe, and give your leg a chance to straighten out.' I went home and did as I was told, and am so well that, so far as I know, one leg is as good as the other." 163

> The less mind there is manifested in matter the better. When the unthinking lobster loses its claw, the claw grows again. If the Science of Life were understood, it would be found that the senses of Mind are never lost and that matter has no sensation. Then the human limb would be replaced as readily as the lobster's claw,—not with an artificial limb, but with the genuine one. Any hypothesis which supposes life to be in matter is an educated belief. In infancy this belief is not equal to guiding the hand to the mouth; and as consciousness develops, this belief goes out,—yields to the reality of everlasting Life. S&H 488:1

> And one of them smote the servant of the high priest, and cut off his right ear. And Jesus answered and said, Suffer ye thus far. And he touched his ear, and healed him. Lk. 22:50-1

"I must relate another sacred experience of our Leader's healings. One day when she had finished her lesson in the class of which I was a member, she asked me to wait after the other members had gone, and as she was standing in the classroom at 571 Columbus, a gentleman called to see her, bringing with him his sister, who greatly needed healing. Mrs. Eddy met them at the door of the room, and asked him to wait downstairs, while she talked with his sister. The belief was insanity, and she looked terrified. Our Leader told me that her delusion was that a serpent was coiled around her body and was crushing her. I stood in amazement, watching Mrs. Eddy's face as she turned and looked at the woman who fell on the floor screaming, 'It's crushing me; it's killing me.' Our Leader looked upwards, as if she had seen the face of an angel in her communion with God. In a moment she said to the woman, 'Has it gone?' And the poor woman looked up and her whole body was shaking and quivering as she answered, 'Yes!' I watched the changes of expression that came over her face, from fear to peace and joy. And O, the love that was expressed in our Leader's face as she looked down on her, stretched out both arms and lifted her up saying, 'Get up darling.' Then our dear teacher took that needy one's head on her shoulder and patted her face, as she lovingly talked the truth to her. Mrs. Eddy then went out of the room and talked to the mother who took her home, and asked me to come and have supper with her, and to sing to her. During the evening she turned to me and said, 'You saw what happened to that lady today? Well, she will never be insane in this world again.' And she has not." 164

And they came over unto the other side of the sea, into the country of the Gadarenes. And when he was come out of the ship, immediately there met him out of the tombs a man with an unclean spirit, Who had his dwelling among the tombs; and no man could bind him, no, not with chains: Because that he had been often bound with fetters and chains, and the chains had been plucked asunder by him, and the fetters broken in pieces: neither could any man tame him. And always, night and day, he was in the mountains, and in the tombs, crying, and cutting himself with stones. But when he saw Jesus afar off, he ran and worshipped him, And cried with a loud voice, and said, What have I to do with thee, Jesus, thou Son of the most high God? I adjure thee by God, that thou torment me not. For he said unto him, Come out of the man, thou unclean spirit. And he asked him, What is thy name? And he answered, saying, My name is Legion: for we are many. And he besought him much that he would not send them away out of the country. Now there was there nigh unto the mountains a great herd of swine feeding. And all the devils besought him, saying, Send us into the swine, that we may enter into them. And forthwith Jesus gave them leave. And the unclean spirits went out, and entered into the swine: and the herd ran violently down a steep place into the sea, (they were about two thousand;) and were choked in the sea. And they that fed the swine fled, and told it in the city, and in the country. And they went out to see what it was that was done. And they come to Jesus, and see him that was possessed with the devil, and had the legion, sitting, and clothed, and in his right mind. . . Mark 5:1-15

The treatment of insanity is especially interesting. However obstinate the case, it yields more readily than do most diseases to the salutary action of truth, which counteracts error. The arguments to be used in curing insanity are the same as in other diseases: namely, the impossibility that matter, brain, can control or derange mind, can suffer or cause suffering; also the fact that truth and love will establish a healthy state, guide and govern mortal mind or the thought of the patient, and destroy all error, whether it is called dementia, hatred, or any other discord.   *Science and Health* 414:4

"A student told Mrs. Eddy of a case of bronchial trouble that she had been endeavoring to heal without success. Mrs. Eddy leaned over the desk and shook her finger at her, saying, 'What are bronchial tubes for?' Then she answered her own question, 'They are to used to sing praises to the Lord, and for nothing else.' The student's patient was healed in that hour." 165

The National Christian Scientist Association held their 1888 meeting in Chicago, June 13, at Central Music Hall, just eight days after the C.S.A. meeting in Boston, where attempts to oust Mrs. Eddy from leadership of her church had failed. While Mrs. Eddy was to attend the meeting, she was not slated to speak. However, George B. Day, a disaffected student, had put her on the program as the primary speaker. Robert Putnam, in his *Association Notes*, relates, "Just as the meeting was about to start, he handed her a copy [of the program] and she was astounded to find out what he had done. He assumed she would refuse to speak, then he would take her place and announce his departure from the movement. However, she detected his plan, rose to the occasion and delivered her famous speech, *'Science and the Senses.'*" Despite this treacherous act, brought to her notice moments before she was supposed to speak in front of nearly four thousand attendees, she rose to the occasion through her ever reliance on the Almighty, and extemporaneously delivered what is known as one of the most famous and inspiring addresses of her earthly career. (A brief synopsis of her address, *Science and the Senses*, appears on page 98 of *Miscellaneous Writings*.)

"Well," Mrs. Eddy said, "God's leading seemed to be more toward the stage than away, so I went thinking there would be some provision. When I got onto the platform, everyone of that vast audience arose as one man, spontaneously, and unexpectedly to the audience even. It was said there that no one had ever known of such a thing before. When I got onto the stage, the thought of my subject came to mind—*Science and the Senses*. It was almost just what I dreamed a short time previously; I could not tell exactly when, nor just about the dream. Then the audience sang, "Nearer My God to Thee;" and I felt full of the Spirit and I was just ready; my fear had all left me, you see, and I talked to them for an hour, and then I said I should weary them, but they called out for me to 'go on,' and I talked a half hour more." One must wonder what power it was that enabled her voice to be heard distinctly by even those in the remotest areas of the immense auditorium. The audience was inspired by this great lady whose book had healed so many of them.

"When I got through, there was a great rush toward the stage, and the detectives and policemen were about to open a way out, but there were a lot of people down in front holding up their hands, and being held up by others, and calling upon me to help them. I said to the police, or those in charge, 'Wait, there is work here yet to do,' and I received acknowledgements from many afterwards saying they had been entirely healed of their diseases, one of a so-called hopeless case of diabetes and others too numerous to mention. Then the police cleared the way to my hack where an immense crowd were striving to see me . . . . 'I tell you this,' she said, 'because in this way you may see that if we trust in the Lord, He will uphold us.'" 166

> *. . . my speech and my preaching was not with enticing words of man's wisdom, but in demonstration of the Spirit and of power: That your faith should not stand in the wisdom of men, but in the power of God. Howbeit we speak wisdom among them that are perfect: yet not the wisdom of this world, nor of the princes of this world, that come to nought: But we speak the wisdom of God in a mystery, even the hidden wisdom, which God ordained before the world unto our glory: Which none of the princes of this world knew: for had they known it, they would not have crucified the Lord of glory. But as it is written, Eye hath not seen, nor ear heard, neither have entered into the heart of man, the things which God hath prepared for them that love him. But God hath revealed them unto us by his Spirit: for the Spirit searcheth all things, yea, the deep things of God. For what man knoweth the things of a man, save the spirit of man which is in him?*

even so the things of God knoweth no man, but the Spirit of God. Now we have received, not the spirit of the world, but the spirit which is of God; that we might know the things that are freely given to us of God. Which things also we speak, not in the words which man's wisdom teacheth, but which the Holy Ghost teacheth; comparing spiritual things with spiritual. But the natural man receiveth not the things of the Spirit of God: for they are foolishness unto him: neither can he know them, because they are spiritually discerned. But he that is spiritual judgeth all things, yet he himself is judged of no man. For who hath known the mind of the Lord, that he may instruct him? But we have the mind of Christ.   I Cor. 2:4-16

The following is a correlation to the experience Mrs. Eddy had at the meeting in Chicago when she addressed the CS Association.

... There is nothing covered, that shall not be revealed; neither hid, that shall not be known. ... Also I say unto you, Whosoever shall confess me before men, him shall the Son of man also confess before the angels of God. But he that denieth me before men shall be denied before the angels of God. And whosoever shall speak a word against the Son of man, it shall be forgiven him: but unto him that blasphemeth against the Holy Ghost it shall not be forgiven. And when they bring you unto the synagogues, and unto magistrates, and powers, take ye no thought how or what thing ye shall answer, or what ye shall say: For the Holy Ghost shall teach you in the same hour what ye ought to say.   Luke 12:2,8-12

Mrs. Eddy had much antagonism to meet during this time because of those trying to wrest control of her church. However, this was a turning point in the growth and acceptance of the Cause of Christian Science providing national recognition, wonder and acceptance through the newspapers of the day. Reporters in attendance to record the event were so struck by her uplifting message that many were unable to write. Over a dozen people were healed during her address that day. Below is another example of her inspiration healing others that day.

Emilie B. Hulin of Brooklyn, New York related the following.

"I was seated in the gallery near the stage, where I had a good view of the platform and the audience. I noticed a woman on crutches coming down the main aisle with great difficulty. She was seated in the front row opposite the stage. At the conclusion of Mrs. Eddy's remarks, which took for their topic the spiritual meaning of the Ninety-First Psalm, the woman referred to, arose in her seat and with outstretched arms said something to Mrs. Eddy,

97

who leaned over the platform and said something in reply which I could not hear. Immediately this woman laid down her crutches and walked out straight and erect."

After Mrs. Eddy returned to her home in Boston, she also spoke of the same healing to members of her household as one of the healings that had occurred during or following her address in Chicago. 167

Another attendee relayed the following upon seeing this same woman healed right in front of her by Mrs. Eddy's compassionate outreach.

"I cannot tell you of the awe that fell on me or the impression I received, and I then determined to learn more of this wonderful truth at the fountainhead." 168

Janet T. Coleman relates her experience that day in Chicago. "She had spoken to her students the first day alone [a business meeting of the N.C.S.A.], and to me she seemed more like a man as she spoke to us; her strength, her manner, impressed me with great strength; the next day she spoke in Music Hall to the multitude. Many were healed; that day I saw her as a woman.

That night as I was getting into bed, had not laid down, when at the foot of the bed I saw Jesus' form rise up in white, then our Leader in white rose up beside Him. She put out her arms and embraced Him. He melted into her, then she rose up beyond my gaze. I became so cold, although it was quite warm weather; it took a long time for me to get normal. I came down to Boston a short time after and I went to see our Leader at Commonwealth Avenue [her home at the time]. I was ushered into her parlor upstairs. Two traitors sat there; will not name them. I told Mrs. Eddy that I had something to tell her. At first she said I could go on, then changed her mind and said for me to go into her little room with her. So I did. After I finished, she told me not to speak of it to any one, not even to her students; it was too far beyond the age at that time. When *Christ and Christmas* came out, the picture CHRISTIAN UNITY expressed more what I saw at Chicago." 169

> . . . *the Lord hath created a new thing in the earth, A woman shall compass a man.* Jer. 31:22

Christ and Christmas—"Christian Unity"
(First Edition-1893)

"Mrs. Eddy told Miss Mary Eaton (one of her students): '[Her] return to Concord after her visit to Chicago was like the triumphant entry into Jerusalem followed by the crucifixion.' Miss Eaton replied: 'Are you not the same to this age as Jesus was to his age?' Mrs. Eddy replied: 'Yes, and more, eighteen hundred years of progress!'"[14]

The advent of Jesus of Nazareth marked the first century of the Christian era, but the Christ is without beginning of years or end of days. Throughout all generations both before and after the Christian era, the Christ, as the spiritual idea,—the reflection of God,—has come with some measure of power and grace to all prepared to receive Christ, Truth. Abraham, Jacob, Moses, and the prophets caught glorious glimpses of the Messiah, or Christ, which baptized these seers in the divine nature, the essence of Love. *S & H333:16-26*

"Susie Lang . . . tells how she was puzzled during her first class with Mrs. Eddy by the question of evil's origin and could get no solution, though Mrs. Eddy patiently analysed it for her three times. Ashamed to ask again before the class, Miss Lang approached the teacher privately afterward and was answered in 'four powerful words'—we can only guess at what they were—but they 'stirred my consciousness to its very depths, keeping it in a state of fermentation for several hours, and then the inward voice spoke to me so clearly, so emphatically, the mystery was solved and I stepped out, as it were into another world." 170

There is no power apart from God. Omnipotence has all-power, and to acknowledge any other power is to dishonor God. *Science and Health 228:25-27*

"At the end of the Primary class which he had completed with her just a week or two before, [Charles F.] Kinzel had come to her and told her that his wife would be having a baby shortly after he arrived back in Kansas. Mrs. Eddy had told him to have no fear, she would give the case her prayer and support. Now he wrote that the birth had been swift and easy. Four hours later his wife had risen and dressed the child, and twenty hours later she had got up for good. If it were not for the healthy little newcomer, it would be difficult to realize that anything had happened. Twenty-two years later Kinzel wrote Mrs. Eddy confirming the incident and telling her that the daughter, now a healthy young woman, was studying in Boston." 171

Shall I bring to the birth, and not cause to bring forth? saith the Lord: shall I cause to bring forth, and shut the womb? saith thy God. Isa. 66:9

Calvin A. Frye was Mrs. Eddy's secretary and "right-hand man" for 28 continuous years. During this time he was at her disposal virtually every moment of the day with the exception of *one* half-day vacation! An entire book could be written, and should be, on this remarkable, loyal follower of Mrs. Eddy's. Those enemies of Christian Science that sought to harm Mrs. Eddy through wicked methods of mental malpractice, theosophy, etc., would also seek to attack her most dedicated and faithful workers. Calvin Frye was often at the forefront of these attacks because of his closeness and importance to Mrs. Eddy in assisting her in her founding of her church. She raised Calvin from death no less than five times over this period! These instances are recounted in this book at the time chronologically that they occurred. 172

Calvin Augustus Frye

The first healing Mr. Frye experienced at Mrs. Eddy's hand however was not a recovery from such serious circumstances. This is evidenced in the letter Mrs. Eddy wrote to her attorney.

April 13, 1907

General Frank S. Streeter
My dear Counsellor:

When Mr. Frye came to the college of mine in Boston as resident physician about 20 years ago my husband Dr. Eddy was with me. At his decease I put my accounts into Mr. Frye's keeping and he became my bookkeeper and secretary. His mother was taken to an insane asylum immediately after Mr. Frye was born. After he had been with me a short time I noticed symptoms of aberration, and my grocer and meatman called on me for bills that I thought Mr. Frye had paid, for I had given him the money therefor, but the poor man could not account for it and I gave again the money to discharge the debts over again, and told the butcher and grocer it was all right. Then I healed Mr. Frye of his heredity and have never dealt with a *more honest* person than he has been in all my business since then. I name this to you to prepare you for falsehoods on this score if it is brought up.

Respectfully yours,
M.B. Eddy 173

Heredity is not a law. The remote cause or belief of disease is not dangerous because of its priority and the connection of past mortal thoughts with present. The predisposing cause and the exciting cause are mental. *Science and Health 178:8*

What mean ye, that ye use this proverb concerning the land of Israel, saying, The fathers have eaten sour grapes, and the children's teeth are set on edge? As I live, saith the Lord God, ye shall not have occasion any more to use this proverb in Israel. Behold, all souls are mine; as the soul of the father, so also the soul of the son is mine: . . .
Ezek. 18:2-4

The first account of Mrs. Eddy bringing Calvin Frye back to life was when she lived at 385 Commonwealth Avenue, in Boston, during the late 1880's. Mr. Frye had started down to the kitchen to get a piece of pie, stubbed his toe at the top of the stairs and fell headlong down the stairs. The students worked for him, but they were frightened and believed he had broken his neck, because his head wobbled so. Mrs. Eddy sensed the situation and appeared on the scene. She declared in a commanding way *from the top of the stairs,*

'Calvin Frye, come up here.' After calling him three times she turned her back on the situation and he rose up and followed her. 174

Mrs. Eddy had not only raised him from the dead but had healed Calvin Frye of a broken neck as well. Later the others asked him what he was doing between the time he fell and was raised. He said he was in the kitchen eating pie. 175

What remarkable spiritual dominion and authority! She commanded, from the standpoint of power and authority of the Christ, that her student obey the mandate of Mind, God, and rise up and follow.

> *And they were all amazed, and spake among themselves, saying, What a word is this! for with authority and power he commandeth the unclean spirits, and they come out.* Luke 4:36

The following account is by Mrs. Helen Andrews Nixon of Boston, who studied with Mrs. Eddy in 1889: "In the autumn of 1888 Mr. Nixon, our son Paul, aged six, and I called upon Mrs. Eddy by appointment in her home on Commonwealth Avenue, Boston. A few months' study of Science and Health *with Key to the Scriptures*, and many remarkable demonstrations of healing by means of its teachings, had convinced me that its author must, of necessity, be a good and very wise woman, but I was not anticipating the impression Mrs. Eddy's presence made upon me. Standing beside her as she greeted me, I felt I was in the presence of one who was like Jesus. That she understood me better than I understood myself and could read my thoughts I felt sure. I felt like a little child and was not afraid to have her see my innermost thoughts, for such inexpressible tenderness and love radiated from her. No other human being had I ever met like her." 176

Mrs. Eddy at times had to respond to news articles written about her. The following is in response to an article.

"The doctor in Springfield, alluded to as one of my physicians, has not the degree of M.D. He was a student of mine, but may at present be figuring under one of the many cognomens belonging to the mind-traffic (her reference to one of the many prevalent species of mental or mind cure taking place at the time—all plagiaristic attempts of Mrs. Eddy's work), which are obsolete in Christian Science. This item could be published with authority, namely, that I healed him instantaneously of a severe bronchial affection, which he said had afflicted him for more than twenty years, and was growing rapidly worse. His expectoration was of such an alarming nature that he told me he emptied his spittoon daily, to prevent his daughter from seeing the discharge from his throat." 177

"When Judge Hanna [An ardent early worker of the C.S. Movement who held more positions of trust and responsibility than perhaps any other student] said he just needed a vacation. Mrs. Eddy told him to go up into the tower room at 385 Commonwealth Avenue and work for himself [mentally] for six hours. He did and then he didn't need any vacation." 178

"Mrs. Eddy once went to call on a patient. After she looked at the sick one, she turned her back on him and went and looked out the window, saying, 'Dear heavenly Father, forgive me for looking at matter.' The patient was healed."179

Thou wilt keep him in perfect peace, whose mind is stayed on thee: because he trusteth in thee.   Isa. 26:3

"One day a student manifested a belief of sickness in the class [at the Massachusetts Metaphysical College]. Mrs. Eddy promptly said to him, calling him by name, 'Stand up!' When he indicated he would like to but felt he could not, she spoke still more sharply, 'Stand up!' This was repeated once more, and the student stood. Then Mrs. Eddy gave him an audible treatment there before us all. I cannot repeat exactly what she said; that would be too much to expect of anyone in that room for we all were profoundly moved. But at the end of the treatment the student sat down once more, *healed.*" 180

Walking in the light, we are accustomed to the light and require it; we cannot see in darkness. But eyes accustomed to darkness are pained by the light. When outgrowing the old, you should not fear to put on the new. Your advancing course may provoke envy, but it will also attract respect. When error

---

"A milliner, whom I knew, who told me of her healing, had been confined to her room with consumption. She was sitting all wrapped up at the window one day with her last will and testament in her lap, thinking of nothing but her approaching end. At this time Mrs. Eddy's carriage drove into the street. As it passed, Mrs. Eddy looked at this woman and her sympathy and love went out to her. The invalid thought, 'What is it that this woman has that I have not?' At once the thought came to her, 'I will try Christian Science.' Then, although it was winter and the snow was on the ground, she went to the closet and put on her coat, rubbers, and hat. Although she had not been out of doors all winter, she hurriedly went down to the Christian Science Reading Room, where she asked questions about Christian Science. At this time she was so uplifted that she returned home and prepared her husband's dinner. When he came in, he thought his wife was out of her mind, and it took her a few days to convince him that all was well." 181

. . . thou hast delivered my soul from death: wilt not thou deliver my feet from falling, that I may walk before God in the light of the living? Ps. 56:13

"Rev. Norcross was a Congregational minister serving his church in Bloomington, Illinois, when he volunteered his services to this new church. The Scientists were happy to have a pastor (like other people), and it was the second of September in 1888 when Norcross preached his first sermon in the Christian Science church. That same month Rev. Norcross enrolled in the Massachusetts Metaphysical College and attended the Primary Class taught by Mrs. Eddy which convened on September 17.

"The teacher found him to be earnest and sincere although limited by his years of theological training:

His belief in the power and comprehensiveness of his theological teaching vanished in one outburst, when in the classroom Mrs. Eddy put some question to him, and then worked him down to where all his arguments rested upon a single point, respecting which she asked a

105

question that she knew he must answer rightly if he would be honest with himself and with her. he did not disappoint her expectation, and when the answer came, he burst out with the statement, 'then all my years of theological study don't amount to that' (snapping his fingers). Mrs. Eddy laughed until the tears ran down her cheeks, and all the class burst into merriment, but the beauty of the event was that everyone felt how charged Mr. Norcross was with honesty of purpose, in the manliness of his admission. The merriment of the class was most kindly, for it spoke for the realization that here was an honest and fearless man, and he, too, feeling the love of all, smiled and then broke into a hearty laugh." 182

... the Jews sought the more to kill him, because he not only had broken the sabbath, but said also that God was his Father, making himself equal with God. Then answered Jesus and said unto them, Verily, verily, I say unto you, The Son can do nothing of himself, but what he seeth the Father do: for what things soever he doeth, these also doeth the Son likewise. For the Father loveth the Son, and sheweth him all things that himself doeth: and he will shew him greater works than these, that ye may marvel. For as the Father raiseth up the dead, and quickeneth them; even so the Son quickeneth whom he will. John 5:18-21

Of old, the Jews put to death the Galilean Prophet, the best Christian on earth, for the truth he spoke and demonstrated, while to-day, Jew and Christian can unite in doctrine and denomination on the very basis of Jesus' words and works. The Jew believes that the Messiah or Christ has not yet come; the Christian believes that Christ is God. Here Christian Science intervenes, explains these doctrinal points, cancels the disagreement, and settles the question. Christ, as the true spiritual idea, is the ideal of God now and forever, here and everywhere. The Jew who believes in the First Commandment is a monotheist; he has one omnipresent God. Thus the Jew unites with the Christian's doctrine that God is come and is present now and forever. The Christian who believes in the First Commandment is a monotheist. Thus he virtually unites with the Jew's belief in one God, and recognizes that Jesus Christ is not God, as Jesus himself declared, but is the Son of God. This declaration of Jesus, understood, conflicts not at all with another of his sayings: "I and my Father are one,"—that is, one in quality, not in quantity. As a drop of water is one with the ocean, a ray of light one with the sun, even so God and man, Father and son, are one in being. The Scripture reads: "For in Him we live, and move, and have our being." *Science and Health* 360:28

"A girl who had a scabby trouble on the top of her head so that her hair never grew there and who had been treated by specialists in Europe and this country without help, was taken by her parents to see Mrs. Eddy. Our Leader called the little girl to her and took her on her knee and talked with her about God, and then she told the parents to wash her head with water and to forget that there had been anything wrong with her and treat her as if she were all right. They did this and the condition was healed and her hair grew out naturally." 183

In the *Christian Science Journal* for September, 1891 there appeared a paragraph by Mr. J.B. Harrington describing a "miraculous" recovery of *Science and Health*.

"April 5th, [18]'91, fire destroyed the Edson Block, in which we were located. The building was completely demolished except a *small* portion of the floor of our Reading Room, upon which stood my table with the Science literature *unharmed*. The fire consumed all else in the room, but kindled not upon the sacred pages of *Science and Health*, or any of the other writings of our beloved Teacher and Leader."

Mrs. Eddy's letter of appreciation was truly inspiring:

175 Poplar St., Roslindale, Mass.
June 18, 1891

Mr. J. B. Harrington:

I address you as my student because you study the little Book that our Heavenly Father has written through me for you and for all mankind. . . .

You may not learn through language my feelings when I took that sacred Book rescued by the Divine hand from the devouring flames, and through it saw the meaning of this rescue in the type before me.

I have received presents from my beloved students that I prize beyond all things that I ever before possessed. But dear friend, your gift to me of my last revised *Science and Health* saved from the fire that consumed all around it, but kindled not on its sacred pages, is a gift dearer to me than aught else this world contains.

Just before the Book arrived one of my noblest and best students gave me a large diamond cross, eleven diamonds sparkling on its significant form. They said to me when presenting it: 'The cross is illumined.' Prophetic words! This Book, my book of books, taken by the finger of God out of elements of matter that would have destroyed it, illumines my life, its struggles, its victories.

I cannot thank you, for pen or tongue cannot express my thanks. But my heart speaks to you. Oh! do you hear it saying, Heavenly Father reward his life, give him victory over sense and self and crown him with what the world cannot give and thieves cannot break through and steal...

I am very truly yours in Christ,

Mary B. G. Eddy 184

And I saw another mighty angel come down from heaven, clothed with a cloud: and a rainbow was upon his head, and his face was as it were the sun, and his feet as pillars of fire: And he had in his hand a little book open: and he set his right foot upon the sea, and his left foot on the earth,

And the voice which I heard from heaven spake unto me again, and said, Go and take the little book which is open in the hand of the angel which standeth upon the sea and upon the earth. And I went unto the angel, and said unto him, Give me the little book. And he said unto me, Take it, and eat it up; and it shall make thy belly bitter, but it shall be in thy mouth sweet as honey. And I took the little book out of the angel's hand, and ate it up; and it was in my mouth sweet as honey: and as soon as I had eaten it, my belly was bitter. And he said unto me, Thou must prophesy again before many peoples, and nations, and tongues, and kings.   Rev. 10:1,2,8-11

This angel or message which comes from God, clothed with a cloud, prefigures divine Science. To mortal sense Science seems at first obscure, abstract, and dark; but a bright promise crowns its brow. When understood, it is Truth's prism and praise. When you look it fairly in the face, you can heal by its means, and it has for you a light above the sun, for God "is the light thereof." Its feet are pillars of fire, foundations of Truth and Love. It brings the baptism of the Holy Ghost, whose flames of Truth were prophetically described by John the Baptist as consuming error.

This angel had in his hand "a little book," open for all to read and understand. Did this same book contain the revelation of divine Science, the "right foot" or dominant power of which was upon the sea,—upon elementary, latent error, the source of all error's visible forms? The angel's left foot was upon the earth; that is, a secondary power was exercised upon visible error and audible sin. The "still, small voice" of scientific thought reaches over continent and ocean to the globe's remotest bound. The inaudible voice of Truth is, to the human mind, "as when a lion roareth." It is heard in the desert and in dark places of fear. It arouses the "seven thunders" of evil, and stirs their latent forces to utter the full diapason of secret tones. Then is the power of Truth demonstrated,—made manifest in the destruction of error. Then will a voice from harmony cry: "Go and take the little book. . . . Take it, and eat it up; and it shall make thy belly bitter, but it shall be in thy mouth sweet as

honey." Mortals, obey the heavenly evangel. Take divine Science. Read this book from beginning to end. Study it, ponder it. It will be indeed sweet at its first taste, when it heals you; but murmur not over Truth, if you find its digestion bitter.
Science and Health 558:9-23 *next page*

gave them power and authority. . . Luke 9:1

DOMINION
1892-1910

"Pleasant View" was the name of her cherished home in Concord, New Hampshire. Much of the maturing of her church came about during her life at Pleasant View, a period spanning seventeen years (1892-1908). Her exercise of spiritual dominion and demonstration of God's infinite power in the minutae of daily life and the growth of her church was always inspiring, a lesson to all who had the privilege of her instruction, or benefit of her healing ability.

Pleasant View

Ira O. Knapp, one of Mrs. Eddy's most trusted and valued students relates an interesting sidelight on discipline in her church regarding one of the members.

"One of the early cases that came before (the Directors) was a charge of immoral conduct against a First Member who was a student of Mrs. Eddy's. From the evidence submitted, the Directors were convinced that the charges were sustained. They, therefore, removed the individual from membership in the church, and took his practitioner's card out of the *Christian Science Journal.* (thereby depriving him of his livelihood) That punishment in no wise healed the individual, but made him so rebellious that he threatened a lawsuit in revenge.

"When Mrs. Eddy heard of this case, she asked the Directors to restore her student to full church membership, including his office as a First Member, and to replace his card in the *Journal.* This resulted in a complete healing of the individual." 185

> *. . . as ye would that men should do to you, do ye also to them likewise. For if ye love them which love you, what thank have ye? for sinners also love those that love them.*
>
> *But love ye your enemies, and do good, and lend, hoping for nothing again; and your reward shall be great, and ye shall be the children of the Highest: for he is kind unto the unthankful and to the evil. Be ye therefore merciful, as your Father also is merciful. Judge not, and ye shall not be judged: condemn not, and ye shall not be condemned: forgive, and ye shall be forgiven:. . . .* Luke 6:31,32,35-37

James F. Gilman was the artist, along with Mrs. Eddy, that was responsible for the pictures in *Christ and Christmas.* In his recollections he showed how one benefited from receiving a rebuke from Mrs. Eddy the right way. He recounts the experience the day following his rebuke from her, when he met again with her.

". . . I heard the gentle rustle on the stairs that I had learned to know, followed by her appearance in the doorway. Instantly I felt that she perceived the state of my mind upon seeing me, as I arose and advanced a step to meet her and receive her extended hand of welcome. She retained the hold upon my hand as she stood near in her precious spiritual way, and with earnest solicitation said yearningly like a mother, 'It seems hard to bear, I know. You won't feel hard toward me, will you? I felt I must be severe because you needed it; but it was hard for me to be so.' I was silent; words failed me for the moment, but Mrs. Eddy continued to look for hoped-for audible signs of submissive acceptance of her rebuke as proceeding from motives of love on her part, and thus to plead with me as a mother with a son she would save. I finally found voice to say that there was 'nothing but gratitude in my mind for her faithfulness toward me,' to which she joyfully responded, 'I am so glad!' 'Oh,!' she said with great feeling, 'you know what burdens I have borne through the necessity I have felt for rebuking students, but could not receive my rebuke as coming from true love for them. This is the great test of the true student. If they are found unwilling to bear this test, they are not worthy to be found in this work. It is the resentment that rebuke uncovers or excites that makes up the burden—*the terrible burden* that I have had, and still have to bear in this pioneer work of Christian Science. It was nothing but a constant joy to me to minister to the needs of humanity in the healing work. It was when I began to teach and be faithful with students that I began to know of suffering and sorrow.'" 186

> Jesus taught by the wayside, in humble homes. He spake of Truth and Love to artless listeners and dull disciples. His immortal words were articulated in a decaying language, and then left to the providence of God. Christian Science was to interpret them; and woman, "last at the cross," was to awaken the dull senses, intoxicated with pleasure or pain, to the infinite meaning of those words. *Miscellaneous Writings 99:32*

At times Mrs. Eddy's demeanor was totally different. As the occasion required she rose "in the strength of the spirit" rebuking error in the treatment of a student or situation, taking on the appearance of someone considerably taller than when one would see her in other circumstances.

Julia Bartlett confirms this in her reminiscence when she said, "I never saw a grander demonstration of Truth than I witnessed as a young student when I saw our Leader stand before one who had for a long time seemed to be held by a very stubborn error. When it did not yield, she gradually rose to a greater and greater power until she seemed a tower of strength, not sparing the error the sharp cutting rebuke necessary for its destruction, unitl this woman was free, and she has since been a faithful worker in the Cause of Christian Science."[15]

———————

"On going downstairs to breakfast one morning, I met Miss Morgan, the housekeeper, and she told me that the farmer (who served Mrs. Eddy with milk) when he came that morning seemed to be very solemn and said his well was frozen and the well from which he obtained water for his cattle was empty. [Mrs. Eddy had instructed her students to work several weeks for no rain at this time because of the necessity of finishing the roof work on The Mother Church, which was under construction.] On the day before, he was obliged to go to a brook or river, which was frozen and some distance away. He had taken barrels in his wagon which he filled with ice and snow from the river and took home to melt, so as to have water for his cows. This was very hard work. It took a long time and he was much distressed. During that day I mentioned his difficulties to Mother, telling her just what happened. She smiled and said, 'Oh, if he only knew;' then after a moment's silence, 'Love fills that well.' The next morning when the farmer brought the milk, he was overjoyed and told Miss Morgan what a wonderful thing had occurred. That morning early, when he had gone out to attend the cattle, he found the well full of water, and in spite of the bitter cold day, with all the ice and snow around, the well was full of water. He said it must have been Mrs. Eddy's prayers that had done it all. She must have had something to do with it for it was a miracle. He had a great reverence for Mrs. Eddy although he was not a Scientist. That day, when we were at dinner, I told Mother what had happened, and just what the man had said. Oh, the joy and sweetness, the illumination and love of her face is ever to be remembered; her expressions of praise and gratitude to God were glorious, and she said, 'Oh, didn't I know.' She gave us a lesson in Christian Science which has blessed us ever since." 187

Mrs. Eddy turned to Gilbert Carpenter (at one time a secretary in her home) and said in explanation, "Oh, Mr. Carpenter! Isn't God good! Oh, trust in the dear, good God!" To him this seemed a present-day fulfillment of the words of Scripture (II Kings 3:17):

For thus saith the Lord, Ye shall not see wind, neither shall ye see rain; yet that valley shall be filled with water, that ye may drink, both ye, and your cattle, and your beasts. 188

In the reminiscences of Edward P. Bates [one of the truly inspiring accounts of how God works in the affairs of men— when true spiritual understanding demonstrates "thy will be done in earth as it is in heaven" concerning his considerable part in the construction of the original edifice of The Mother Church, we read his recollection of a conversation with Mrs. Eddy.

"Dinner was duly served and while at dinner, she stopped eating and said, 'Mr. Bates, the Directors were up here yesterday and I told them that, but for you, the church would never have been built.'

"I replied, 'Mrs. Eddy, but for you the church would never have been built.'

"She said again, 'Mr. Bates, but for you the church would never have been built.'

"I again replied, 'But for you, Mrs. Eddy, the church never would have been built.'

"The third time she said, 'Mr. Bates, if you had not come and helped me, the church never would have been built.'

"I replied, 'Mrs. Eddy, but for your demonstrations the church would never have been built.' There was no further conversation of this nature at the table, and after dinner we retired again to the library and were alone for some time.

"After a general conversation, she looked me straight in the eye and said, 'Mr. Bates, are you prepared for what is to come?' I could not think what she meant, and asked her. She said, 'Are you prepared for the treatment you will receive?' I could not imagine what she meant. I supposed that everybody would be so glad the church was built and we could hold services in our own temple that they would rejoice with everyone who had anything to do with its construction. She went on to say, 'You came here in answer to prayer. I prayed God for three months to send me a man to finish the church. He heard my prayer and sent you and you followed my demonstration and the church is finished; — but they will hate you for helping Mother.' This seemed incomprehensible. She went on to say, 'They will shun you; they will try to ruin you morally, physically, financially and spiritually.' Of this I had ample proof within a few weeks."
189

114

"This shows us what Mr. Bates had to deal with for being faithful; but Mrs. Eddy knew the treatment very well for she had received it a thousand times more severely than Mr. Bates. She knew how M.A.M. (malicious animal magnetism) operated through her materially minded students to deny her and they still are. Bates continued, "Before my leaving, she said, 'We have built the church; it will be easy for branch churches to build their structures as we have cleared the way. If The Mother Church had not been finished at the time I designated, it would have remained a monument to the error and my students would have died sudden and unnatural deaths. You have helped me to save them.' " 190

. . . "It was during the month of March that I began to realize what Mrs. Eddy meant when she said, 'The students will shun you,' et cetera. I found, in an audience of over one thousand students, there were hardly fifteen or twenty of them that would speak to me at all, and many of them took deliberate pains to shun my personality. It went about the church currently that the Bateses were animal magnetism and that if people wanted to be well and live, they must shun the Bateses. Mrs. Eddy never wrote nor taught that any one person or any one set of persons embodied animal magnetism. We bore this as well as we could, but it continued with gradually less pressure until I was appointed President of the church for the third term, when it nearly died out. I remember well that many students came to me and took my hand, saying that they had been abusing me both orally and mentally and wanted to be forgiven. I told them that I had nothing against them and was glad if they wanted to do right instead of wrong." 191

"Mrs. Eddy once said to Miss Shannon [Clara M. Sainsbury Shannon, C.S.D., was a worker in Mrs. Eddy's home from 1894-1903], 'You have wonderful physical health, nothing seems to touch you.' However, there came a day, Miss Shannon recounted, when she experienced a severe attack of diphtheria. She did not want Mrs. Eddy to know how ill she was, and thus be a burden to her, and she went to the Buswells at Christian Science Hall, Concord. On arrival, she was found to be very ill and was put to bed. They wanted to send to Boston for James A. Neal [a fellow Christian Scientist and practitioner], but there was no time for that. When it seemed that Miss Shannon could not live another ten minutes, Mrs. Eddy drove up to the door, and enquired after the patient. Mrs. Buswell told her of the condition. Mrs. Eddy said, 'Go and tell her there is nothing to fear; that Love is taking care of her, and that I am praying for her.' When Miss Shannon received this message all fear left her and she felt instantaneous relief. She knew she was healed. She fell asleep, and did not wake until 8 o'clock the next morning. She had not slept the previous night. She dressed and came down to breakfast with Mr. and Mrs. Buswell, and found two letters from Mrs. Eddy telling her to return. Miss Shannon was perfectly well and walked back to Pleasant View after breakfast. She told Mrs. Eddy how her words had healed her." 192

> *The nobleman saith unto him, Sir, come down ere my child die. Jesus saith unto him, Go thy way; thy son liveth. And the man believed the word that Jesus had spoken unto him, and he went his way. And as he was now going down, his servants met him, and told him, saying, Thy son liveth. Then inquired he of them the hour when he began to amend. And they said unto him, Yesterday at the seventh hour the fever left him. So the father knew that it was at the same hour, in the which Jesus said unto him, Thy son liveth: and himself believed, and his whole house.* John 4:49-53

"An interesting experience may be related [from Edward Everett Norwood, another student of Mrs. Eddy's]: Sometime before this I had withdrawn from the Methodist church, and felt their prayers and appeals quite forcibly—the mesmerism of old theology. In fact for some time I was utterly miserable—knew the cause—but could not seem to meet it. At this time, in response to Mrs. Eddy's invitation, to 'Please write again and let me know how you are getting along,' I wrote her, and mentioned the mental darkness. I have not forgotten the wonderful freedom that came to me three days later when she read my letter, and the claim was instantly healed. I rejoiced with joy unspeakable, and thanked God."193

> *And the chief priests and scribes sought how they might kill him...*
> Luke 22:2

A member of Mrs. Eddy's household had an appointment with the dentist and Mrs. Eddy needed her just when the appointment was scheduled [for some very important work] and would not let her go. She said that if she had, she would have been allowing mortal mind to rob [that *time* that] should be sacrificed for the whole world's good. The need was met without the dentist and the tooth filled with substance [,metaphysically]. 194

> Divine Love always has met and always will meet every human need. It is not well to imagine that Jesus demonstrated the divine power to heal only for a select number or for a limited period of time, since to all mankind and in every hour, divine Love supplies all good. *S&H 494:10*

"One day, while I was taking Mrs. Eddy's dictation, she sent me with a message to Mr. Frye, who was in his room. When I reached the door, which was open, I saw him lying on his back on the carpet, apparently lifeless. I returned to our Leader and told her about it saying, 'It seems as though he has fainted.' She immediately rose and we both went to his room. She kneeled beside him and lifted his arm, which fell inert. Then she began to talk to him. I had been praying for him, but what she said to him was a revelation, to which I listened in wonder. Such heavenly words, and tenderness, such expression of love I had never heard, telling him the truth of man's relationship to God. After a while he opened his eyes, and as soon as Mother saw that he was becoming conscious, her voice changed, and most severely she rebuked the error that seemed to be attacking him. Her voice and manner were so different, according to the need, that I was deeply impressed.

"Presently she told him to rise on his feet, and gave him her hand to help him up. Then she turned round and went out of the room down the passage where she had been sitting. Then she called out, 'Calvin, come here!' And he followed her. She spoke to him for several minutes, striving to wake him up—at times, thundering against the error. Then she said, 'Now you can go back to your room.' He went from the passage towards his room, but before he entered, she called him again and talked to him, and this was repeated several times.

"I said, 'Oh, Mother, couldn't you let him sit down a few minutes?' She said, 'No, if he sits down, he may not waken again—he must be aroused—he is not quite awakened yet!' She began to talk to him again and reminded him of the time when Martha [Morgan] and Mrs. Frye together drove out and spent the day

117

there, and she began to remind him of the experiences of that day. That reached him, and she said, 'You haven't forgotten, Calvin?' and he said, 'No, Mother!' and laughed heartily. Then she talked more of the Truth to him and told him he could go back to his room and this time 'watch.'

"She explained to me that when you speak the truth to anyone, if the truth you speak causes him to laugh, cry, or get angry, you have reached the thought that needed correction.

"Mr. Frye was a changed man after that experience, to which he never referred. To me, such a demonstration was a glorious inspiration and lesson." 195

As has been mentioned, Mrs. Eddy rarely appeared in public without someone being healed by her constant reflection of God's infinite love, and never did she preach without some needy person receiving benefit from her inspiring sermon or address. The following account when Mrs. Eddy was speaking from the pulpit is provided by Edward P. Bates, C.S.B., a faithful student of Mrs. Eddy's.

"During this address several healings took place; one in particular, an account of which was published in the *Journal* a few months afterwards. A man came in with two crutches, listened to her and went out without them. When he reached the house he was visiting on Tremont Street, his friends asked him where his crutches were; he said he did not know, he had never seen them since he went into that church and heard that woman talk. The janitor looked for the crutches but never found them." 196

"The day preceding our Leader's first address in The Mother Church (May twenty-sixth, 1895), Mother went from Concord to Boston, and remained in The Mother's Room at the Church all night. The next morning, Sunday, during the singing of the second hymn, she was conducted up the aisle of the church to the reader's platform by Mr. E. P. Bates, and she stood at the reader's desk and addressed the congregation. You will find that wonderful and inspiring address on page 106 of *Miscellaneous Writings*. Her words were a great arousal and I learned that thirteen people were healed while she was speaking—there may have been others of whom I did not know." 197

And he came down with them, and stood in the plain, and the company of his disciples, and a great multitude of people out of all Judaea and Jerusalem, and from the sea coast of Tyre and Sidon, which came to hear him, and to be healed of their diseases; And they that were vexed with unclean spirits: and they were healed. And the whole multitude sought to touch him: for there went virtue out of him, and healed them all. Luke 6:17-19

"Mr. G. of Boston told me that his wife's eldest brother had a rupture which he had seen, and which was so bad that the man could not stand on his feet with it, and that he always had to wear a truss for support. This man went to the original Mother Church to one of the meetings at which Mrs. Eddy spoke, and was healed during the service." 198

The following illustrates Mrs. Eddy's wisdom in listening to God regarding every detail of her life and the formation and growth of her church. God told her what was needed in the by-laws of her church just as much as when she needed to purchase a piece of property, because she was always *listening*.

"Mrs. Eddy made a practice of doing things quickly when it was revealed to her that they should be done. In response to a demonstration, we saw the owner of 95 Falmouth Street for the first time on Christmas Eve. Christmas morning before eleven o'clock we had a contract for the house and had paid part of the purchase money as per agreement. We knew before we had finished the original Mother Church, judging from the constant growth of our audiences, that we should need a larger building and we should need all the property on that block for the purpose. Later on we purchased 97 Falmouth Street, all in one day. 99 Falmouth Street hung along a while until Mrs. Bates received a telegram from Mrs. Eddy: 'Buy Ninety-nine at once or you will never get it.' The party who was to furnish the money for the purchase lived in a distant city, but Mrs. Bates, in response to this order, went to the real estate agent and bought the house that day. Next we bought number 101 in a similar manner." 199

The following story is a healing that took place after Mrs. Eddy's second address in The Mother Church and appeared in the columns of the *Journal* (Vol. xiv, p.550) a year later.

"The father of one of my students who has long been connected with one of the banks in the city, went into the vice-president's room one day about four weeks ago, and found the vice-president sitting there apparently much dazed about something. The caller was greeted by the question, 'Do you know anything about Christian Science?' My friend said, 'Yes; but why do you ask?' The vice-president replied: 'Because an old friend of mine, a man I have known for years, has just been here, and he told me what seems to me to be a miracle. This man had been a pronounced invalid for years and had grown so irritable that his family could scarcely live with him. He was unable to walk without support. Last January he was visiting in Boston not far from the Christian Science Church there. Sunday morning, hearing the chimes, he asked to what church they belonged. On being informed that it was the Christian Science Church, and that the worshippers in that church claimed to heal the sick, he went to the service. He said he had not been in there long when a woman came in who was announced as Mrs. Eddy, and she gave a talk. She had not talked long, until all of a sudden he felt he was healed. He did not miss his canes until after he reached the house of his friend. The next day he bought *Science and Health*, a book written by the same Mrs. Eddy who spoke in the church. Since then he has been an ardent student of that book. This is his story,' said the vice-president, 'and I don't believe even he realizes the transformation that has taken place in him. I assure you I never saw so great a change in any person. His face was radiant with health and happiness and for two hours he has talked on Christian Science. I did not know he could be so enthusiastic on anything.'. . . " 200

> Then said Jesus to those Jews which believed on him, If ye continue in my word, then are ye my disciples indeed; And ye shall know the truth, and the truth shall make you free. John 8:31,32

> . . . be not conformed to this world: but be ye transformed by the renewing of your mind, that ye may prove what is that good, and acceptable, and perfect, will of God. Rom. 12:2

"One of Mrs. Eddy's students had worked for herself without success and had another student work for her without success; and she was nearly passing on. Mrs. Eddy sent a message to her which read as follows: 'God gave you an abiding sense of Life that needs not to be fought for. Remember this and you will live forever.'

"She recovered at once." 201

There are so many instances of God's protection of Mrs. Eddy. Mortal mind (evil) was always trying to kill her or use others to kill her, but her divinely appointed mission to humanity under God's precious care always protected her.

"Clara Shannon has told of a time that [Dr. Ebenezer] Foster-Eddy (Mrs. Eddy's adopted son) was driving Mother along State Street when the city of Concord was doing work on the street and had a big hole dug in the middle. The doctor drove right into the hole and out again, and Mrs. Eddy was thrown out of the carriage as it went down and back up. The wheel was just about to come over her neck and face, and she said afterward, 'Love stopped that wheel, and would not let it come over me.'" 202

> *And we have known and believed the love that God hath to us. God is love; and he that dwelleth in love dwelleth in God, and God in him.*
> I John 4:16

"At Pleasant View, dominion over weather, storms, etc., was just the same as over other seeming material conditions. After a prolonged drought, the inharmonious condition was met by our Leader's watching and praying, the effect being rain when there was not a cloud visible in the sky. At other times heavy, dark clouds appeared when there was no rain. Also Truth was demonstrated to quell storms.

"During part of the year, cyclones were sometimes experienced at Concord, and one day Miss Morgan came to see me and said that the clouds were gathering, and there was going to be a dreadful storm, and she called me to look through the windows of her room, which was at the end of the house, looking towards the stables. Above, I saw dark clouds which seemed to be coming towards us very rapidly, and as Mother had told me whenever I saw a cyclone or storm coming I must let her know, I went to her room immediately and told her. She rose and went to the verandah at the back of the house; by that time, the clouds had reached overhead. She then went into the front vestibule and looked on that side of the house. Then she returned to the verandah, and I heard her say, 'The children in Boston!' (meaning her students-the Directors) I ran downstairs to the front door, opened it and went outside, looked up and saw the clouds hanging over the house—very heavy black clouds, and in the middle, right over the house was a rift; they were dividing—part were going one way and the other part in the opposite direction. This seemed to be such a strange phenomenon that I went in, closed the door, and went upstairs to Mother, on the verandah, and told her what I saw. I said, 'The clouds are dividing just overhead!' She said, 'Clouds—what do you mean? Are there any clouds?' I said, 'No, Mother!' She was looking up, and I could see by the expression on her face that she was not seeing clouds, but was realizing the Truth. I saw the black clouds turn to indigo, to light grey, to white, fleecy clouds, which dissolved, and there were no more, and she said to me, 'There are no clouds to hide God's face, and there is nothing that can come between the light and us. It is divine Love's weather.' That was early in the evening; the wind had been blowing terrifically, and Mr. Frye and another gentleman were in the attic trying to pull down a large American flag. It was a 'Fete' day, and a gentleman had sent his flag to Mrs. Eddy; it was very large. She had it hoisted, and Mr. Frye and his friend were trying to pull it down, and the strength of the two men was not sufficient to pull down the flag, but suddenly the wind subsided and the flag yielded. Next morning early, when the mail was delivered, the postman was amazed to see that nothing had been disturbed in the garden as, from a short distance down the road and in the town, there was a great deal of damage. The lesson I learned then, through that experience, has since helped me through many storms by sea and on land.

"Blizzard: Sometime, during the winter, just before the hour at which Mrs. Eddy took her daily drive, there would be a heavy snow storm which would develop into a blizzard and snow drifts, so that one could scarcely see the opposite side of the road. One day, when it seemed very severe, and this error had to be overcome, from blinding snowstorm, in a short time, a beautiful afternoon was experienced; it stopped snowing and drifting, the sun came out, and everything was covered with new white snow—it was

122

perfect; and we had every proof that error was trying to interfere and deprive our Leader of the little recreation that her drive afforded. Thank God for that victory." 203

He maketh the storm a calm, so that the waves thereof are still.
Psalm 107:29

"Another day when there was a snow storm, and the snow was falling heavily, she went into the garden in the same clothing which she was wearing indoors—without coat or hat. She asked someone to tell her when the snow had reached a pile above her head. She stood there until this friend told her that it had gone as high above her as it could, when she came in and brushed the snow off wherever it had accumulated, and thus proved that cold and inclement weather could not do her any harm." 204

"At one time, some of the students at Mrs. Eddy's Pleasant View home in Concord were sitting in front of a window working against a storm which was approaching; suddenly Mrs. Eddy came up behind them and said, 'You are not meeting it because you are mesmerized by the appearance.' Then she swept them aside, took up the case herself, and in a short time they saw the blue sky appear through the center of the storm cloud." 205

"Mrs. Eddy's maid was working in the room where Mrs. Eddy was and all of a sudden it got very dark and it surprised her so much that she looked out of a window back of Mrs. Eddy and saw a most terrible storm. There were black clouds shaped like funnels rolling around and coming straight towards Mrs. Eddy's home. She had never seen anything like it. Then she went out of the room about her work and when she came back a short time afterwards, Mrs. Eddy said to her; 'Have you looked out of the window?' No, she had not, but she did and there was all sunshine and clear skies. The storm had disappeared." 206

Henrietta Chanfrau [at one time a worker in Mrs. Eddy's home in Concord—Pleasant View] relates in her *Reminiscences of Mary Baker Eddy*, another instance when Mrs. Eddy raised Calvin Frye from death.

"One morning about ten o'clock, Mr. Frye was taken with a belief of suffering and apparently was passing on. Mrs. Eddy was told of it and immediately came to his room where several of us were gathered. She walked straight up to where he was lying on his bed and, standing over him, called out, 'Calvin, rise up! They are trying to kill your Leader!' She repeated this two or three times. Suddenly he sat up, looked about him, and was restored immediately to health. Then she told him to come with her to her study, where she talked with him alone for about half an hour. This was a most remarkable experience, and I shall always recall it when I wish to think of what absolute Christian Science healing is." 207

During the founding of her church Mrs. Eddy would frequently rely on the services of attorneys in finding the exact wording or law that was required to fit a particular need.

"When the Boston attorneys failed to find a law by which our church could obtain a charter, I called in the services of the Hon. Reuben Walker, now Judge of the Supreme Court of the State of New Hampshire. I asked him to find for us a law to fit the case. He said that he knew of no such law upon the statute books. I asked him upon what was human law based. He reflected and then said, 'Upon the divine law. But,' he said, 'if the Massachusetts abstracter of law can find no such statute, how can I?' To this I replied, 'God has somewhere provided such a law and I know you can find it.'

"Three days later my secretary visited him, and found him lost in a pile of law books he had been examining. His greeting was, 'I have found the law.' It was a statute which was enacted to suit the needs of the Methodist Church, and fully met our requirements." 208

There is to-day danger of repeating the offence of the Jews by limiting the Holy One of Israel and asking: "Can God furnish a table in the wilderness?" (Ps. 78:19) What cannot God do?
Science and Health 135:17

124

In 1897, Mrs. Eddy invited her followers to visit her at Pleasant View, July 4th, Independence Day. Many were the followers that traveled that day by train or carriage. One of the attenders, a Mrs. Jessie Cooper, brought her nine-year-old son and seven-year-old daughter all the way from Kansas City. The daughter had been suffering severely from a boil on her curly-haired head. Following Mrs. Eddy's words to those that had come, she received them through the port-cochere where she was seated on the porch. When Mrs. Cooper and her children reached Mrs. Eddy quite an impression was made upon the mother whose account was preserved below.

"I wish I could make the world know what I saw when Mrs. Eddy looked at those children. It was a revelation to me. I saw for the first time the real Mother-Love, and I knew that I did not have it. I had a strange, agonized sense of being absolutely cut off from the children. It is impossible to put into words what the uncovering of my own lack of the real Mother-Love meant to me.

"As I turned in the procession and walked toward the line of trees in the front of the yard, there was a bird sitting on the limb of a tree, and I saw the same Love, poured out on that bird that I had seen flow from Mrs. Eddy to my children. I looked down at the grass and the flowers and there was the same Love resting on them. It is difficult for me to put into words what I saw. This Love was everywhere, like the light, but it was divine, not mere human affection.

"I looked at the people milling around on the lawn and I saw it poured out on them. I thought of the various discords in this field, and I saw, for the first time, the absolute unreality of everything but this infinite Love. It was not only everywhere present, like the light, but it was an intelligent presence that spoke to me, and I found myself weeping as I walked back and forth under the trees and saying out loud, 'Why did I never know you before? Why have I not known you always?' . . .

"When we got back to the hotel, there was no boil on my child's head. It was just as flat as the back of her hand. . . .

"Each time I saw Mrs. Eddy I had a wonderful revelation of God. I know she was no ordinary woman. God had anointed her with the oil of gladness above her fellows, . . . " 209

Thou lovest righteousness, and hatest wickedness: therefore God, thy God, hath anointed thee with the oil of gladness above thy fellows.
Ps. 45:7

During the construction of Christian Science Hall in Concord, N.H., Mrs. Eddy was attentive to all the details of the construction of the edifice until its completion. ". . . I inspected the work every day, suggested the details outside and inside from the foundations to the tower, and saw them carried out. One day the carpenter's foreman said to me: 'I want to be let off for a few days. I do not feel able to keep about. I am feeling an old ailment my mother had.' I healed him on the spot. He remained at work, and the next morning said to Mr. George H. Moore of Concord, 'I am as well as I ever was.'" 210

In February of the following year Mrs. Eddy gave an address in Christian Science Hall, this church of her home community. "When the time came for Mrs. Eddy to speak, she stepped forward gracefully to the desk designed for her, and read the 91st Psalm, without using glasses." (this was in her 78th year) 211

Frequently, those who were of the greatest service to Mrs. Eddy were under the most severe attacks. Mrs. Eddy accomplished so much good during her time here and evil was trying all the while to stop her. It could never stop her directly, because she was ever alert to its methods, so it attempted to harm her through those who were most important to her, her most faithful and helpful students. Calvin Frye, as was mentioned, was a frequent target of this malicious mental influence. Ira O. Knapp and Flavia S. Knapp were two of her most trusted students. Mrs. Eddy intended for Mrs. Knapp to teach the Normal Class, taking over the teaching of classes previously taught by herself.

"The critical attacks upon Flavia Knapp were less deserved and more insidious, and her struggle against this error was severe. Mrs. Knapp was a fine practitioner with many remarkable healings to her credit. Late in February [1898] she told briefly of some of these healings in a very impressive testimony in the Mother Church ending with her own healing, contrasting the thirteen years of her invalidism with her thirteen years of Christian Science practice. After she had resumed her seat she rose again and in a

126

tone never forgotten by some of her auditors she said, 'For which of these works do ye stone me?'

"Mrs Knapp had struck at the root of the error assailing her, but a very short time later, after prolonged exposure to bitterly cold weather while responding to a patient's call, the animal magnetism manifested itself as pneumonia, and she passed away on the fifteenth of March.

"About this time Mrs. Eddy had requested that her household not bring her any messages about death, so the news of Mrs. Knapp's illness and death was withheld from her until too late. When she heard of it she sent a telegram to one of Mrs. Knapp's students, Miss Isable Harrington, requesting her to come to Pleasant View as she wished to ask her about Mrs. Knapp:

When Miss Harrington arrived, Mrs. Eddy greeted her tenderly. They sat in Mrs. Eddy's sitting-room while Miss Harrington told her about Mrs. Knapp's illness and passing. Mrs. Eddy listened intently and finally said with emphasis, 'When will my people learn when to speak and when not to speak! She was my best student. I needed her. Why, I could have healed her just like that,' and she snapped her fingers in the air. When the call was over, Mrs. Eddy went to the head of the stairs with Miss Harrington, kissed her cheek tenderly, and thanked her for coming and for her service to the field." 212

"Mrs. Eddy's followers in the 1890's performed the marvelous healings that Jesus' disciples had wrought more than nineteen hundred years earlier. In both cases the understanding and spirituality of the Leader were manifested through their students, but perhaps the nineteenth century disciples were more aware of this fact. Members of Mr. Buswell's class were aware of it, and it is altogether possible that many of them had experiences similar to that of two Canadian students, Mr. and Mrs. Higman, as described in Mrs. Higman's letter to her teacher:

Ottowa, July 16, 1898

Dear Mr. Buswell:

Your kind letter received. Every word you say to us we value and heed.

About six weeks ago on Monday next a girl was brought to me far gone in consumption. It was a most discouraging case, if one allowed the senses to judge. I had to say to myself, 'Surely you would not let her die because it looks like a failure before you start?' I said, 'No; whatever the result, my duty is clear.' After one week there was a slight improvement; in two weeks I said to her mother (a poor woman and a widow), 'The money you used to spend on cod-liver oil will buy *Science and Health* in a few weeks.' She consented, and paid me for it. I wrote to her while in Concord, and today she is well,—not half well, but perfectly recovered,—no cough, happy and *well*. This girl and a man I have tried for a long time to cure of drunkenness, both appeared to my consciousness very clearly while the Mother [Mrs. Eddy], in class that day said, "Make drunkenness appear hateful to a man. Show him the loathsomeness of it, and he is cured. Destroy the fear of sickness and your patient is cured.' Both of these cases are well today, and they were the only ones I had in mind while she spoke. When I tell you I had tried my best for four months to sober this man for his wife and children's sake, you will believe as I do, that the illumination of Mrs. Eddy's thought shone through mine and did the work. . . .

Elizabeth Higman   213

Edward E. Norwood relates in his reminiscences the incredible spiritual insight that Mrs. Eddy had, and in some measure conveyed, if only temporarily, to those in her class—in a sense lifting the "veil" of matter and providing a glimpse of the real world of Spirit.

"I had prayed earnestly for a great unfoldment of good, a clearer and broader vision, and suddenly, during the second day's lesson it came. . . . Suddenly it did seem a veil was lifted or a window opened, and I could see, in one of those supreme moments (that never leave one where it found him) the reality of things—the majestic oneness of the spiritual universe—its vast quietness—the infinite Mind—the eternal stillness, which is really primal energy. And as I looked, the symbols around me, the personalities, the class, all externals, seemed to fade, and a wondrous sense of reality appeared—and ah, my friends, it was awesome! I understood somewhat what our Leader means by 'The unlabored motion of Mind,' and that what mortal mind calls activity is lethargy, inaction, inertia, and is the seeming obstruction in the way of the operation of divine law. I realized, to some extent, the joy and activity of what is forever going on in Mind, and all that hides it is the misty curtain of false belief, which lifts at intervals. I got such a glimpse of the Way—the road our Leader trod—the first one since Jesus walked in it, and my heart yearned to go on! But anon the veil dropped down, and I was back again. . . .

128

"Upon relating this once to Mr. Armstrong, (then publisher of Mrs. Eddy's books) he told me of a similar experience when, just before the class, Mrs. Eddy called him to Pleasant View to consult about substitute First Reader (in Judge Hanna's absence). She told him about the coming Class, and what she hoped it would do for the world. He said as she talked, the wonderful vista opened, and for a few moments he saw what *she* saw, and he said, 'I never dreamed of such heaven on earth.' And this was the mental state in which that God-blest woman abode more or less all the time!" 214

> *. . . we have not followed cunningly devised fables, when we made known unto you the power and coming of our Lord Jesus Christ, but were eyewitnesses of his majesty. For he received from God the Father honour and glory, when there came such a voice to him from the excellent glory, This is my beloved Son, in whom I am well pleased. And this voice which came from heaven we heard, when we were with him in the holy mount. We have also a more sure word of prophecy; whereunto ye do well that ye take heed, as unto a light that shineth in a dark place, until the day dawn, and the day star arise in your hearts: Knowing this first, that no prophecy of the scripture is of any private interpretation. For the prophecy came not in old time by the will of man: but holy men of God spake as they were moved by the Holy Ghost.* II Pet. 1:16-21

The rays of infinite Truth, when gathered into the focus of ideas, bring light instantaneously, whereas a thousand years of human doctrines, hypotheses, and vague conjectures emit no such effulgence. *Science and Health 504:23*

> *Thy kingdom come. Thy will be done in earth, as it is in heaven.*
> Matt. 6:10

Another simple reference to a healing performed by Mrs. Eddy was in a letter to Augusta E. Stetson, another of her students, who was later on to establish an enormously successful church in New York.

". . . Oh! I was glad to hear that *you*, at least, demonstrated *Christian* Healing. When I united the joint of Gill's *toe*—in a minute, and he said, Why could not your students have done this? I made an excuse as best I could. . . ." 215

A version of this healing was also preserved as follows:

"Gill had an example of what she meant when he injured his ankle in jumping from the train by which he commuted daily between Lawrence and Boston. For several days he suffered intensely but managed to hobble to the *Journal* office each day. Finally he sent a telegram to Mrs. Eddy that the condition was so much worse he would be unable to come to work that day. She wired him in return that his duty was in Boston and that he should report at once to her. He arrived, as he later told a Lawrence friend, in such acute pain that he was totally unfit for work. When Mrs. Eddy came into the room, she spoke to him briefly, then turned and gazed out the window silently. Suddenly the ankle snapped back into place with a loud crack. When Gill returned home that night, the Lawrence friend who had been greatly disturbed by the situation in the morning met him walking easily and naturally." 216

> To-day the healing power of Truth is widely demonstrated as an immanent, eternal Science, instead of a phenomenal exhibition. Its appearing is the coming anew of the gospel of "on earth peace, good-will toward men." This coming, as was promised by the Master, is for its establishment as a permanent dispensation among men; but the mission of Christian Science now, as in the time of its earlier demonstration, is not primarily one of physical healing. Now, as then, signs and wonders are wrought in the metaphysical healing of physical disease; but these signs are only to demonstrate its divine origin,—to attest the reality of the higher mission of the Christ-power to take away the sins of the world. *Science and Health 150:4*

"Mrs. Eddy had some full-grown trees brought from the woods and planted in her front garden (on each side of the gate near the street) at Pleasant View. Large holes were dug to receive the roots, and after they were planted, piles of stones were placed around each tree on the ground to keep the roots in position. For days and weeks people came and looked over the front fence at them to see if they were still alive, expecting to see the leaves wither. But no, the trees grew and flourished, and they may still be there; I do not know. One other tree, an elm, which was growing on the lawn in front, Mother had removed to the back of the house. This also flourished." 217

"It is related once, when some of the Scientists were at Pleasant View, Mrs. Eddy started out on her drive. One of her horses became quite restive, dancing around. Mrs. Eddy called out sharply, 'Mind your own business,' and he quieted at once." 218

"One day Mrs. Eddy was choosing a pair of horses at Pleasant View. When she returned from the stables, she told Louis, the man who had charge of the horses, to bring the new one up to the verandah so she could see it well. She said to me, 'Stand beside me, and I will teach you how to choose a good horse!' Then one of them was brought for her to look at, and she told me to notice the horse's eyes, that the whites of them showed, and that was a vicious horse; so she told the man to take it away. The next one she refused for the same reason. The third she decided to keep; there was no white visible, and as she spoke to the horse, he seemed to feel her kind thought, and bowed his head up and down, showing every sign of pleasure; they were friends at once.

"In writing on the subject of horses, I must mention Jerry and Jean, who were very much attached to her, and seemed to know her well. When she returned from her drive and got out of her carriage, she would often go to the end of the verandah nearest to the horses' heads, and speak to each one. Jerry was nearer to the verandah than Jean, and she would pat his neck or face and speak to him, and then Jean would put his head over Jerry's back as if he did not wish to be left out, and then she would speak to him. It was very beautiful to see her tenderness and love to those horses, and when she came out to get into the carriage, they seemed to recognize her each time." 219

"Ira O. Knapp was a Director of The Mother Church. His wife had passed on from pneumonia and he hadn't been able to free himself from the sense of loss. He visited Mrs. Eddy with his son Bliss and she immediately perceived his depressed sense. She gave him an audible treatment which completely healed him. She told him that they should have treated his wife for animal magnetism, not for pneumonia, as that was only the decoy, and if they had, she would have been healed.

"Mr. Knapp spoke of the seeming wall of partition between him and his wife. Mrs. Eddy said, 'But there is no wall. I see right through that wall.' Then she proceeded to tell him exactly what his wife was doing at that very moment. This shows Mrs. Eddy could see beyond the veil. . . . Jesus, in the story of Dives and Lazarus, was telling what he saw beyond the veil. Jesus spoke with Moses and Elias on the Mount of Transfiguration. . . ." 220

131

"An old school friend of Mrs. Eddy's who was down and out called on her one day, and she talked with him. Before he left, she gave him a prayer that she had given the students, and asked him to say it each day. After two weeks, he came back completely healed. Then Mrs. Eddy gave him $500.00 (about $7500 today) to set him up in business. The prayer was, 'O divine Love, give me higher, holier, purer desires, more self-abnegation, more love and spiritual aspirations." 221

"Another experience I would like to mention was with little Ruth Clarke. Mr. Clarke had charge of Pleasant View Estate, and lived in Pleasant View Cottage, and the infant was the daughter of his adopted son. She was too young to talk, being less than a year old. As she had no mother living, she had never been taught the word, 'mother;' and her grandmother, Mrs. Clarke, she was taught to call 'grandma' although indistinctly. She had been shown Mrs. Eddy's picture and told to call her 'best Auntie.' She had never seen our Leader, but one morning she was brought into her sitting room and told that it was 'best Auntie.' Our Leader, who was sitting in her rocking chair, raised her arms to take the child from the one who was holding her and who repeatedly said to her, 'Say best Auntie.' Little Ruth looked at Mother and tried to go to her, and as she did so, she said, 'No, no, Mama.' It was the first time she had ever said that word and did it of her own accord. Mrs. Eddy was so pleased and grateful, and she became very attached to that little girl. It was so sweet that she recognized the Motherhood that was expressed to her in such love." 222

"There was also, in an insane asylum that Mrs. Eddy used to drive past, a mentally deranged man who had a sore on his leg. Every day when he saw Mrs. Eddy's carriage coming, he would run to the gate and pull down his sock so that our Leader would see the sore. This man was evidently saner on one point than the average individual. Mrs. Sargent told us that one day when she was at Pleasant View she heard Mrs. Eddy tell her sister Victoria Sargent, that this man had been healed of his sore and of his insanity." 223

132

"Many of the students were very young; some were fairly new students of Science, and all were dedicated and sincere. Some Mrs. Eddy had never met, while one acquaintance dated back to 1862. Miss Emma Morgan had met Mrs. Patterson in Portland, Maine, when both were patients of Dr. Quimby, but she had not found the healing she sought at that time. It was twenty-two years later in Minneapolis, Minnesota when she finally found complete healing by reading *Science and Health*. When she, then Mrs. Emma Thompson, traveled to Boston in 1886 to attend the Massachusetts Metaphysical College, she was surprised to learn that Mrs. Eddy was the Mrs. Patterson she had known twenty-four years earlier.

"Mrs. Thompson's little daughter Abigail accompanied her mother on that and several subsequent trips to Boston and became quite well acquainted with Mrs. Eddy. On one occasion the child was suffering severely from a serious, hereditary disease and was healed instantaneously by the Leader. She grew up totally devoted to both Mrs. Eddy and Christian Science." 224

> *What mean ye, that ye use this proverb concerning the land of Israel, saying, The fathers have eaten sour grapes, and the children's teeth are set on edge? As I live, saith the Lord God, ye shall not have occasion any more to use this proverb in Israel. Behold, all souls are mine; as the soul of the father, so also the soul of the son is mine. . .* Ezek. 17:2-4

"In January, 1902, when in the home of Mrs. Mary Baker Eddy, she said to me (Miss Mary Eaton): 'Christian Science is nothing personal with me: it is a revelation from God. There is but one Leader and that is God!' Some one in the room said to her, 'You cannot deny that you are a Leader to this age,' and she replied, 'I cannot deny that, but I can only be a Leader in as much as I allow God to lead me, whereas others allow self to lead.'"[16]

> *Except the Lord build the house, they labour in vain that build it....*
> Ps. 127:1

"A well known actor was healed physically, and his testimony appeared in the *Christian Science Journal*. Afterwards, [one day] he

133

was walking along a street in Concord with a big cigar in his mouth. Mrs Eddy passed in her carriage and looked at him. He took the cigar out of his mouth and threw it away, and was completely healed of the desire to smoke." 225

"One day Mrs. Eddy was going out for her afternoon drive when a tall, gaunt man, who appeared far gone in consumption came up to her gate, held out his hands to her and shouted, 'Help me!' Mrs. Eddy said a few words to him out of the carriage window; talked to him for about two minutes and then drove on out of the gate. On her return she exclaimed, 'What a need that man had!' Next day she received a letter from the man telling Mrs. Eddy that he was conscious he had been healed as soon as the carriage drove on." 226

"A lady came to the door at Pleasant View with a box of American Beauty roses and begged Lydia [Hall; another of Mrs. Eddy's workers in her home] to accept them and give them to Mrs. Eddy; and say that she would call in the afternoon to see Mrs. Eddy. Lydia waited until the midday meal before bringing them in and showing them to Mrs. Eddy, who gave a wave of her hand and said, 'Take them away; what a mockery!'

"Lydia took them to the kitchen and all day long suffered severely. As night drew on and she was tucking Mrs. Eddy into her swing on the front veranda, no amount of tucking in seemed right and she had to come back constantly to do it over. Mrs. Eddy finally said, 'Lydia, you are suffering and have been suffering all day.' She replied saying, 'Yes, Mother.' Then Mrs. Eddy said, 'What have you done with those roses?' 'I took them to the kitchen, Mother.' 'Are they destroyed?' 'No.' 'Go to the kitchen immediately and take the roses and put them in the fire.'

"Lydia said that this was a most difficult thing for her to do. However, she complied with Mrs. Eddy's instruction. Immediately she was released from the pain and was her normal self again.

"As she came in about an hour later to make preparations for the night, Mrs. Eddy said to her, 'You are free?' 'Yes, Mother, I am.' 'Lydia, do you know what that means? That was theosophy. They believe that if they can get something into your hands they can use you as an avenue. Now be on your watch.'" 227

134

. . . when Saul inquired of the Lord, the Lord answered him not, neither by dreams, nor by Urim, nor by prophets.   Then said Saul unto his servants, Seek me a woman that hath a familiar spirit, that I may go to her, and inquire of her.   And his servants said to him, Behold, there is a woman that hath a familiar spirit at Endor.   And Saul disguised himself, and put on other raiment, and he went, and two men with him, and they came to the woman by night: and he said, I pray thee, divine unto me by the familiar spirit, and bring me him up, whom I shall name unto thee.   And the woman said unto him, Behold, thou knowest what Saul hath done, how he hath cut off those that have familiar spirits, and the wizards, out of the land: wherefore then layest thou a snare for my life, to cause me to die? And Saul sware to her by the Lord, saying, As the Lord liveth, there shall no punishment happen to thee for this thing.   I Sam. 28:6-10

"When I read the chapter on *Miscellaneous Writings* on 'Love Your Enemies,' a particular experience which our Leader had in 1899, and which I recorded, is recalled by which I saw the carrying out of her teaching in that chapter, exemplified in her life. One of her former students who had manifested great enmity against her and was persecuting her and falsifying her character was dealt with in the following manner.

"One morning as our dear Teacher was writing letters, she called me and said,'To whom do you think I have just written?' From the look on her face I said, 'I suppose someone to whom no one else would write!' And then she said, 'It is so and so [Mrs. Josephine Woodbury]. and I have invited her to come to see me. I have given her two days from which to select the time most convenient to her, and have asked her to telegraph and let me know the day.' She read the letter through to me and told me to enclose a stamped telegraph form. I said, 'Oh, Mother, how could you write to her, when you know she is doing all she can to harm you, and not hiding it , but talking about it?' She said to me, 'You must learn to love that woman.' I said, 'Do you love her?' 'Yes, and I am trying to bless her! If you and I do not love her, who can or will?'

"To that letter Mrs. Eddy received no reply. When the second day named came, before going out for her drive she put on her special best dress and ordered the carriage to be at the door to take her for her drive an hour earlier that usual, in order to be home early before her guest arrived. Before leaving, our Leader ordered another carriage to be sent to the station to meet her. Just as she was putting on her gloves before entering her carriage, she called me from my writing and said, 'Will you promise something?' I said, 'Of course , I will if it is something I can do.' She said, 'If Mrs. [Woodbury] comes before I return I want you to greet her kindly.' I said, 'Yes, Mother, I will.' Then she said, 'Lovingly?' with a note of interrogation in her voice. My answer was, 'I will try.' Then she said, 'Just heavenly?' I answered, 'I will go upstairs and ask God to help me to do that and to show me how.' Lastly she repeated, 'Now remember what I say—kindly, lovingly, just heavenly!'

"I went to my room and prayed earnestly to divine Love to help me, for, as it was right for her to feel that, it was right for me to manifest it. In a short time I felt such a desire that she should come, and willing to welcome her in the most heavenly way that I knew, because I knew what a blessing there was awaiting her through an interview with our Leader and great good would result.

"Our Leader returned from her drive and hour earlier than usual, and when she got out of her carriage, she said, 'Has she come yet?' I said, 'No, Mother.' 'Never mind,' she said, 'I will wait in the drawing room for her.' In the meantime the carriage had been sent a second and a third time to meet three trains in succession. The last time it was late and too dark for her to have come, and our Leader sat in her sitting room, and said, 'Oh, what a benediction of love she would have received! It would have saved and comforted her!' I too felt sorry for her to have lost such an opportunity and a great blessing. I learned a lesson of love such as I have never forgotten." 228

> . . . I say unto you, Love your enemies, bless them that curse you, do good to them that hate you, and pray for them which despitefully use you, and persecute you; That ye may be the children of your Father which is in heaven: for he maketh his sun to rise on the evil and on the good, and sendeth rain on the just and on the unjust. For if ye love them which love you, what reward have ye? do not even the publicans the same? And if ye salute your brethren only, what do ye more than others? do not even the publicans so? Be ye therefore perfect, even as your Father which is in heaven is perfect.   Matt. 5:44-48

> . . . be ye all of one mind, having compassion one of another, love as brethren, be pitiful, be courteous: Not rendering evil for evil, or railing for railing: but contrariwise blessing. . . .   I Pet. 3:8,9

There were other instances where Mrs. Eddy showed her students the efforts of mental malpractice or hatred.

"A lady whom our Leader had healed of consumption, and afterwards taught, came to Mrs. Eddy seven years later and told her that the old claim had returned, and was worse than ever. Mrs. Eddy told her that it was not the old claim of consumption from which she was suffering but a law of mental malpractice that Christian Science does not heal, and she must handle it as a law of malpractice, and not as a disease. The claim was met.

"Then those of us who have had the privilege of reading Mr. Bliss Knapp's book about his father and mother, will remember that Mrs. Eddy told the students who treated Mrs. Knapp, that had they handled malpractice instead of the disease, they would have healed Mrs. Knapp." 229

> *Therefore rejoice, ye heavens, and ye that dwell in them. Woe to the inhabiters of the earth and of the sea! for the devil is come down unto you, having great wrath, because he knoweth that he hath but a short time. And when the dragon saw that he was cast unto the earth, he persecuted the woman which brought forth the man child. ... And the dragon was wroth with the woman, and went to make war with the remnant of her seed, which keep the commandments of God, and have the testimony of Jesus Christ.* Rev. 12:12, 13, 17

"Judge Ewing was sent by Mrs. Eddy on a lecture tour that took him around the world giving his lecture CHRISTIAN SCIENCE, THE RELIGION OF JESUS CHRIST. On his return he found himself called on to give a lecture in Lynn, Mass. It was a stormy night and when he got on the platform he immediately felt he was up against an antagonistic audience doubtless composed of the then very large, active body of Spiritualistic sympathizers in that town who were strongly opposed to Christian Science.

"It seemed useless for him to try to give his regular lecture to such an audience; so in his usual friendly way of taking an audience into his confidence, Judge Ewing decided the only way was to get nearer to them. He got down from the platform and stood right in front of the audience. He began to talk to them about Lynn, assuring them from his own travel experiences that their town was well known all over the world for its wonderful footwear that for years had been sent out everywhere. After enlarging on this for a while, he gave them the real reason why Lynn would live forever in the hearts and minds of men—it was the place in which *Science and Health* was written by Mrs. Eddy.

"Then, allowing Spirit to speak through him, he told in beautiful, sympathetic language of some of Mrs. Eddy's struggles, privations and difficulties in bringing forth her book, and emphasized that it was her deep love for mankind that enabled her to stand and overcome all that she had to meet.

"By the time he was through talking about Mrs. Eddy there was hardly a dry eye in the place; and so he knew that the opposition was broken and he could deliver his regular lecture on Christian Science. He got back on to the platform and did so.

"The following morning he took the first train for Concord, N.H., where he had an appointment with Mrs. Eddy. Immediately Mrs. Eddy began to thank him for all the things he had said about her the night before and assured him how true they were. She quoted whole statements he had made and the Judge began to puzzle how she could have gotten hold of them, because he himself had come in on the train that brought the newspapers; so she could not have read the reports yet (and the phone was not available then). How was she able to repeat his own statements in his own words?

"Finally he burst out with, 'How do you know what I said?' And Mrs. Eddy replied, 'Suppose I told you that I heard you?'" 230

> God hath revealed them unto us by his Spirit: for the Spirit searcheth all things, yea, the deep things of God. For what man knoweth the things of a man, save the spirit of man which is in him? even so the things of God knoweth no man, but the Spirit of God. Now we have received, not the spirit of the world, but the spirit which is of God; that we might know the things that are freely given to us of God.
>
> I Cor. 2:10-12

"Another instance of the way our Leader met hate, I will share with you. A travelling salesman—selling shoes, came to Asheville [N.C.], in 1901. He told me this story: He said that he had not known Mrs. Eddy, and knew nothing of her teaching but what he had read in the papers, and these were unfriendly comments by people who derided our dear Leader and her work. The man said he hated Mrs. Eddy with a hatred that was insane for there was no reason for it. He hated her as he had never hated anything or anybody else. One day in 1900—in the late part of the summer, he had a vacation, and being in the neighborhood of Concord, N.H., he decided he would go to Concord and get a look at this woman he hated so. He stood outside of her driveway to see her come out, at the hour of her daily drive. He was gloating over the opportunity to satiate his hate. Mrs. Eddy's carriage came towards him. She saw him and greeted him with a gentle bow, as she looked deep into his eyes, with that searching, lingering look that we all knew, whoever saw her. The man told me that in that moment he felt all baptized in Love—such a Love as he had never felt before, and could not have believed possible,—it was not of earth but of heaven. Much to his own surprise, he suddenly crumpled up and wept like a child. When he regained his composure, he went back to town, got a copy of *Science and Health*, began to study it, and was healed of something—I have forgotten just what it was.

"On page 16 of *Message for 1901*, line 24, Mrs. Eddy asks: 'Shall it be said of this century that its greatest discoverer is a woman to whom men go to mock, and go away to pray?'

"The date of this *Message to The Mother Church* is 1901, and it was in the late summer of 1900 that the travelling salesman of whom I have just told, saw Mrs. Eddy and was healed of his hate and later became a Christian Scientist." 231

> And while he yet spake, behold a multitude, and he that was called Judas, one of the twelve, went before them, and drew near unto Jesus to kiss him. But Jesus said unto him, Judas, betrayest thou the Son of man with a kiss? When they which were about him saw what would follow, they said unto him, Lord, shall we smite with the sword? And one of them smote the servant of the high priest, and cut off his right ear. And Jesus answered and said, Suffer ye thus far. And he touched his ear, and healed him. Luke 22:47-51

"The following extracts from the diary kept by Calvin Frye tell an interesting story:

> August 6, 1900. When Mrs. Eddy was out on the swing this morning, she told me to go and tell Joseph Mann for him and me to constantly hold the thought, the sun will not appear for three days and three nights, and there will be a constant rain; the clouds will be continually replenished. It is a very hot

sunny day. Suddenly at 10 o'clock tonight a severe thunder shower came up with almost a cyclone. We united in that thought and in less than five minutes the wind (which was filled with water like mist) came down to a gentle breeze. Mother then told me to tell Joseph, no thunder and lightning, but continuous gentle rain. In a few moments the thunder died away in the distance and there was a steady gentle rain. Today, Aug. 7, there has been a gentle rain most of the day without thunder.'..." 232

"Mrs. Eddy drove into Concord one day and stopped at the Christian Science Hall, and Mr. Calvin Frye, her secretary, went in with a letter, leaving the carriage door open. A gentleman who was standing in front of the hall had called at Pleasant View earlier in the day to see Mrs. Eddy but was told that she could not see him, and that an appointment or an opportunity might be arranged later. As he went away from the house he was very discouraged and said, so that a worker heard him. 'There may not be any later.' This man stepped to the carriage, took off his hat, and said, 'Mrs. Eddy? Mrs. Eddy said, 'Yes.' 'May I ask you a question?' 'Certainly!' she said. Then he said, 'Can you tell me about God, who is He, where is He, and what is He?' Mrs. Eddy told him that God was his Mind, his Life, and continued talking just three minutes. Then the man looked at the clock, which they could both see, and said, 'I have learned more in these three minutes about God than I have in all the rest of my life.' He raised his hat and said Good-bye, and the carriage drove off. Mrs. Eddy afterwards told her students that she saw he was suffering from jaundice and that as she talked with him, she saw the unhealthy color fade from his face like the shadow of a cloud vanishing away, and his face became perfectly normal. She added, 'He was healed, but he did not recognize it while we were talking.' Next day the man wrote he was completely healed, ant that he took the train home that same night." 233

"This noon when Mrs. Eddy was telling of her healing the boy of a carious shin bone, she said, 'I know that if he died, he would awake to find that he had not that disease and I wanted to wake him fully to it *before he died.*'" 234

140

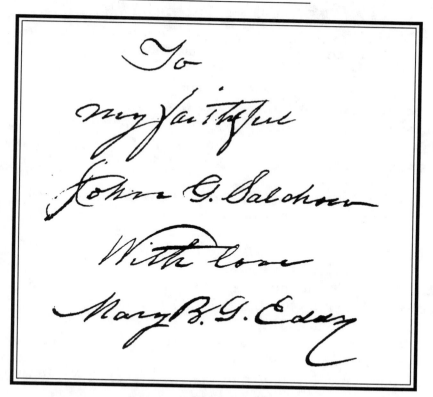

Inscription to Salchow

"John Salchow in Junction City had an interesting dream about this time involving Mrs. Eddy and a boat he owned. It seemed he was instructed to get his boat ready because Mrs. Eddy wanted to go out in it, but, dreamlike, his much-enlarged boat was filled with people all vying for postions to see the Leader. Dutifully, John was willing to serve and went to the stern cabin to handle the rudder, but found his dutifulness rewarded when the door swung open a few inches and gave him a good view of Mrs. Eddy walking toward the boat with a parcel in her hand:

It seemed as if the burden of the whole universe was on her shoulders and as if she would be crushed before she could take another step, but still she came on, her eyes looking upward and beyond the world. It was the most heartrending sight I had ever seen. When she had reached the spot where the man had spoken to me she caught sight of me through the opening in the door. It seemed then as if the whole scene changed, her burdens fell away and she came tripping directly to the door of the cabin. Without noticing anyone else, she handed the parcel to me (it was a copy of *Science and Health*) with the words, "To our faithful boy," and then turned and walked away.

"At a later date when John Salchow was serving Mrs. Eddy at Pleasant View he felt that his dream had been fulfilled when she presented him with a copy of *Science and Health* inscribed 'To my faithful John [G. Salchow With love Mary B. G. Eddy],' — although he had never told her about his dream."   235

> . . . *whosoever shall exalt himself shall be abased; and he that shall humble himself shall be exalted.*   Matt. 23:12

"Mrs. Eddy was well aware of the constant suggestions of animal magnetism (the devil, or evil), which most of her students accepted unwittingly. But the following incident was an eye-opener for Calvin C. Hill.

"One day when I was with Mrs. Eddy she rang for her personal maid and requested that she bring some article to her. The maid returned, bringing something totally different from what Mrs. Eddy had asked for. Mrs. Eddy looked at her earnestly and said, 'Dear, that isn't what I told you to bring [naming the article], and I told you where to find it. Now please get it.'

"Turning to me Mrs. Eddy remarked, as I recall her words, 'That is what animal magnetism does to the members of my household, and they will say, 'Mother sometimes forgets!'. . . Shortly after I left her I met this same maid in the hall, and she said to me, 'Mother sometimes forgets what she asks for!'"   236

> *They which are the children of the flesh, these are not the children of God: but the children of the promise are counted for the seed.*
> Romans 9:8

"One day when the *Message for 1901* was about half finished, Clara [Shannon] *felt* the insidious wickedness that was striking at Mrs. Eddy's life and was doing her utmost to counteract it:

> Miss Shannon was keeping her Watch [the term designating the time an individual spent in prayerful work knowing the

142

truth about a particular subject and working to know the nothingness of evil and that it could not interfere] in another room, and Calvin Frye and Joseph Mann were with Mother, who was having a struggle as Miss Shannon knew. She could hear the two men talking with Mother, and Miss Shannon was praying to God, sometimes on her knees, for Life and strength, Truth and Love to be manifest there, for Miss Shannon felt something awful was approaching mentally.

Finally, the sound of the men's voices ceased. Miss Shannon said she *heard* that *silence*; it was the most awful sound she had ever heard. She went into Mother's room, and there lay Calvin Frye and Joseph Mann stretched on the floor, flat on their faces. Then she looked at Mother; her head had dropped, her jaw dropped. and *every sign* of *death*.

Miss Shannon shouted truth at her, shook her, called her, quoted the book *Science and Health*, reminded her that *Mother had written this book!* Finally, consciousness began to return, and Miss Shannon told her to stand on her feet, and putting her hands under Mother's arm-pits, held her up, — a dead weight. Finally and suddenly Mother *laughed!*

Miss Shannon looked up and gave thanks when she heard this, and asked what the laugh meant. Mother said, "Your face! If you could see your face, you would laugh too."

"Mrs. Eddy picked up her pad of paper and continued her writing as if nothing had happened which was not as easy for Clara Shannon to do. She returned to her room across the hall, but left the door ajar and kept looking in on Mother quietly. After two or three times Mrs. Eddy rebuked her saying sharply: 'Go and handle your fear! You are afraid I shall have another attack. Go and handle your own fear!'

"In her earnest intensiveness Miss Shannon had become unconscious of the 'unconscious' men on the floor and knew not when they recovered and departed.

"When the *Message* was completed Mrs. Eddy said to Miss Shannon, 'Oh what a lot of love it took to do that! The mesmerists did not want the world to have that Message, but love meant it to be given.' She also told Clara that the 1901 Message was Christian Science in a nutshell." 237

Heal me, O Lord, and I shall be healed; save me, and I shall be saved: for thou art my praise.
                                    Jer. 17:14

"Mother told me that one day she was called to help a family where several members were ill and she had to remain for some days. Before going to them she left a pot containing a plant with a beautiful flower on the window-sill of her sitting room. On returning home, when she went into the room, there was the plant all withered, and the earth cracked; the sun had been pouring in through the glass of the closed window and had dried up the earth. A friend who was with her saw it. She then went to the next room to open windows, and in a short time she heard the friend exclaim. When she went to see the reason for this exclamation, she found the plant had revived without being watered, and the leaves and flower were just as beautiful as when she had left them. This was the result of the truth she had been realizing." (The truth that God, and all of God's ideas reflect infinite Life, never subject to mortal law, decay or death.) 238

Mrs. Eddy made the divine law of the Kingdom of Heaven practical in her everpresent radiance of God's love.

> Behold, the tabernacle of God is with men, and he will dwell with them, and they shall be his people, and God himself shall be with them, and be their God. And God shall wipe away all tears from their eyes; and _there shall be no more death_, neither sorrow, nor crying, neither shall there be any more pain: for the former things are passed away.
> Rev. 21:3,4

"I must not forget the goldfish in the fountain basin. There was a large number of them. The dogs from the street used to come and drink water from the basin to quench their thirst in the severe heat, and they would snap at the little goldfish. Our Leader designed a cover for the basin of the fountain, which was of copper wire, with diamond-shaped holes through which the dogs could reach the water to drink, but the holes were not big enough to let them reach the goldfish.

"The food for the goldfish sent from Boston periodically in small boxes looked like oblong sheets of white blotting paper or rice paper, about six inches wide. Daily when Mother reached home after her drive, my duty was to have the little box of food ready for her. She would take a few sheets and we would go to the fountain together, and she would break them in pieces and feed the fish, which, on hearing her voice, would swim to the top of the

144

water with wide open mouths.

"One day, when she put her hand in the water, her diamond marquise ring which was on the under side of her finger sparkled as the sun shone on it, and the fish were frightened and darted away. She did not move her hand but called out, 'Come, little fish, come to Mother—you are not afraid,' and they all returned and swam in and out between her fingers, regardless of the sparkling ring.

"Another day when I handed her the food, she said, 'You stay here. Don't come with me. I will go on tip-toe, very quietly, and see if they will feel my thought and come for the food.' She walked over the grass to the fountain very quietly and did not speak. Immediately the fish rose to the surface. Then she beckoned me to join her, signing to me not to speak, and I saw the fish waiting for their food, which she gave them." 239

"Mrs. Laura E. Sargent told the following story to the class she taught in the Metaphysical College [1913]: Mrs. Eddy in one of her homes had two canaries named Benny and May. One day someone moved the chair against one of the birds, May, which was on the floor, and broke its leg, so that it was held together just by a piece of skin. The bird was put back in its cage, and shortly afterwards a visitor came in. The other bird, Benny, kept flying between the cage and the visitor, and chattering to attract her attention, and when she asked our Leader what was the matter with the bird, Mrs. Eddy told her to look in the cage. She did so and exclaimed, 'Why, this bird's leg is broken!' Our Leader asked her to come back in three days, and when the lady returned three days later she found the bird's leg was perfectly healed, and little May was hopping about on her perch." 240

"[Nemi Robertson] wrote a letter to Mrs. Eddy at a time when she was exercised in her mind about a patient who showed great resentment toward Mrs. Eddy. Although she had not actually mentioned the patient, the reply from Mrs. Eddy contained the advice: 'Turn you patient's thought *to God*, and let *Love* show me to him just as I really *am*!' The patient was healed." 241

"One day a beautifully dressed student called on Mrs. Eddy expecting her to pour out spiritual thought to her. Instead, Mrs. Eddy started talking on her own plane of thought, commenting on her fine clothing and remarking, 'What a beautiful hat you have on!' And that practically ended the conversation." 242

"A student once said to Mrs. Eddy that since coming into Christian Science she had lost fear to such an extent that she did not have the slightest fear of walking down Columbus Avenue alone at eleven o'clock at night. Mrs. Eddy replied, 'Do not tempt the Lord your God.'" 243

"Mr. and Mrs. Riley were asked to pay a call on Mrs. Eddy shortly after they had lost both a son and another dear one. Since Mrs. Eddy was having much to meet in the Field at the time, they were determined not to let their own grief appear in the interview and sought to clear their thoughts of the grief entirely. When they went to see her, so far as they knew they had eliminated this from their thoughts; but Mrs. Eddy was keen to read thought and in the midst of the conversation said, 'Now, in regard to death: Suppose you were sitting in this chair and I was sitting in that one conversing with you, and suddenly an archer should shoot an arrow into your heart from that window.'

"'You would experience a sudden shock, a commotion within, nothing more. I would try to continue our conversation, but I, believing the arrow had killed you, could no longer converse with you; so you would arise from your chair, *leaving no body* in the chair, and go among those you could converse with, while I would have to bury my belief of you which was still in the chair.' She declared that death was just like that." 244

Needless to say this insight by Mrs. Eddy was of great help to the Rileys in completely removing any lingering sense of grief they may have had for their loved ones.

"One time there was a state fair at the back of Pleasant View, Mrs. Eddy's home, and there was a man [Oscar Norin] who dived from a high place into some shallow water. Mrs. Eddy, with Judge and Mrs. Ewing in the carriage drove down to see him dive, and he came up to [Pleasant View] afterwards to speak to her and she took him into the drawing-room and began to talk to him about hearing voices when a child, and Miss Shannon wondered why she did this. Then Mrs. Eddy went on to speak about fear, and said: 'You are able to dive because you have overcome fear.' He said, Yes, he had no fear whatever, he had practiced for a long time taking higher and a higher dive till he could do it without fear. Then Mrs. Eddy said: 'Use that overcoming of fear on your eyes.' The man had dark glasses on and said: 'Well, I damaged one eye so that the eyeball had to be taken out, and that is why I wear these glasses, because the eye is unpleasant to look at.'

Concord State Fair—highdiver Oscar Norin
with Mrs. Eddy in carriage

"The cabman who took this man to the station told afterwards that when the man got to the station he took off his glasses and his eye was completely restored, so that both eyes were the same. (I heard from another source that Mrs. Eddy once told her class that she had healed a man of blindness whose eyeballs were gone and

147

had restored his sight at the same time. Someone in the class asked why, if sight was mental, she needed to restore his eyeballs, and she pointed out that if he had gone around telling people he could see things when he did not have any eyes to see with, they would have thought he was crazy, and would have shut him up.)" 245

> *Now we know that God heareth not sinners: but if any man be a worshipper of God, and doeth his will, him he heareth. Since the world began was it not heard that any man opened the eyes of one that was born blind. If this man were not of God, he could do nothing.*
> John 9:31-33

At another time Mrs. Eddy made the comment that God restores that standard of perfection that mortal mind calls for, and that such things must be humanly manifested.

In August, 1902, Mrs. Eddy wrote to a student, "I want you to give most of your time to healing. This department of Christian Science is the one in which no student has equalled me. It is the one to which every student should aspire to more than any other." 17

"I would like to read an excerpt given to me in the very early days by Mr. James Neal, the beloved student and friend of our Leader. I have given this before, but I find it so valuable that I cannot resist sharing with you our Leader's own interpretation of "Christmas Morn" in healing a patient.

> Thou gentle beam of living Love,
> And deathless Life!
> Truth infinite is you, as God sees you,
> As you see yourself.

"Still I quote our Leader:

> I have taken this hymn and raised a patient who was at the point of passing on in [the] hospital. I held her as a 'gentle beam.' Of what? 'Living Love'—as far above all the strife, all the striving, as far above the conditions that brought her there. 'Or cruel creed'—the doctor's verdict. So far above all cruel edicts, creeds of mortal belief. 'Or earth-born taint'—so far above any taint of inheritance. 'Fill us,' fill her, today, right now, 'with all Thou art.' With what? With 'living Love, and deathless Life, Truth infinite.' Thou all of her. Thou all of me. Fill us, be Thou our all of Life always." 246

"When Professor Herman S. Hering became interested in Christian Science, he read in *Science and Health* (118:23), where Mrs. Eddy said, '. . . yeast changes the chemical properties of meal.' He said it was too bad that such an intelligent woman as Mrs. Eddy should make such a mistake. Not long afterwards another man at the same college came to him and told him that he had just made the discovery that yeast changes the chemical properties of meal. Later Professor Hering met Mrs. Eddy and asked her how she knew that yeast changes the chemical properties of meal when it had not been discovered. She said that she did not know it, that she just wrote down what God told her."   247

> . . . *there is a spirit in man: and the inspiration of the Almighty giveth them understanding.*   Job 32:8

The following is an inspiring account from Elizabeth Earl Jones, C.S.B, a teacher of Mrs. Eddy's day.

". . . As the carriage came alongside Mrs. Hazzard [and Miss Jones], our Leader seemed to feel her rather than see her, for she was looking, as it were, into the far depths of infinity and eternity with, oh! such a solemn, intent expression in her large serious eyes. I had never seen so profoundly serious an expression on any face before. It was half forward, half up look, as if our dear Leader was listening to and communing with things so far above and beyond mortal ken, that is impossible to describe. I remember thinking at the time, what a sin it was to interrupt such sacred communion, and I never did it again. Her eyes looked black and luminous. She wore a purple velvet dress and ermine cape, a small purple and ermine bonnet with a black velvet band under her chin. Her hair was soft, curly and snowy white. She was a rarely beautiful, exquisitely refined, yet forceful woman. She sat erect in her carriage like a lady of the old school. There was a gentle elegance about her and great spirituality. She seemed centuries above even the best of humanity today.

"I do not know how Mrs. Eddy looked at the others, but when she seemed to swoop down from heaven to greet me, she seemed to look clean through me with a sweetly searching, penetrating look, like a great search light turned full upon me. I felt glad, however, to be searched by such wonderful love. I did not know there was such love in all the world. It warmed me through and through, and lifted me high above the plane of human consciousness. I had never been on that plane before, and have never been entirely on the old plane since. The crushing load just melted into nothingness and I felt so happy and free and so strongly uplifted. For days I seemed to walk on air. I cannot describe the uplift and exhilaration of that divine love which dear Mrs. Eddy radiated. Every one and everything I saw seemed to be baptized in that divine love. I can imagine, from this experience, what it must have been to come into the presence of Jesus. There is nothing else like it. It is an experience one can never forget." 248

June 1903
In Front of Christian Science Hall

"Miss [Elizabeth Earl] Jones and Mrs. Hazzard remained in Concord, New Hampshire, the Tuesday and Wednesday after Mrs. Eddy spoke from the balcony at Pleasant View because they wanted to attend the Wednesday evening testimonial meeting in Christian Science Hall. On that Wednesday afternoon, Miss Jones had the privilege of seeing Mrs. Eddy again and of witnessing a healing by her, which, she said, 'was accomplished in much less time than it takes to tell of it.' (See also *Twelve Years With Mary Baker Eddy*, by Irving C. Tomlinson, p. 52)

"Mrs. Eddy always took her drive in the afternoons, except in very bad weather. Often she drove by Christian Science Hall. . . . . . . There must have been ten or twelve of us there. Mr. Irving C. Tomlinson, C.S.D., and his sister lived in a wing at the rear of the house, and a patient was to call for a treatment just prior to our Leader's drive by the Hall. The patient had come for her first treatment in Christian Science. She drove up in a handsome open carriage with a driver and a footman on the top seat in front. The carriage was open, the top folded back, because it was a beautiful early day in June. With great difficulty Mr. Tomlinson and the footman helped the dear little old lady [Mrs. Jeanette Glick] out of the carriage, and she stood all bent over. She could not lift up herself at all. She joined the little group of Scientists on the stoop. . . . Her carriage had just driven off, when, around the bend in the road came an old-fashioned type of closed carriage. The carriage
150

was very small but handsome; the horses were fine bays, and the driver in uniform was Calvin Frye."

Mrs. Eddy taking her daily drive in her carriage

"As Mrs. Eddy drove by, we all waved to her, but she seemed to see no one but this dear little old lady. Mrs. Eddy looked at her with that same lingering, loving, searching look that she had given me the year before, only this time our Leader was not serious but exceedingly happy looking. . . . she had the most heavenly expression on her lovely face. Mrs. Eddy always presented a picture of refined and exquisite lovliness, and she was, even when I knew her, the most beautiful woman I had ever seen. Indeed, I was so intently looking at this beautiful expression on Mrs. Eddy's face, and was so filled with joy at the sight of her countenance, that I forgot the dear little old lady close by who had come for Mr. Tomlinson to treat her. Mrs. Eddy did not seem to see any of us but this little old lady. She looked at her intently with a deep searching look, as if she was discerning and meeting the old lady's innermost need. I knew what she was doing, for once she had looked at me

151

that way. It all happened so quickly—as Mrs. Eddy's carriage passed by and was soon out of sight. Immediately that dear old lady straightened right up and dropped her cane. She was standing erect, and also no longer leaning upon Mr. Tomlinson's arm. I heard her say joyously to Mr. Tomlinson, 'I do not need a treatment; I am healed!' And so she was. Her face was flushed and radiant and she was upright, strong, and free. It all happened in much less time than it takes to tell it. I shall never forget that heavenly expression on our Leader's face.

"This was the kind of healing work Mrs. Eddy did, and it certainly convinced one of the practical truth of her teachings...." 249

> And, behold, there was a woman which had a spirit of infirmity eighteen years, and was bowed together, and could in no wise lift up herself. And when Jesus saw her, he called her to him, and said unto her, Woman, thou art loosed from thine infirmity. And he laid his hands on her: and immediately she was made straight, and glorified God.   Luke 13:11-13

Mrs. Eddy addressing students at Pleasant View-1901

"After the gathering of church members at Pleasant View in 1903, I was leaving the grounds when I saw a young lady apparently much affected. She told me her story: When the Scientists entered

152

the grounds of our Leader's house, she was among the last to go in, and was unable to see or hear our Leader when she spoke to us from the balcony of her home. At first the girl was bitterly disappointed, but then she began to work for more love and humility, and to thank God that others could see and hear, and she felt grateful for that—if any must be crowded out it was herself and not another. She thus mastered the error, and was really very happy. Our Leader, after leaving us, passed through the front door, in order to enter her carriage for her daily drive. In leaving the house, she passed right by this dear girl and stopped, put her hand tenderly on the girl's shoulder, looked deep into her eyes, smiled and said, 'Parting only makes the heart grow fonder.'" 250

"Mrs. Eddy would not tolerate error in any form, error being her term for anything unlike the true sense of harmony and perfection that God is and man perpetually reflects. At one time, when Mrs. Eddy was having her meal brought to her room, the worker who was to bring her meal had a severe cold. She did her best to hide it as she approached the doorway to Mrs. Eddy's room, whereupon Mrs. Eddy looked up, took in the entire mental atmosphere of the worker at a glance, and said in a commanding tone, 'Drop it!' The worker instantly dropped the tray, dishes, dinner and all. After cleaning up the mess, she realized that she was completely free of the cold." 251

The following is an excerpt from the reminiscences of Elizabeth Earl Jones, CSB

"I had the great privilege of coming in contact with our beloved Leader. Mrs. Eddy was not like other people. One felt a power in her presence that shook one to the very base of his or her being. One little girl who, with her mother saw our dear Leader for the first time, came away crying. As she held her mother's hand she sobbed: "Oh, mummie! I want to be good. When you call me, I want to come. I want to do everything you tell me to do. I want to be good." She had been a difficult child, and not inclined to be obedient. She had manifested a lot of human will. But in even a few moments in our Leader's presence, her whole thought was so lifted up and transformed, that she became obedient, loving, and considerate." 252

"Calvin Frye suffered a number of deadly attacks, and on more than one occasion several of the students in the home witnessed Mrs. Eddy's work in bringing him back from death. John Salchow and his sister, who was also working at Pleasant View, were the only two witnesses to one such occurrence in 1903. Whether it was as serious as the other attacks is not known, but Miss Salchow thought it was, for she was the one who found Calvin slumped over his desk, and she was sure he was dead. Mrs. Eddy was summoned immediately, and as John and his sister watched, the Leader brought Calvin back to consciousness in about five minutes." 253

"When one is drunk without wine—mesmerism, apathy—he will talk with a thick tongue something like a drunken man; I can always tell it; they must arouse out of such a sense. I (Mrs. Eddy) was in a street car once when a drunken man came in and sat down. I said mentally, 'You are a fool and don't know it.' I kept thinking that and nothing else; in a few moments that man was perfectly sober; it had roused his dormant sense to the situation, and when he *saw*, that was the end of it." 254

"Mrs. Weller went with Mrs. Eddy to a furniture shop to help her select some chairs. The clerk who was waiting on them wore a bandage over one eye. Mrs. Eddy seemed absorbed in thought while they were being shown the chairs, paying very little attention to them, and when pressed as to which she liked best, she said, 'Any that we can sit on.' Mrs. Weller was annoyed at Mrs. Eddy's indifference, and told the clerk that they would come back the next day and give a decision about the chairs. They were on the second floor of the shop with two doors opening out, one into a stairway, the other to a chute for sliding boxes down to the sidewalk. Mrs. Eddy opened one door and went down the stairs; Mrs. Weller, in her perturbation opened the other door and stepped on the chute, and slid down to the sidewalk where Mrs. Eddy arrived in time to see her picking herself up. Mrs. Weller reproached Mrs. Eddy for her lack of attention to the business at hand, and Mrs. Eddy replied, 'Could I think of chairs when the man was suffering?' When Mrs.

Weller went the next day to see about the chairs, the clerk said, 'Who was that lady with you yesterday? I had an abscess on my eye, and when she went out, I took the bandage off, and there was not a sign of it left.'" 255

"A small but typical example of her [charitable] attitude was recounted by a Methodist minister, E. N. Larmour, who in 1903 was a seminary student and acting pastor of the Methodist Episcopal church at Bow, New Hampshire, Mrs. Eddy's birthplace. Sending out an appeal for funds to repair the church, he received a reply from her offering to give $50 toward a bell if the church could raise enough to meet the balance of the bell's cost. Since they had no intention of adding such a feature, her suggestion at first caused some derision, but soon others pledged the additional funds necessary to buy a 900-pound bell. Notified of this Mrs. Eddy sent a check for $100 [about $1500 today]. Young Larmour, puzzled, made a special visit to Pleasant View, ... and she explained to him that $50 was for the bell, $50 for the repairs; having stimulated them to effort beyond their original intention, she was now responding to their original request. On the same occasion, noting the heavy glasses without which Larmour 'could not see a thing,' she asked him why he was wearing them and added ironically, 'For style?' When he returned from Pleasant View, he found himself wholly unable to read until he laid his glasses aside—for good, as it turned out. Fifty years later his wife wrote that his eyesight was perfect for the rest of his life. Mrs. Eddy's 'charities' sometimes took a very unexpected form." 256

> Sight, hearing, all the spiritual senses of man, are eternal. They cannot be lost. Their reality and immortality are in Spirit and understanding, not in matter,—hence their permanence.
> *Science and Health 483:23-26*

"At the time the church in Concord, N.H. was being erected, Mrs. Ella Peck Sweet went into the building and slipped on a board or something, and hurt herself. Some of the workers at Pleasant View tried to help her, but without much success. Mrs. Eddy asked them what was the matter with Mrs. Sweet. They answered that she was all right. Our Leader said: 'But she is not all right.' She then asked Mrs. Sweet what the trouble was, and the latter replied that it was all right, it was being met. Mrs. Eddy said: 'It is not being met!' Then our Leader asked her how she was working, and Mrs Sweet answered that she was knowing that there were no accidents in Mind. Mrs. Eddy replied, 'That would not heal you. You were brought here to help me; you are one of my best workers,' and [then] pointed out to her that the trouble was only an argument to interfere with her usefulness to Mrs. Eddy. By the time our Leader finished talking to her, Mrs. Sweet was healed."

"It was in this conversation that Mrs. Eddy said to Mrs. Sweet: 'I will say this for your comfort that if you were brought here with every bone in your body broken, you would respond to my treatment."257

> *All that hate me whisper together against me: against me do they devise my hurt. An evil disease, say they, cleaveth fast unto him: and now that he lieth he shall rise up no more. Yea, mine own familiar friend, in whom I trusted, which did eat of my bread, hath lifted up his heel against me. But thou, O Lord, be merciful unto me, and raise me up, that I may requite them. By this I know that thou favourest me, because mine enemy doth not triumph over me. And as for me, thou upholdest me in mine integrity, and settest me before thy face for ever.* Ps. 41:7-12

> *I will extol thee, O Lord; for thou hast lifted me up, and hast not made my foes to rejoice over me. O Lord my God, I cried unto thee, and thou hast healed me. O Lord, thou hast brought up my soul from the grave: thou hast kept me alive, that I should not go down to the pit.* Ps. 30:1-3

In 1904 the International League of Press Clubs produced what was to be a journalistic masterpiece. The volume *Bohemia* was to have articles expressly prepared for it by men of distinction, presidents, ex-presidents, kings, admirals, etc. One of these few specially selected "men" of distinction was a woman, Mary Baker Eddy. [The *Concord Monitor* stated, "It is a notable fact that Mrs. Eddy's is the only contribution in the book which deals with other than a literary or personal theme, and this will be taken as another indication of the widening scope of her recognition and influence. . .] Although it was desired to make a special presentation of this

156

volume to Mrs. Eddy, she graciously declined as her work for the world and her church consumed her every moment. One of the editors of this famous publication later found out just how valuable Mrs. Eddy's time was.

Arthur Talmadge Abernathy had come in contact with Mrs. Eddy in his editorial capacity, and at a later date made an impromptu social call at Pleasant View when he found himself in Concord with free time. In response to his message asking for an interview, the busy Leader sent down her message on a card: "I am very busy. I would rather give you a thousand dollars than a minute of my time." In a light, jesting mood Mr. Abernathy returned the card with the penned note: "My initials are A.T.A."

A.T. Abernathy may have expected to be received. but he was not expecting what he *did* receive which left him stunned and somewhat ashamed. As he was leaving the house a messenger handed him Mrs. Eddy's engraved card, "With compliments of" in Mrs. Eddy's handwriting above her name. Her handwriting was also on the accompanying check made out to Mr. Abernathy for one thousand dollars. (This represented the staggering sum of about $15,000 in equivalent value of today's money!)258

The integrity of the upright shall guide them: Prov. 11:3

"A lady came to me for healing, she had been advised by her cousin to take up Christian Science . . . . This lady told me how her cousin had become interested in Science. The cousin lived in Providence, R.I., and had been a theosophist. She evidently thought it was quite right to silently mentally rob the minds of others, until she learned the way in Christian Science, and realized that the most sacred thing in the world is the individual's right to the privacy and absolute freedom of his own mentality untouched and uncontrolled by any one, even by his best friend, unless he asks for help, or unless a situation arises where he cannot ask for help, and his friend knows that his help would be desired. So this lady who was at that time a theosophist, needed healing, and attempted to draw in secret upon Mrs. Eddy's healing power. For three days, at the same hour, she went into what she called 'the silence,' and concentrated her thoughts upon Mrs. Eddy in order to draw Mrs. Eddy's thought upon herself. The first day she felt absolutely nothing. The second day it was the same. The third day, as soon as she began her attempted mental trespass into our Leader's mentality, she felt a great flood of Love and light,—she had never dreamed of such love—it was a revelation to her—and she seemed to hear the *sweetest* voice say to her, 'Don't dear.' It waked her up to see the error of the whole thing she had been believing in and practicing, and the experience showed her how Christlike was Mrs. Eddy's thought and method of working and practicing. She purchased *Science and Health* at once, gave up theosophy, and became a devoted Christian Scientist." 259

Of course Saul, on his way to Damascus, had his thought illumined by the Lord in a similar manner. (see Acts 22)

"Mrs. Eddy possessed the ability to read the unspoken thoughts of her pupils. For example: A student called at her home for an interview and was told that Mrs. Eddy would see her in a few moments. While the student was looking out of the window as she waited for Mrs. Eddy, she saw an intoxicated man across the street. She began to ponder the case, and asked herself, 'Where is that seeming error? Am I drunk or is that man drunk? Is the error in me or is it in him?' Immediately Mrs. Eddy, who had entered the room unobserved, said aloud, 'No, that error is not in your thought.'"260

"One morning Mrs. Eddy was examining us in her study, putting various questions to us. Finally she said, 'Dear ones, you have answered well. Now that you have been so patient with Mother, what can she do for *you*?' We were all surprised at the question, but Mr. Strang [Lewis Strang, at one time a secretary to Mrs. Eddy], I believe it was, spoke up finally, 'Mother, will you prophesy for us?' Her face clouded for just an instant, and then she said, 'To perform the demonstration of prophecy always includes a temptation of animal magnetism [Mrs. Eddy's term for mortal mind, or another word for evil, the devil.]. Now I have always found this rule of help: When you are about to prophesy, always handle animal magnetism first, and then you will find the times in His hands, and all need for prophecy will be gone. Why? Because *faith in God* will have taken its place!'

"But the next day she referred to this again, and said, 'My dear students, God has told me this much for you: At the end of this [twentieth] century , Christian Science will be the only universally acknowledged religion in the world, because the other religions have no demonstrating basis. But much work remains undone, much self-denial waits for us all before this end can be fulfilled. The main thing is for us to handle M.A.M. [malicious animal magnetism] that would make us fold our hands till this manifests itself. But Truth demands work, work, work! Never forget that!'" 261

Another example of Mrs. Eddy's effective healing work in raising Calvin Frye from death took place in 1905. George Kinter recorded the following account in his reminiscences. What is interesting also, is that Calvin had been dead for well over an hour before being revived.

"One winter night the three rings (Mrs. Eddy utilized a bell system which rang in the appropriate room of the individual she needed to see.) which were Frye's special summons to Mrs. Eddy's room sounded throughout the house unheeded. Then Kinter's five-ring signal rang out sharply and he flew to answer it. Taking a shortcut through Frye's room, he was surprised to see Calvin in a chair but apparently [unconscious]. Mrs. Eddy, apprised of this, sent him back to rouse Frye, but Kinter now discovered that the motionless figure was stone cold and rigid, with no perceptible pulse, breath, or other sign of life.

"By this time Mrs. Eddy had rung for Laura Sargent, who arrived to find her already out of bed and advancing in her nightdress toward Calvin's room, regardless of the icy cold of the house. Paying no slightest attention to Kinter's and Mrs. Sargent's protests, Mrs. Eddy bent over the sitting figure and began at once to make 'bold audible declarations' of truth.

"For more than an hour she continued to call upon Frye in one way or another to 'wake up and be the man God made!' Mrs. Sargent meanwhile had rung for the maid, who brought a double blanket in which they wrapped Mrs. Eddy, while Kinter with an aching back supported her in the half-stooping position in which she bent over Frye's inert form, completely oblivious of what they were doing for her or of anything except the need to rouse him. At last he moved slightly and began to murmur. They could pick out broken phrases: 'Don't call me back. . . . Let me go. . . . I am so tired.'

159

To which Mrs. Eddy replied that she would indeed continue to call him back from the dream-state in which he had been—that he loved life and its activities too well to fall asleep, that he was freed from the thralldom of hypnotism and alive to God, his Saviour from sin and death.

"In another half hour Calvin had recovered and everybody went to bed. The next morning no mention was made of the night's events. Frye was in his usual place, and life proceeded normally." 262

> Now a certain man was sick, named Lazarus, of Bethany, the town of Mary and her sister Martha. . . . When Jesus heard that, he said, This sickness is not unto death, but for the glory of God, that the Son of God might be glorified thereby. Now Jesus loved Martha, and her sister, and Lazarus. When he had heard therefore that he was sick, he abode two days still in the same place where he was. Then after that saith he to his disciples, Let us go into Judaea again. . . . Our friend Lazarus sleepeth; but I go, that I may awake him out of sleep. Then said his disciples, Lord, if he sleep, he shall do well. Howbeit Jesus spake of his death: but they thought that he had spoken of taking of rest in sleep. Then said Jesus unto them plainly, Lazarus is dead. . . . Then when Jesus came, he found that he had lain in the grave four days already. Now Bethany was nigh unto Jerusalem, about fifteen furlongs off: And many of the Jews came to Martha and Mary, to comfort them concerning their brother. Then Martha, as soon as she heard that Jesus was coming, went and met him: but Mary sat still in the house. Then said Martha unto Jesus, Lord, if thou hadst been here, my brother had not died. But I know, that even now, whatsoever thou wilt ask of God, God will give it thee. Jesus saith unto her, Thy brother shall rise again. Martha saith unto him, I know that he shall rise again in the resurrection at the last day. Jesus said unto her, I am the resurrection, and the life: he that believeth in me, though he were dead, yet shall he live: And whosoever liveth and believeth in me shall never die. Believest thou this? She saith unto him, Yea, Lord: I believe that thou art the Christ, the Son of God, which should come into the world. And when she had so said, she went her way, and called Mary her sister secretly, saying, The Master is come, and calleth for thee. As soon as she heard that, she arose quickly, and came unto him. . . . When Jesus therefore saw her weeping, and the Jews also weeping which came with her, he groaned in the spirit, and was troubled, And said, Where have ye laid him? They said unto him, Lord, come and see. Jesus wept. Then said the Jews, Behold how he loved him! And some of them said, Could not this man, which opened the eyes of the blind, have caused that even this man should not have died? Jesus therefore again groaning in himself cometh to the grave. It was a cave, and a stone lay upon it. Jesus said, Take ye away the stone. . . . Jesus saith unto her, Said I not unto thee, that, if thou wouldest believe, thou

160

shouldest see the glory of God? Then they took away the stone from the place where the dead was laid. And Jesus lifted up his eyes, and said, Father, I thank thee that thou hast heard me. And I knew that thou hearest me always: but because of the people which stand by I said it, that they may believe that thou hast sent me. And when he thus had spoken, he cried with a loud voice, Lazarus, come forth. And he that was dead came forth, bound hand and foot with graveclothes: and his face was bound about with a napkin. Jesus saith unto them, Loose him, and let him go.   see John 11:1-44

Edward Norwood assisted Mrs. Eddy in putting together the chapter "Fruitage" in *Science and Health*. During his involvement with this he relates a fascinating experience, one which was repeated during the building of The Mother Church.

"It may be of interest to note that during this time, my watch, a very good one, began to gain in time, until it was three hours a day. Regulating did it no good, so I let it go, and as soon as the work was finished, it resumed its normal condition. Mr. Armstrong told me he had the same experience in the building of The Mother Church, and the jeweler told him, 'It is *you*, not the watch.'"   263

And I saw another mighty angel come down from heaven, clothed with a cloud: and a rainbow was upon his head, and his face was as it were the sun, and his feet as pillars of fire: And he had in his hand a little book open: and he set his right foot upon the sea, and his left foot on the earth, And cried with a loud voice, as when a lion roareth: and when he had cried, seven thunders uttered their voices. And when the seven thunders had uttered their voices, I was about to write: and I heard a voice from heaven saying unto me, Seal up those things which the seven thunders uttered, and write them not. And the angel which I saw stand upon the sea and upon the earth lifted up his hand to heaven, And sware by him that liveth for ever and ever, who created heaven, and the things that therein are, and the earth, and the things that therein are, and the sea, and the things which are therein, that <u>there should be time no longer:</u> But in the days of the voice of the seventh angel, when he shall begin to sound, the mystery of God should be finished, as he hath declared to his servants the prophets. See Chapter 10, Book of Revelation

---

Because of the incredible healing work performed by Christian Scientists and the phenomenal growth of Christian Science, Mrs. Eddy and her church garnered much attention from the newspapers of the day. "Yellow" journalism was rampant in her day, and because of the unjust attacks upon her there was much to meet in setting the record straight. As always Mrs. Eddy responded with love, constantly blessing those who would harm her.

"In the days when our dear Leader was being held up for ridicule by the pulpit and press, because of ignorance of Christian Science, a newspaper reporter called to see her and asked her to tell him what a Christian Science treatment was. He intended to quote her in the press, and then ridicule her words and ideas. Mrs. Eddy paused several moments and then answered: 'A Christian Science treatment is an absolute acknowledgement of the the ever-presence of infinite perfection.'

"The reporter thought over Mrs. Eddy's words, but could make nothing out of them, so did not quote her and ridicule her. Years later, the same newspaper man lay dying with a serious throat infection; he could not speak, and his wife thought him unconscious. She was talking with someone in an adjoining room, when she was startled to hear her husband repeating slowly in a perfectly clear, strong voice: 'A Christian Science treatment is an absolute acknowledgment of the ever-presence of infinite perfection.' He had remembered what Mrs. Eddy told him, and in his hour of extremity it came back to him with a spiritual realization that healed him completely." 264

> For the word of God is quick, and powerful, and sharper than any twoedged sword, piercing even to the dividing asunder of soul and spirit, and of the joints and marrow, and is a discerner of the thoughts and intents of the heart. Heb. 4:12

> So shall my word be that goeth forth out of my mouth: it shall not return unto me void, but it shall accomplish that which I please, and it shall prosper in the thing whereto I sent it. Isa. 55:11

"As it became evident that a greater attack (this was during the time of the 'Next Friends' suit) than ever before was building up, Mrs. Eddy wrote [Edward] Kimball, 'To be honest and wise is the acme of Christian Scientist's attainment at this period; I pray importunately for wisdom.' ... Three years earlier young Calvin Hill, after one of his frequent trips to Pleasant View, had written her that the 'calm assurance that God, good is the only power, which

I have always seen in you from my first visit, has given me renewed strength and confidence that honesty, fidelity and truth lived, must, will ultimately triumph.' Now, on February 21, he wrote her that her last talk with him a few days before had brought him an instantaneous healing of an unnamed difficulty. . . .

"Calvin Hill added: 'This manner of healing is on par with the accounts of the way Jesus healed.'" 265

"A healing which I recall with much interest occurred in the year 1907, at the time of the 'Next Friends Suit,' when many newspapers were sending their reporters to Concord in the hope of securing interviews with Mrs. Eddy. Since it would have taken nearly all her time if she had seen all these representatives of the press, she appointed me [Irving C. Tomlinson] as a receiver and giver of messages. At this time there were three or four reporters particularly determined to see Mrs. Eddy. They had been sent to Concord to 'dig up' the truth about her. The orders from the city desk were positive; they were, 'Use whatever methods are necessary, but get the facts!' If Mrs. Eddy was dead and someone was impersonating her, if she was mentally incompetent and physically in ill-health, they were to bring back the story, sparing no one.

"As one of these men remarked later: 'We hoped that something of a sensational nature would be uncovered. If Mrs. Eddy was merely living in a saintly retirement, working and praying for mankind, it was not news. But if any of the other rumors about her were true, it would be a great story.' This man said they were a belligerent lot of old-timers, and they hoped and expected to 'dig up' a lot of scandal; that they were news hounds baying on the trail.

"Having been in Concord for some time, covering the occurrences surrounding the suit, and trying to get whatever information they could about Mrs. Eddy, this reporter said they were all greatly amazed at the kind and loving treatment accorded them. 'If ever anyone has a right to hate someone, surely the Christian Scientists had a right to hate us,' he said. 'We had no reverence and no decency. We did not believe anything but the worst about anybody, and we wanted if possible to hold Mrs. Eddy up to scorn and ridicule, to expose and denounce her.'

"The chief man among this group, representing a big New York newspaper, was known as a particularly hard-boiled reporter and a steady drinker. He had been afflicted for some years with a cancerous growth of the the throat, which was extremely painful and at times overwhelmed him completely.

"One evening as they were all sitting in his room at the Eagle Hotel, drinking and smoking, bored with their stay, this man was suffering with his throat; he had lost his voice entirely and was unable to speak a word. Mrs. Eddy had asked me to call these men by telephone and inform them that it was impossible for her to see them. But she cautioned me at the same time, 'Be sure to ask for the leading man and speak directly to him.' (God told her who to talk to!)

"The telephone rang and one of the younger reporters answered the call. According to instructions, I asked to speak to the head man, whose name he mentioned, but was told that this man, was too ill to come, could not come, and could not speak if he did come to the telephone, and could not speak anyway. Remembering Mrs. Eddy's instruction I said, 'Tell him to come to the telephone; he can hear what I say even if he can't talk.'

"Accordingly, the suffering newspaper man came to the telephone, showing decided anger (as I was later informed). He listened for a few moments. Those in the room, of course, could not hear what was being said, but when this man turned away from the telephone, he not only could speak perfectly, but was healed.

"The healing stirred these men. They sat around, looking at each other, unable to comprehend what had happened and more startled by it than anything else. They had of course heard that Christian Scientists claim to heal the sick, and they knew that their comrade had been healed.

"One can imagine the consternation and excitement produced by this sudden transformation of one of their number. These men had believed Mrs. Eddy to be only a humbug, and the reputed healings of Christian Science to be a great hoax. Their whole position was overthrown by this proof offered before their very eyes. They packed their bags and left.

"Some years later a relative of this man called at my office in Boston, and gave me the following message: 'My uncle requested me to see you and to tell you that in his last days he turned to Christian Science, and he knew that he owed a debt of gratitude to Mrs. Eddy for his healing in Concord.'" 266

164

For the kingdom of heaven is like unto a man that is an householder, which went out early in the morning to hire labourers into his vineyard. And when he had agreed with the labourers for a penny a day, he sent them into his vineyard. And he went out about the third hour, and saw others standing idle in the marketplace, And said unto them; Go ye also into the vineyard, and whatsoever is right I will give you. And they went their way. Again he went out about the sixth and ninth hour, and did likewise. And about the eleventh hour he went out, and found others standing idle, and saith unto them, Why stand ye here all the day idle? They say unto him, Because no man hath hired us. He saith unto them, Go ye also into the vineyard; and whatsoever is right, that shall ye receive. So when even was come, the lord of the vineyard saith unto his steward, Call the labourers, and give them their hire, beginning from the last unto the first. And when they came that were hired about the eleventh hour, they received every man a penny. But when the first came, they supposed that they should have received more; and they likewise received every man a penny. And when they had received it, they murmured against the goodman of the house, Saying, These last have wrought but one hour, and thou hast made them equal unto us, which have borne the burden and heat of the day. But he answered one of them, and said, Friend, I do thee no wrong: didst not thou agree with me for a penny? Take that thine is, and go thy way: I will give unto this last, even as unto thee. Is it not lawful for me to do what I will with mine own? Is thine eye evil, because I am good? So the last shall be first, and the first last: for many be called, but few chosen. Matt 20:1-16

"On several occasions I [Miss Adelaide Still] saw Mrs. Eddy subdue a storm and I well remember the first time that I witnessed this demonstration. It was the 3rd of August, 1907, between 4:30 and 5:30 p.m. The sky was overcast with heavy clouds and it was very dark. Mrs. Eddy sat in her chair in the study at Pleasant View watching the clouds with a smile and a rapt expression on her face. It seemed to me that she saw beyond the storm and her present surroundings and I do not think that she was conscious of my presence. In a few moments the clouds broke and flecked and the storm was dissolved into its native nothingness. About a half an hour later I had occasion to go to her room again when she said to me, 'Did you see the sky?' I said, 'Yes, Mrs. Eddy.' Then she said, 'It (meaning the cloud) was never there. God's face was never clouded.'" 267

And when they had sent away the multitude, they took him even as he was in the ship. And there were also with him other little ships. And there arose a great storm of wind, and the waves beat into the ship, so that it was now full. And he was in the hinder part of the ship, asleep

165

on a pillow: and they awake him, and say unto him, Master, carest thou not that we perish? And he arose, and rebuked the wind, and said unto the sea, Peace, be still. And the wind ceased, and there was a great calm. And he said unto them, Why are ye so fearful? how is it that ye have no faith? And they feared exceedingly, and said one to another, What manner of man is this, that even the wind and the sea obey him?

Mark 4;36-41

"Chestnut Hill" was her home for the last three years of her sojourn here. Located in Brookline, Massachussetts. Mrs. Eddy was nearer the everyday affairs of her church. While this was a necessary move for her because of business and tax reasons at the time, it broke her heart to have to leave her beloved "Pleasant View." Nonetheless, demonstrations of her nearness to God resulted in many proofs of her healing power and illustrations of God's law, refuting the claims of mortal law and material sense.

Chestnut Hill

At one time a new student of *Science and Health* had just received a healing and her thought being so moved she rushed to Boston to see Mrs. Eddy and thank her for her work. Upon reaching her home she was disappointed to find that Mrs. Eddy had become too busy to see visitors. Although she could not see the author of *Science and Health*, she asked to view a portrait that she heard hung in one of the rooms of Mrs. Eddy's home. As she was ushered into the parlor she found herself face to face with the beloved woman she had come to meet. Mrs. Eddy said that she had been extremely busy writing when God impelled her to come downstairs—she did not know why. She lovingly embraced her visitor, and before she left she had enrolled in Mrs. Eddy's next class. 268

"A man in the landscaping business who was a student of Christian Science came East from Kansas City. Mrs. Eddy hired him to come to Chestnut Hill with his crew and do some work on her place. The first day he came all prepared and Mrs. Eddy would not permit him to start. This experience was repeated the second day. Since this meant a great expense to him, he was disturbed and spent the entire second day in the study of *Science and Health*. When he arrived at Chestnut Hill the third day his thought was right and Mrs. Eddy permitted him to go to work." 269

> *Study to shew thyself approved unto God, a workman that needeth not to be ashamed, rightly dividing the word of truth. But shun profane and vain babblings: for they will increase unto more ungodliness.* II Tim. 2:15,16

Adam Dickey, in his memoirs of Mary Baker Eddy showed how every detail of ordinary life was looked after by Mrs. Eddy. There was a fruit tree on the grounds of Chestnut Hill that was dying, and was slated to be cut down. When Mrs. Eddy heard of it she directed that it be left and taken care of as best as possible. She took up the situation in Christian Science and very shortly the tree was again thriving. 270

Perhaps one of the most inspiring accounts of Mrs. Eddy's healing ability is related by Adam H. Dickey in his reminiscences, an instance where she raised Calvin Frye from death, and when he had been dead for over half an hour. What is also remarkable is the fact that this healing took place when Mrs. Eddy was eighty-eight years of age! (Another version of this account can be read in *Twelve*

167

"One evening, shortly after Mrs. Eddy had retired, Mrs. Sargent came to my door in great trepidation, informing me that she had found Calvin Frye unconscious on the lounge in his room and that she had been unable to arouse him. I hurriedly accompanied her and found Mr. Frye stretched on the lounge in a most uncomfortable attitude, speechless and eyes closed, apparently breathless and with no pulse or indication of life whatever. We continued our efforts to arouse him but with no success. We called him, shook him, and used every means at our command. Finally another worker came in and united his efforts with ours, but we could gain no response of any kind in our efforts to call Mr. Frye back. We hesitated about letting our Leader know of his condition but we saw that inasmuch as we were making no headway, we must inform her of the circumstances.

"This was done by Mrs. Sargent. Mrs. Eddy was in bed but she hurriedly rang her bell for her maid and started to arise and dress herself, when she was seized with a sudden determination, and dropping back into bed she said, 'I cannot wait to dress. Bring him to me.' Mrs. Sargent said, 'But Mother he is unconscious. We cannot arouse him.' She said, 'Bring him to me at once.' On receiving this instruction, the one who had come to our aid lifted the senseless form of Calvin Frye and placed him in a low rocking chair. Then we dragged him around through the hall, through Mrs. Eddy's study, into her bedroom. She sat up in bed with a shawl or some kind of robe over her shoulders and we drew Mr. Frye right up to her side where she could both touch and speak to him. It was an interesting moment. The workers stood around the small room and watched the proceedings. Our Leader reached out her hand and placed it upon Mr. Frye's shoulder and addressed him in a loud voice, 'Calvin, Calvin, wake up! It is Mother who is calling you. Wake up, Calvin, the Cause needs you. Mother needs you, and you must not leave. Calvin, Calvin, wake up. Disappoint your enemies. You shall not go. I need you here. Disappoint your enemies, Calvin and awake!' All this time Mr. Frye's head was hanging limp on his shoulders. I had hold of the back of the rocking chair in which we had placed him to steady him. I placed my hand on his head to lift it up. Mrs. Eddy instantly stopped me and said, 'Do not touch him, leave him entirely to me.' Again she repeated her calls to him to arouse himself and remain with her. It was now

168

something like half an hour since Calvin had first been found, and while those who were looking on at our Leader's efforts to arouse him had not the slightest doubt that she would succeed in awakening him, yet the time seemed to pass without any perceptible response to her work. This did not discourage her. She redoubled her efforts and fairly shouted to Mr. Frye her commands that he waken. In a moment he raised his head and drew a long, deep breath. After this his respiration became regular and he was restored to consciousness. The first words he uttered were, 'I don't want to stay. I want to go.' Mrs. Eddy paused in her efforts and turning her gaze to the workers about the room, said, 'Just listen to that.' She again turned to Mr. Frye and in her commanding tones insisted that he awake and remain here.

"Never shall I forget the picture that was before us in that small bedroom the light shining on the half-scared faces of the workers, and our Leader's intense determination to keep Mr. Frye with her. I had heard of similar occasions when rumors reached the workers in the field that at different times our Leader had restored prominent students to life after experiences of this kind, but of this incident I was an eye-witness and from the very first my attention was not diverted for one second from what was going on, and I am simply relating this event as it occurred.

"It had been rumored that Mrs. Eddy's power of healing was lost but those who were present on this occasion have a different story to tell. Our Leader rose to the occasion like a giant and in commanding tones she demanded that her servant should live and he responded. When Mr. Frye became fully conscious she turned him over to one of the workers who remained with him through the night. The next morning he was about his accustomed duties. Not one in the house that I know of said anything to Mr. Frye concerning his experiences. We do not know whether he realized how far he had gone or whether indeed, he knew of the work that had been done for him. No questions were asked him as we felt it would not be well to recite the experiences to him, but the fact remains that Calvin Frye had passed through what mortal mind calls death, and the grave had been cheated of its victim by our Leader's quick and effective work." 271

Irving C. Tomlinson, a student who was also present at this time, had this to say about the incident.

169

It is most inspiring to recall that throughout the entire experience Mrs. Eddy manifested tremendous spiritual strength and poise. Those of us who were present on that occasion can testify that this remarkable woman had lost none of her healing power in her eighty-eighth year. She spoke in strong, clear tones. There was no fear, no doubt, no discouragement; only absolute confidence, only perfect assurance of the victory of Truth. The following morning Mrs. Eddy was up at the usual hour, and at nine o'clock when I entered her study, I found her busily occupied in reading her Bible. She called my attention to verses 7 and 8 of Psalms 138 which she marked in pencil:

Though I walk in the midst of trouble, thou wilt revive me: thou shalt stretch forth thy hand against the wrath of mine enemies, and thy right hand shall save me. The Lord will perfect that which concerneth me: thy mercy Lord, endureth for ever: forsake not the works of thine own hands.

"Mr. and Mrs. James Morton from California, were devoted workers in the rank of Christian Scientists. Mr. Morton suddenly passed on although Mrs. Morton had help, yet she did not seem to be able to get above the awful grief she was suffering. She went to Mr. [Adam] Dickey for help. He asked Mrs. Eddy if he brought Mrs. Morton to her study door, would Mrs. Eddy just speak a word to her.

"Mrs. Eddy consented. As Mrs. Morton appeared in the doorway of our Leader's study, our dear Leader gave her one of her wonderful, searching looks. Every bit of grief vanished, and a sense of peace and holy joy came over Mrs. Morton."   272

Gilbert C. Carpenter [a secretary to Mrs. Eddy at one time] relates, that while Mrs. Eddy was taking her daily carriage drive one afternoon she noticed a piece of fur placed under the harness of one of the horses. She was told that it was placed there to protect a chafed spot on the horse's shoulder. Upon the return from her drive, and after the horses were unharnessed it was seen that the sore was entirely healed. She *never* permitted mortal mind or error to dictate anything in her experience, even the smallest details did not escape her scrutiny and her constant expression of divine love.

"[At another time] Jerry, the horse, was limping; and Mrs. Eddy called for the carriage to stop. She put her head out of the window and said to Jerry, 'You go right along about your business and do not pay any attention to anything said to you; you listen to me,' And that was the end of Jerry's limping." 273

"Laura Sargent has recorded that when she told Mrs. Eddy, after Mr. Kimball's [a student of hers that had taken over some of the teaching responsibilities] death, that she thought she had seen him in the library, Mrs. Eddy simply confirmed that he was fetching a book." 274

"She said she never lost a case. A few months before she left us in 1910, a worker in Mrs. Eddy's home fell on a meat hook and tore her face open from her chin to her eye. The other workers were not able to handle it. It was a very serious situation and they thought they should tell Mrs. Eddy. They did so and *instantly* every trace of the torn face disappeared as if it had never happened. It might be noted that the workers in Mrs. Eddy's home were some of the finest healers in the Cause and this was a case that did not respond to their work." 275

Three times a day Mrs. Eddy took time to work for the Cause of Christian Science and for all the world. There were those in Germany, it is related, that tried for three years to bring about the first world war. But Mrs. Eddy was working, and this evil intent could not be accomplished then.

Similarly, it was not until right after Mrs. Eddy's passing [December 3, 1910] that three monumental events took place in this country, which have served to keep the populace in bondage to political and financial enterprise ever since. Was it merely coincidental that two of these three major developments were also significant planks in Karl Marx's *Communist Manifesto*, serving to erode individual rights and liberty, giving socialism its first stranglehold on this country?, what many believe to be the culminating ultimate social and political evil.

These few paragraphs but chronicle an isolated item of interest. These events were the following:

1) The Federal Reserve Bank—a centralized banking system
2) a graduated tax system
3) the popular election of senators.

Additionally, the formation of the League of Nations (the forerunner of the United Nations), was about this time. The first step in the destruction or subordination of this God-inspired and ordained nation to international interests, subverting our sovereignty and nationalism to outside interests was put in place.

What evil Mrs. Eddy kept at bay while she was here we may never fully know or appreciate. James Gilman relates the following on this topic (*Recollections of Mary Baker Eddy*, p.48); "... malicious animal magnetism had been trying all over the land to precipitate evil leading into all sorts of sin and destruction, seeking to lay its work to Christian Scientists, but said she, 'I have been holding it back.'" (As was mentioned in the beginning of this book, a whole volume could be written on what work Mrs. Eddy did for the world in holding crime and evil in check.)

"Mrs. Eddy once told her household: 'If I should be taken from you, the students will have to do a great deal of work for the universal welfare, to make up for what I have done.'

"They say our dear Leader went aside three times a day to pray for the whole wide world. ... Mrs. [Sue Harper] Mims told me that Mrs. Eddy did not need that anyone should tell her the affairs of the nations, because her spiritual insight was such that she knew the conditions of every Court in Europe. The world was her patient, and she knew the needs of her patient. She gave us the [*Christian Science*] *Monitor* partly to make world-workers of us. We must know the needs of our patient (the world) and meet them spiritually and daily."[18]

The *Christian Science Monitor* was once the most prestigious newspaper this country ever produced. Unfortunately today it is a mere shadow of its former glorious heritage.

> The government of a nation is its peace maker or breaker. I believe strictly in the Monroe doctrine, in our Constitution, and in the laws of God. *Miscellany 282:1-4*

Mortal mind's tendency towards socialism or communism is not new. We see that shortly after our beloved Master's resurrection these evil tendencies went unchecked in the work and practices of even the apostles.

> . . . a certain man named Ananias, with Sapphira his wife, sold a possession, And kept back part of the price, his wife also being privy to it, and brought a certain part, and laid it at the apostles' feet. But Peter said, Ananias, why hath Satan filled thine heart to lie to the Holy Ghost, and to keep back part of the price of the land? Whiles it remained, was it not thine own? and after it was sold, was it not in thine own power? why hast thou conceived this thing in thine heart? thou hast not lied unto men, but unto God. And Ananias hearing these words fell down, and gave up the ghost: and great fear came on all them that heard these things. And the young men arose, wound him up, and carried him out, and buried him. And it was about the space of three hours after, when his wife, not knowing what was done, came in. And Peter answered unto her, Tell me whether ye sold the land for so much? And she said, Yea, for so much. Then Peter said unto her, How is it that ye have agreed together to tempt the Spirit of the Lord? behold, the feet of them which have buried thy husband are at the door, and shall carry thee out. Then fell she down straightway at his feet, and yielded up the ghost: and the young men came in, and found her dead, and, carrying her forth, buried her by her husband. And great fear came upon all the church, and upon as many as heard these things.   Acts 5:1-11

Nowhere did Christ Jesus advocate communism or socialism; he advocated Christian charity as being blessed; a giving of the heart, willingly, the choice of individual demonstration. But never did he *force*, or murder (mentally or otherwise), those who chose to do what they would with their own possessions, as in the case of Ananias and Sapphira above.

"Often [Mrs. Eddy] spent the whole day alone in her rooms attended only by Adelaide Still, and there were times when even Adelaide was excluded. Perhaps Miss Still enjoyed a respite, for she sometimes felt overburdened by being constantly on call. But Laura Sargent and Martha Wilcox at times grew concerned on days when Mrs. Eddy was long alone.

"One day when [she] asked to be left alone and not to be

disturbed, they both listened attentively for a summoning bell, but none rang. After several hours had elapsed and she had not come out nor called for anyone Laura and Martha began to worry that something had happened. Finally, after a good deal of deliberation, they decided to go in. As they listened at the door they *heard voices*, and as they opened the door to see if everyone was all right, Mrs. Eddy said: 'Girls, why did you disturb me? I was talking with Jesus.'" 276

> *And after six days Jesus taketh with him Peter, and James, and John, and leadeth them up into an high mountain apart by themselves: and he was transfigured before them. And his raiment became shining, exceeding white as snow; so as no fuller on earth can white them. And there appeared unto them Elias with Moses: and they were talking with Jesus.* Mark 9:2-4

Mrs. Eddy devoted every moment of her time to the nurturing of her "child," her church. She was perhaps the most unselfed woman this world has known. She rarely took time for her own pleasure, except that she derived so much pleasure from helping those around her. It was not until the last year of her life that she spent any time on demonstrating other aspects of the unreality of matter and the allness of Spirit for her own benefit. Some fascinating examples have survived that illustrate the possibilities of rising above the pull of the flesh or mortal sense.

"But you say Jesus walked on the water. No, Mrs. Eddy did not walk on water, but there are accounts of her overcoming gravity. But, of course, you don't know about that do you? And Mrs. Eddy did this in an age with strong beliefs about material law, giving great weight to thought contrary to spiritual law. Our Lord could appear or travel anywhere, overcoming distance and time. (see John 6:21-26) Evidence shows that Mrs. Eddy did this also. There are instances of workers at Pleasant View seeing Mrs. Eddy at the top of the steps, a moment later in the kitchen, and a moment later way out in the yard." 277

The compiler learned of an interesting fact during the final editing of this book. According to the testimony of one who was in possession of letters from Ira O. Knapp to his son, Bliss Knapp, Ira Knapp related an interesting account where Mrs. Eddy did in fact walk on the water.

It seems one day when Mrs. Eddy and Mr. Knapp were on

the coast at Red Rock, near Lynn, Mass., Mrs. Eddy was caught out on the rocks as the tide was coming in. Mr. Knapp saw what had happened, since he was closer to the shoreline. He started looking around for a small boat in which to go out and convey Mrs. Eddy back to the shore. However, Ira Knapp could find nothing to accomplish this and Mrs. Eddy walked back herself over the water![19]

Calvin Frye stated in his diary that one day he entered Mrs. Eddy's room and found her floating, suspended up near the ceiling. He was no doubt bewildered and surprised, but Mrs. Eddy allayed his concern, telling her not to be afraid, that all was fine. She subsequently settled down into her chair. [278]

"She once said in class in Columbus Avenue, [in years previous at the] College, 'Were it not for the minds around me, I could step out of this (second story) window, and not fall to the ground.'" [279]

"Mary Baker Eddy's hand disappeared to personal sight of Ella Peck Sweet when she laid her hand on the latter's arm—later became visible. She said, 'Ella, I am showing you things I could not tell you.'" [280]

> Philip opened his mouth, and began at the same scripture, and preached unto him Jesus. And as they went on their way, they came unto a certain water: and the eunuch said,
> See, here is water; what doth hinder me to be baptized?. . . .
> And when they were come up out of the water, the Spirit of the Lord caught away Philip, that the eunuch saw him no more: and he went on his way rejoicing. But Philip was found at Azotus: and passing through he preached in all the cities, till he came to Caesarea. Acts 8:35,36,39,40

"Apocryphal stories abound of what Mrs. Eddy is said to have done with her body while providing such divine instruction to members of her household. To the metaphysician they are enlightening and encouraging, but *not supernatural*.

"Nevertheless, on one occasion some students who were holding her body (and evidently holding her to be *in* body) recorded that they found she could escape from their restraint and reappear instantly on the other side of the room." This is related in detail in the following account. [281]

"One day when Mrs. Eddy had dismissed Adelaide Still and asked not to be disturbed, Laura Sargent and Martha Wilcox grew concerned after quite some time had elapsed with no word from the Leader. After waiting longer and discussing it further, they finally decided to enter her room. They listened first at her door but heard nothing. And when they entered they found nothing. Mrs. Eddy was not there!

"Laura and Martha searched the whole house and the entire household was alerted. Returning to Mrs. Eddy's room following some six or eight hours of searching and consternation, they found her there. After calming the household the Leader asked to see Martha and Laura alone.

Mrs. Eddy about 1907-1908

"When the others were gone and the door was closed, Mrs. Eddy said, 'Girls, come here and put your arms around me.' As they did so Mrs. Eddy disappeared and was standing on the other side of the room looking at them. She then cautioned them about relating this experience to those metaphysically unprepared for it and told them not to put it in writing."   282

"We must also remember that in our Lord's time, there was no resistance to healing. It was not until Mrs. Eddy discovered [Christian] Science and showed us *how* to heal, that mortal mind perverted this and started mental malpractice and all forms of resistance. Our Lord did not have to deal with the full intensity of this error nor with organized medical belief. Mrs. Eddy said, 'The burden is light, the yoke is easy, and if I can say that, any mortal can; for never mortal before drank my cup....' One's demonstration is determined by the resistance he must overcome."   283

"It is important to understand the age issue in relation to Mrs. Eddy. When she was in her seventies, she looked forty years of age. At that time the malpractitioners were just beginning to argue old-age beliefs and it was only then that she began to show age. She said that it was a claim of animal magnetism that she had not met, not because she could not, but because she did not have sufficient time to do so with the incredible demands made upon her."   284

Her church was organized under the divinely inspired government of the Church By-laws established by her in the *Manual of The Mother Church*. Only in this way could she leave a legacy that would not be subject to the wayward influences of ego and love of position and power.

Mrs. Eddy's church had a board of four directors, and for a time, a temporary board of five directors. Three of the five members of this male element constituting the Board at the time of her passing had conspired to wrest control of her church from her. They thought that they were better prepared to run the church and the burgeoning Christian Science movement than a "little gray haired old lady." Their disloyalty and lack of spiritual demeanor were indicative of why God always inspired her in taking the necessary steps to preserve the integrity of what she had founded for the future of mankind in the affairs of her church.

"General Frank S. Streeter, who was one of the ablest lawyers in New England, perhaps even in the United States, once asserted, according to his son's testimony, that Mrs. Eddy knew more law than he did. Most probably Mrs. Eddy would have said that it was God who knew all law and it was He that told her what to do. But some of her Boston officials felt that they knew better. A good deal of 'mental murder' was going on among her directors and other officers by the last quarter of 1910. That is, they were thinking and discussing their belief that Mrs. Eddy will pass away before long. Some of them were also discussing how the organization would function without her controlling hand.

"Archibald McLellan was the lawyer on the Board of Directors and perhaps the one most concerned about some of the by-laws in the *Manual*. He was well aware, as he had once told Mr. [William Dana] Orcutt, that Mrs. Eddy 'has left us nothing to conceive or originate—simply to carry on and to execute.'

"There were even a number of things which they could not carry on if they adhered to the by-laws in the *Manual* because Mrs. Eddy's approval was required, often *in writing*. So a campaign began to induce Mrs. Eddy to change some of the by-laws that restricted the directors. Adelaide Still was present on one occasion when one of the directors (probably Mr. McLellan) tried to get Mrs. Eddy to remove these restrictions from the *Manual*, but she refused.

"It may have been after this interview that she said to Mr. Dickey, in a voice filled with earnestness and pathos, that if she could find one individual, who was spiritually equipped, she would place him at the head of her church government. After she had said this she asked Mr. Dickey to take a pencil, and then dictated very slowly so that he would not miss one word:

> I prayed God day and night to show me how to form my Church, and how to go on with it. I understand that He showed me, just as I understand He showed me Christian Science, and no human being ever showed me Christian Science. Then I have no right or desire to change what God had directed me to do, and it remains for the Church to obey it. What has prospered this Church for thirty years will continue to keep it.

"While Mrs. Eddy was talking with Adam Dickey, Mr. McLellan was explaining the dilemma he foresaw to William Rathvon." 285

Rathvon and McLellan conspired with Clifford P. Smith, then First Reader of the Mother Church, in a plan to tell Mrs. Eddy that they would commit her to an asylum if she did not sign their proposed new by-law establishing them as an executive committee over the Board of Directors, replacing Mrs. Eddy, giving them authority to supervise the Board of Directors, and make or change any by-laws. They attempted to recruit Judge Septimus Hanna in their plan to usurp Mrs. Eddy's leadership. He told them that they were to go to her and immediately confess their plan and their disloyalty to her, and if they didn't, he would! They refused claiming that they had progressed too far to turn back now. Judge Hanna told Mrs. Eddy. Shortly after she told her faithful student, Ira O. Knapp, one of the directors at the time, he passed on.

"Mr. Knapp said he has a photostat of a letter Mr. Frye wrote and that Mrs. Eddy signed, where she said a cabal was formed, a triumvirate, to get themselves put above the Directors by having a change made in the *Manual* and thus to nullify the *Manual*. Mrs. Eddy evidently was not certain she could defeat their purposes. However, there was one way she could defeat them and that was by allowing herself to pass on. Then the *Manual* could not be changed. She chose this course and chose her own time to go. Thus she gave her life for the *Manual* and her Church, as Jesus gave his life to show the way and reveal the Christ."   286

There are indications that she knew as early as three years before her passing [March 10, 1907] when she would be "delivered up," necessitating the protective measures in the *Manual*. In fact in 1903 she had said to her students: "It was not the material cross that killed Jesus, but it was the desertion of his students that killed him." Several days before she left us she dictated to her trusted student Laura Sargent, "It took a combination of sinners that was fast to harm me," and signed it in her own hand. (see Doris Grekel's *The Forever Leader*, page 583-4.)

> But, behold, the hand of him that betrayeth me is with me on the table. And truly the Son of man goeth, as it was determined: but woe unto that man by whom he is betrayed! And they began to inquire among themselves, which of them it was that should do this thing.
> And there was also a strife among them, which of them should be accounted the greatest. And he said unto them, The kings of the Gentiles exercise lordship over them; and they that exercise authority upon them are called benefactors. But ye shall not be so: but he that is greatest among you, let him be as the younger; and he that is chief, as he that doth serve. For whether is greater, he that sitteth at meat, or he that serveth? is not he that sitteth at meat? but I am among you as he that serveth. Luke 22:21-27

The directors even altered her *Manual* within days *prior* to her passing, illegally, without her consent, although purporting all the while the changes had been authorized by Mrs. Eddy. [Mrs. Eddy always made changes in her own handwriting, when it concerned her own writings.]

"Ira O. Knapp passed on three weeks before Mrs. Eddy did. Bliss Knapp [Ira Knapp's son] asked Adam Dickey if Mrs. Eddy said anything about his father's passing. Mr. Dickey said he told her there was a vacancy on the Board. She didn't ask who it was. Evidently she knew. She then offered the position to Calvin Frye. He declined. She then offered it to Adam Dickey. He accepted. As both Calvin and Adam were her secretaries, she would not have appointed them if she had intended to stay [here, on this mortal plane]. On the Sunday before her passing, at the song service in her home, she said to continue to hold the service, 'even though I will not be with you.' She passed on the following Saturday night. They had thought that she meant she would stay in her room." 287

> Certain students, being too much interested in themselves to think of helping others, go their way. They do not love Mother, but pretend to; they constantly go to her for help, interrupt the home-harmony, criticise and disobey her; then "return to their vomit,"—world worship, pleasure seeking, and sense indulgence,—meantime declaring they "never disobey Mother"! It exceeds my conception of human nature. Sin in its very nature is marvellous! Who but a moral idiot, sanguine of success in sin, can steal, and lie and lie, and lead the innocent to doom? History needs it, and it has the grandeur of the loyal, self-forgetful, faithful Christian Scientists to overbalance this foul stuff.
>
> When the Mother's love can no longer promote peace in the family, wisdom is not "justified of her children." When depraved reason is preferred to revelation, error to Truth, and evil to good, and sense seems sounder than Soul, the children are tending the regulator; they are indeed losing the knowledge of the divine Principle and rules of Christian Science, whose fruits prove the nature of their source. A little more grace, a motive made pure, a few truths tenderly told, a heart softened, a character subdued, a life consecrated, would restore the right action of the mental mechanism, and make manifest the movement of body and soul in accord with God. *Miscell. Writings* 353:27-19

Two days before her passing, Thursday, December 1, 1910, an interesting scene took place.

"... Mrs. Eddy's helpers thought she was suffering from a cold. When it came time for her drive they said to her, 'Don't you think it would be wise, Mother, to stay at home today?' Mrs. Eddy answered as she had for many years when her students voiced the lying suggestion instead of the scientific reality of being: 'That's right, talk with the devil!' Mrs. Sargent opened her Bible and, after silently reading the passage she had opened to, she *thought*, 'I wish I might ask Mother what this means.' As Mrs. Eddy was arranging her bonnet she said, 'Laura, do not bring your questions to me, take them to God. You lose your answer if you take them to me.'

"Laura Sargent accompanied her on her drive that day, and recorded one of the Leader's last messages for her followers. During the drive Mrs. Eddy appeared to be thinking deeply and said aloud: 'Oh! If the students had only done what I had told them to do, I should live and carry on the Cause.'

"When they returned from the drive Mrs. Eddy appeared very weak, to those in her household. She asked for a pad which Ella Rathvon brought to her, and on it she wrote her last written message: 'God is my life.'" 288

"The Great Pyramid in Egypt has been called 'The Bible in Stone.' Mrs. Eddy referred in *Christian Healing* to 'the great pyramid of Egypt,—a miracle in stone.' She also left a pamphlet on her desk on December 3, 1910, which was entitled *The Latter Days: with Evidence from The Great Pyramid*. She left this pamphlet *open* on her desk the day of her passing. It was opened to page 32. The passage marked on page 32 read: 'By the same standard of interpretation, the termination of The Grand Gallery 1,910 inches, gives the 3rd of December, 1910, [the day of her passing] as the end of the present era, which we accept as an approximation only, though possibly a very close one.'" 289

For centuries Bible scholars and historians have agreed that the Great Pyramid contains an historical and prophetic "road map," confirming many waymarks in Bible history and prophecy.

"The message I am about to impart is not only an important message for all Christian Scientists, but in my estimation it is the most important incident in Mrs. Eddy's experience which proves without any doubt the infallibility of her complete demonstration of the revelation of Christian Science. . . . Twenty-five years ago I had the privilege of visiting all of the historical landmarks pertaining to Mrs. Eddy's revelation of Christian Science.

Mrs. Eddy's Bed chamber-Chestnut Hill

". . . Our last stop of this tour was Mrs. Eddy's bedroom. . . . This room was homespun and expressed simplicity. . . . I was impressed to see several pictures of Jesus hanging on the walls. It was at this moment that my guide turned to me and said that she felt impelled to tell me what happened to Mrs. Eddy on December 3, 1910 [the day of her passing]. She went to the door of the bedroom to see if we were alone and then proceeded to tell me the following incident, which was told to her by Miss Adelaide Still, one of three persons watching with Mrs. Eddy in the final hours of her human experience. She told me that Miss Still had requested her not to repeat what she was about to tell me, because she had promised those in authority at the Boston headquarters of the Christian Science church never to speak of this experience to anyone. I can assure you that by this time I was not only awed but more than moved by what she was relating.

"On the night Mrs. Eddy passed her three valued and beloved workers were with her. They were Miss Adelaide Still, Mrs. Laura Sargent, and Mr Calvin Frye. On this eventful day in December, 1910 the furnace had ceased to function and a repair man had been summoned to fix it. When he arrived, Mr. Frye and Mrs. Sargent went downstairs to the first floor to admit the repair man. Mr. Frye accompanied him to the basement while Mrs. Sargent waited in the front hall. Miss Still was left sitting by Mrs. Eddy's bed. In a short while the furnace was in working order and Mr. Frye and Mrs. Sargent hurried to the second floor to return to their post by Mrs. Eddy's side. As they neared the bedroom they noticed that Miss Still was standing in the doorway. Approaching her side they looked into the bedroom and beheld Mrs. Eddy by the side of the bed smiling at them. Then Mrs. Eddy turned and pointed to the bed where they saw the form of the one they had called Mother. As their gaze turned again to Mrs. Eddy she was shaking her head back and forth as if to say, 'I am not there; I have risen.' Then as these three watched, the vision of their beloved Leader gradually faded from their sight.

"At that moment, as I stood there looking into Mrs. Eddy's bedroom, I felt a wave of insight into the magnitude of Mrs. Eddy's mission I had never felt before. They had witnessed the ascension of their Leader! ... Before we returned to the entrance hall on the main floor, my guide, who had told me her name (which I have forgotten), expressed the importance of what she had related to me. She repeated that she felt impelled to tell me this incident, which she had heard from the lips of Adelaide Still—who was her sister." 290

Prior to Mrs. Eddy leaving this experience [recorded in January, 1896], "she explained to [Calvin] Frye that, while David died and was buried and Jesus died but his body was raised again, the demonstration for her would 'not be in death even, but a body transformed by the renewing of Mind [Mind with a capital 'M' is one of the synonyms for God—see pg. 587, Science and Health].'" 291

And the angel answered and said unto the women, Fear not ye: for I know that ye seek Jesus, which was crucified. He is not here: for he is risen, as he said. Come, see the place where the Lord lay. And go quickly, and tell his disciples that he is risen from the dead; and, behold, he goeth before you into Galilee; there shall ye see him: lo, I have told you. Matt. 28:5-7

"It was the third day after Mrs. Eddy's passing. In the room with the body, which lay on the bed, were Mrs. Elizabeth Norton and a Miss Grace Collins. In the room next to them were Mr. Frye and two of the Directors [of The Mother Church]. There was a great noise—almost like an explosion. The directors went to investigate—they went through the house and to the cellar and could find no cause for or results of the detonation. Immediately following this noise Mrs. Eddy appeared to Mrs. Norton and Miss Collins. She walked across the room and disappeared through the wall. She appeared as youth, dark hair, and most radiant. Mrs. Norton turned to Miss Collins and said: 'Grace, did you see what I saw?' Grace said, 'Yes.' Mrs Norton told the directors what they had seen and the directors said it must not be told yet." 292

Jesus, when he had cried again with a loud voice, yielded up the ghost. And, behold, the veil of the temple was rent in twain from the top to the bottom; and the earth did quake, and the rocks rent... Matt. 27:50,51

Prior to her passing Mrs. Eddy had stated to a student that it was not old age that was affecting her, but rather a peculiar form of malicious animal magnetism that she had not been able to overcome. This was confirmed in an unsolicited report from the undertakers who were called to Mrs. Eddy's home.

December 6, 1910

To Whom It May Concern:

We were called to the residence of Mrs. Mary Baker Eddy in Chestnut Hill, Mass., at 8:15 A.M., Sunday December 4, 1910, to care for her body. We found it in an excellent state of preservation when first called, and also fifty-eight hours after death. No preserving compounds were used until that time. The tissues were remarkably normal; the skin was well preserved, soft, pliable, smooth and healthy. I do not remember having found the body of a person of such advanced age in so good a physical condition. The walls of the arteries were unusually firm and in as healthy a state as might be expected in the body of a young person. The usual accompaniments of age were lacking, and no outward appearance of any disease, no lesion or other conditions common to one having died at such an advanced age were noticeable.

In the process of embalming we found the body at sixty hours after death, in as good condition of preservation as we always find at twelve to twenty-four hours after death.

This is our voluntary statement made without solicitation or influence of any kind.

Frank S. Waterman
George A. Pierce
Katherine M. Foote   293

January 26, 1911 marked the date that Mrs. Eddy was to be interred in Auburn Cemetery, Boston, Mass. For this occasion those in attendance, all men, had been issued tickets. It was a cold, gray and drizzling day, not a fit place for a woman. Yet, in the procession there was an unidentified woman. Who could she be? It was later presumed to be the funeral director—but she later denied she was at Mt. Auburn!

> *And entering into the sepulchre, they saw a young man sitting on the right side, clothed in a long white garment; and they were affrighted. And he saith unto them, Be not affrighted: Ye seek Jesus of Nazareth, which was crucified: he is risen; he is not here: behold the place where they laid him. But go your way, tell his disciples and Peter that he goeth before you into Galilee: there shall ye see him, as he said unto you. And they went out quickly, and fled from the sepulchre; for they trembled and were amazed: neither said they any thing to any man; for they were afraid.*
>
> Mark 16:5-8

"Bliss Knapp was one of the pall-bearers. He said it did not feel as if there was any body in the casket." 294

EPILOGUE

Having seen the inspired healing results achieved by Mrs. Eddy when Truth is realized, one may wonder to what extent this healing is taking place today. If this is a practical demonstrable science, why doesn't the public hear more about the healing of incurable disease and other maladies through these means? They most certainly are taking place, although not nearly in the volume that this church resounded with a century ago. The efficacy of Christian Science as a permanent dispensation of the Christ power is apparent in the following testimony of a case of A.I.D.S., quoted from Helen Wright's book, God's Great Scientist, vol. III, p. 77.

> A member of our New York City church responded to a request for Christian Science from an A.I.D.S. patient in a hospital in New York City. This week's lesson was "Sacrament." After it was read, the patient asked to be helped out of bed so he could kneel beside the bed and pray. (One of two Sundays in the year that we kneel.) Next day the practitioner was informed no need to come, the patient would die that day. Of course the practitioner went, and went for 48 days, when the patient was pronounced *completely healed* and released.

Thousands upon thousands of healings resulted from the reading alone of *Science and Health*, and this was before Mrs. Eddy passed from the scene over eighty years ago. At one time Mrs. Eddy was asked if she was the woman who wrote *Science and Health*. Her reply was, "Oh, mercy, no. I could never have written such a book." She always gave God the credit. Her meekness, and honesty refused to take credit for that revelation which God alone revealed to her receptive thought.

What is it that heals, that accomplishes this God-inspired transformation in every situation needing healing? It is not person or personality. Mary Baker Eddy in her own words acknowledges this. It is the Christ. When we "Let this mind be in [us], which was also in Christ Jesus...", we reflect the divine nature and the healing is natural, instantaneous.

How do we possess this Christ consciousness?

186

Christ Jesus gave us the answer in his sermon from the Mount.

Blessed are the poor in spirit: for theirs is the kingdom of heaven. Blessed are they that mourn: for they shall be comforted. Blessed are the meek: for they shall inherit the earth. Blessed are they which do hunger and thirst after righteousness: for they shall be filled. Blessed are the merciful: for they shall obtain mercy. Blessed are the pure in heart: for they shall see God. Blessed are the peacemakers: for they shall be called the children of God. Blessed are they which are persecuted for righteousness' sake: for theirs is the kingdom of heaven. Blessed are ye, when men shall revile you, and persecute you, and shall say all manner of evil against you falsely, for my sake. Rejoice, and be exceeding glad: for great is your reward in heaven: for so persecuted they the prophets which were before you.   Matt. 5:3-12

How do we effectively pray in order to help and heal our fellow man, our nation and the world? Again, what better example can we have but what our Master has taught us.

But thou, when thou prayest, enter into thy closet, and when thou hast shut thy door, pray to thy Father which is in secret; and thy Father which seeth in secret shall reward thee openly. But when ye pray, use not vain repetitions, as the heathen do: for they think that they shall be heard for their much speaking. Be not ye therefore like unto them: for your Father knoweth what things ye have need of, before ye ask him. After this manner therefore pray ye: Our Father which art in heaven, Hallowed be thy name. Thy kingdom come. Thy will be done in earth, as it is in heaven. Give us this day our daily bread. And forgive us our debts, as we forgive our debtors. And lead us not into temptation, but deliver us from evil: For thine is the kingdom, and the power, and the glory, for ever. Amen.   Matt. 6:6-13

Mary Baker Eddy in all she wrote and did endeavored to turn her students to the Christ—for only through partaking of his character are we the sons and daughters of God. Only through assimilating this nature can we obey his commands to " Heal the sick, cleanse the lepers, raise the dead, cast out devils," and if obedient to these angel thoughts we are then prepared to do the "greater works" of which he spoke.

And Jesus went about all the cities and villages, teaching in their synagogues, and preaching the gospel of the kingdom, and healing every sickness and every disease among the people.
But when he saw the multitudes, he was moved with compassion

*on them, because they fainted, and were scattered abroad, as sheep
having no shepherd. Then saith he unto his disciples, The harvest
truly is plenteous, but the labourers are few; Pray ye therefore the
Lord of the harvest, that he will send forth labourers into his harvest.*
Matt. 9:35-38

Jesus' promise is perpetual. Had it been given only to his
immediate disciples, the Scriptural passage would read you,
not they. The purpose of his great life-work extends through
time and includes universal humanity. Its Principle is infinite,
reaching beyond the pale of a single period or of a limited
following. As time moves on, the healing elements of pure
Christianity will be fairly dealt with; they will be sought and
taught, and will glow in all the grandeur of universal goodness.
Science and Health 328:28

If the lives of Christian Scientists attest their fidelity to Truth,
I predict that in the twentieth century every Christian church in
our land, and a few in far-off lands, will approximate the
understanding of Christian Science sufficiently to heal the sick
in his (Christ's) name. *Pulpit and Press 22:9-13*

Mrs. Eddy used to tell her household that *Science and Health
with Key to the Scriptures* contained enough Truth to take us out of
the flesh. "But," she added, "the students must not merely read it,
they must study, dig to understand and demonstrate it fully."

"Our present understanding of *Science and Health* is very small."
Mrs. Eddy also said that she had not one student as yet, who has
assimilated one [bit] of what is in that book. And she did not
exclude herself. She told a student but six months before going
away: "I feel I am just really beginning to understand *Science and
Health*."[20] Imagine! The Discoverer, Founder and penultimate
demonstrator of this Science was just *beginning* to understand
what she had written as a "scribe under orders," forty years earlier.

At another time, she told her student, Adam H. Dickey, "When
any practitioner puts *Science and Health* in a patient's hands, it is
Science and Health that does the healing." She said she hadn't
attained *one millionth* of what the book calls for. "It is a wonderful
book and covers eternity," she said.[21]

A fantastic misconception that the public has had regarding
Christian Science is that this denomination has replaced the Bible
with *Science and Health*. Nothing could be further from the truth.
Science and Health with Key to the Scriptures is *complementary* to the

Bible and is meant to be studied with the Bible, for therein lies its value and authority. Its practical healing message for mankind is in bringing the Bible to life, especially for those yearning for the inspiring truths of the Scriptures that bring solace and healing in so many varied situations. It simply illustrates how the Bible, written over 1500 years ago, has relevance to today's sin-filled and disease-weary world and how to rise above this seeming tide of sin, disease and death through the realization of the ever-presence of Life, Truth and Love, here and now.

Since the time of her discovery in 1866 to 1902 it was estimated that more than two million healings had been accomplished in Christian Science.[22]   So we see that healing was relatively commonplace when Mrs. Eddy was with us. In fact, for decades afterward, until the 1940's, healing was still widespread, both in quality and quantity.

During the last 50-70 years the emphasis on healing and spiritual growth through the church has taken a back seat to more secular interests and promotions, and obedience to Mrs. Eddy's commands has been sidelined, resulting in the tragic decline in the church we see today.

Much of today's generation of Christian Scientists have taken the prescription of Christian Science through faith and not through understanding. This has resulted in a laity that knows or *understands* little of the healing truth, but *believes* that it does work. Other impediments to healing have been the love of materialism and sensuality, both antagonistic to spiritual growth.

One wonders if there is any chance for Mrs. Eddy's prophecy regarding Christian Science to come to pass. She told her household, "If the students live up to the teachings of our textbook, Christian Science will be the only *universal religion* by the end of this century." She added: "But if they do not live up to what they know to be Christian Science, this planet will be destroyed about the year 2100."[23]

It is possible that the "1" was transposed in the above quote. In a letter to Bliss Knapp, one of Mrs. Eddy's most devoted students, Bliss states that, "Mrs. Eddy told my family the end would come—regardless—no later than the year 2001. . . " (Private letter dated March 1, 1961)[24]

She explained *why* the above was true in a statement recorded by Elizabeth Earl Jones about 1905. "At the end of *this century*

189

Christian Science will be the only universally acknowledged religion in the world, because the [other] religions have no demonstrating basis. (emphasis added)

"But much work remains undone, much self-denial waits for us all before this can be fulfilled. The main thing for us to handle is [the devilish suggestion] that would make us fold our hands till this manifests itself. But Truth demands work, work, work! Never forget that."

Mrs. Eddy stated, "We need good healers more than anything else. . . ." She mentions to this same individual, "Nothing must be allowed to hinder your healing, this is above all else."

"She healed everything that her thought touched but after a time she saw that she would have to probe the false claim of evil to the bottom before it could be intelligently handled and destroyed. In speaking of this experience she told us that she walked the floor for three days and nights with perspiration pouring from her. In *Miscellaneous Writings,* 222:29 Mrs. Eddy says, 'I shall not forget the cost of investigating, for this age, the methods and power of error.' Again we may ask ourselves, do we appreciate or understand one tithe of her life of love and self-sacrifice? She has shown us in her writings how to meet every phase of [evil] or malicious mental malpractice that can ever come and we owe her undying gratitude, and continuous, watchful, intelligent obedience. Her life on earth was a tragedy just as much as the Master's for her faithfulness in uncovering error caused it to turn its full force of hatred on her."

"Christian Science could not have been a human invention. It must have originated with God. And the works resulting from Mrs. Eddy's discovery prove its divine origin. Only by divine inspiration could the healings wrought in Christian Science ever have taken place. Only by divine revelation could Mrs. Eddy have brought about her own healing, achieved her epoch-making discovery, written *Science and Health,* established her church, and revolutionized the thinking of the world.

"The healing work established by Mary Baker Eddy not only proves the existence of God, but also the truth contained in the Bible. And to those with eyes to see, there is abundant Scriptural testimony clearly showing Mrs. Eddy's place in Bible prophecy."

Mrs. Eddy confirms Mr. Tomlinson's statement above when she wrote to Augusta Stetson on December 17, 1900, "Jesus was the man that was a prophet and the best and greatest man that ever has appeared on earth, but Jesus was not Christ, for Christ is the spiritual individual that the eye cannot see. Jesus was called Christ only in the sense that you say, a Godlike man. I am only a Godlike woman, God-anointed, and I have done a work that none others could do. As Paul was not understood and Jesus was not understood at the time they taught and demonstrated, so I am not. As following them and obeying them blessed all who did thus—so obeying me and following faithfully blesses all who do this. . . ."[25]

On March 13, 1907, she confirms this again when she said, "God talks to me through this book (the Bible) as a person talks to another, and has for forty years."[26]

So much incorrect literature and other information has come from the bosom of her church during the past twenty years that contradict Mrs. Eddy's own statements above. So many of her followers have failed to explore existing biographies and reminiscences, let alone Mrs. Eddy's own published writings, in order to understand what she says on this most important topic.

Why is this important?

The attempt to separate her from her divinely appointed mission, as one chosen of God and as fulfilling the Scriptural commands and prophecies, is the same error that eliminated Christ Jesus as the practical example to mankind when he was elevated to the status of God, thereby depriving mankind of the practical import of the Wayshower. Doing so denies the individuality and authority of that one who is the example to their age.

At the beginning of this book we asked why this marvelous woman is virtually unknown to the general public. The attempts to humanize her life and thus separate her from her discovery have resulted in the decline of Christianly Scientific healing, and the withering of her church; this taking place from within her own church.

Mrs. Eddy states, "Unless Christian Scientists are faithful the healing will be lost sight of just as it was after Jesus' ascension." Healing has declined dramatically since Mrs. Eddy has left us. Why? She has given the answer.

It is not the purpose of this book to delve deeply into why this healing has been lost or diminished, or what is necessary to rejuvenate it, or why her church has been declining. That has been done by others and their works are available from the sources listed in the bibliography of this volume (see listings under

'Covington,' 'Hartsook,' 'Smillie,' and 'Wright' and others).

However, it is important that every conscientious student of the Bible recognize that Christ Jesus' words have not passed away and his command to, "Heal the sick, cleanse the lepers, raise the dead, cast out devils," is and must be for all time. Mrs. Eddy's life work was to *complement* the Master's and provide the map leading mortals out of sense and into Soul, where healing is natural and one can obey the Master's injunction to do the "greater works." She proved his words and did as he commanded; history records her inspired results.

These following paragraphs provide basic reasons for the decline and loss of healing during Jesus' time, and the decline and loss of virtually all spiritual healing in this age. Paul Smillie, in his book, *Mary Baker Eddy, The Prophetic and Historical Perspective*, goes into detail as to why this tragedy has and is taking place and how it can be remedied. We are immensely grateful for his contribution; the thoughts below touch on ideas from his writings.

Someone once asked Mrs. Eddy, "What is prophecy?" She replied, "Prophecy is history written in advance."[27]

One naturally associates Christ Jesus with Christianity and knows and understands his life and character, even his place in Bible prophecy. Without this understanding of the Master's life we have no example to follow, we *can't be* Christians, and Christianity would have no practical value to humanity. Few people however, even those in Mrs. Eddy's own church, understand the import of Mary Baker Eddy's life or her place in history or prophecy in relation to her discovery, and why she is, and *must* be, inseparable from her discovery. Obviously, the same logic applies.

Christ Jesus taught in parables. In communicating spiritual truth one must teach by symbols and by example. (see *Science and Health*, p. 575:13.) If that is deprived the pupil how can they understand the spiritual precept that is to be imparted?

There are two ways to lose the practical import of the way-shower to mankind—through deification of the messenger or through the opposite extreme—apathy, making the individual ordinary, and lack of gratitude for their example. The practical healing import of Christ Jesus' career was lost when his professed followers ceased to understand his prophetic stature. What was it that "made their [the disciples] hearts burn within them" when Jesus spoke to those on the way to Emmaus? It was his recounting

192

of his place in prophecy recorded throughout the Old Testament, which set forth his authority as the Wayshower, the one chosen by God to save Israel, God's chosen people.

Mrs. Eddy's inspired status on the other hand was virtually excommunicated from within her own church and the subsequent attitude of humanizing her has made her ordinary amidst the tide of ingratitude and apathy of her professed followers. Just as Jesus was made God, deified, hence humanity lost the relative example of the divine character to the human experience, so has the practical import of Mrs. Eddy's life and mission been diminished in the Christian Science church, only in the other extreme. Without a proper understanding of the life and character of the one whom God has chosen and sent to benefit mankind there can be no practical realization of what that individual has to bless mankind with.

> *Then said they unto him, What shall we do, that we might work the works of God? Jesus answered and said unto them, This is the work of God, that ye believe on him whom he hath sent.*   John 6:28,29

> *. . . The words that I speak unto you I speak not of myself: but the Father that dwelleth in me, he doeth the works. Believe me that I am in the Father, and the Father in me: or else believe me for the very works' sake. Verily, verily, I say unto you, He that believeth on me, the works that I do shall he do also; and greater works than these shall he do; because I go unto my Father.*   John 14:10-12

The reputation of Jesus was the very opposite of his character. Why? Because the divine Principle and practice of Jesus were misunderstood. He was at work in divine Science. His words and works were unknown to the world because above and contrary to the world's religious sense. Mortals believed in God as humanly mighty, rather than as divine, infinite Love.

. . . Through the magnitude of his human life, he demonstrated the divine Life. Out of the amplitude of his pure affection he defined Love. With the affluence of Truth, he vanquished error. The world acknowledged not his righteousness, seeing it not; but earth received the harmony his glorified example introduced.

. . . The advancing century, from a deadened sense of the invisible God, to-day subjects to unchristian comment and usage the idea of Christian healing enjoined by Jesus; but this does not affect the invincible facts.

Perhaps the early Christian era did Jesus no more injustice than the later centuries have bestowed upon the healing Christ and spiritual idea of being. Now that the gospel of healing is again preached by the wayside, does not the pulpit sometimes scorn it? But that curative mission, which presents the Saviour in a clearer light than mere words can possibly do, cannot be left out of Christianity, although it is again ruled out of the synagogue.

Truth's immortal idea is sweeping down the centuries, gathering beneath its wings the sick and sinning. My weary hope tries to realize that happy day, when man shall recognize the Science of Christ and love his neighbor as himself, — when he shall realize God's omnipotence and the healing power of the divine Love in what it has done and is doing for mankind. The promises will be fulfilled. The time for the reappearing of the divine healing is throughout all time; and whosoever layeth his earthly all on the altar of divine Science, drinketh of Christ's cup now, and is endued with the spirit and power of Christian healing.   *Science and Health 53-55*

Blessed be the Lord God of Israel; for he hath visited and redeemed his people, and hath raised up an horn of salvation for us in the house of his servant David; as he spake by the mouth of his holy prophets, which have been since the world began: That we should be saved from our enemies, and from the hand of all that hate us; to perform the mercy promised to our fathers, and to remember his holy covenant; the oath of which he sware unto our father Abraham, that he would grant unto us, that we being delivered out of the hand of our enemies might serve him without fear, in holiness and righteousness before him, all the days of our life. And thou, child, shalt be called the prophet of the Highest: for thou shalt go before the face of the Lord to prepare his ways; to give knowledge of salvation unto his people by the remission of their sins, through the tender mercy of our God; whereby the dayspring from on high hath visited us, to give light to them that sit in darkness and in the shadow of death, to guide our feet into the way of peace.   Luke 1:68-79

Wycliffe, over 600 years ago, translated "knowledge of salvation," in the above Scripture as, "science of health."

Millions of unprejudiced minds — simple seekers for Truth, weary wanderers, athirst in the desert — are waiting and watching for rest and drink. Give them a cup of cold water in Christ's name, and never fear the consequences. What if the old dragon should send forth a new flood to drown the Christ-idea? He can neither drown your voice with its roar, nor again sink the world into the deep waters of chaos and old night. In this age the earth will help the woman; the spiritual idea will be understood. Those ready for the blessing you impart will give thanks. The waters will be pacified, and Christ will command the wave.   *Science and Health, p. 570:16-25*

194

The COMFORTER
in BIBLICAL PROPHECY

And I will pray the Father, and he shall give you another Comforter, that he may abide with you for ever; Even the Spirit of truth; whom the world cannot receive, because it seeth him not, neither knoweth him: but ye know him; for he dwelleth with you, and shall be in you. . . . But the Comforter, which is the Holy Ghost, whom the Father will send in my name, he shall teach you all things, and bring all things to your remembrance, whatsoever I have said unto you. *John 14:16,17,26*

In the words of St. John: "He shall give you another Comforter, that he may abide with you forever." This Comforter I understand to be Divine Science. Mary Baker Eddy, Science and Health 55:27

What made Christ Jesus unique? Was it not his ability to make the divine law practical in the human experience through his healing ministry? Have Christians followed his example and healed as Jesus healed? Why not? How could they? He left no record of his Christianly Scientific methodology. Why must his method be Christianly Scientific? How else can one demonstrate, infallibly, divine healing, if their method is not consistent and based upon a divine Principle that is repeatable? Christians have not understood the divine method employed by Jesus in the healing of the sick and sinning or they would have been healing in his name during the past 1600 years. This is not because they didn't *want* to heal, but because they could not. There was nothing to scientifically show them how to accomplish what he did. All dedicated Christians would love to heal as Christ healed, for that is the nature of being Christian.

195

Christ Jesus distinctly explained why he did not leave this scientific roadmap showing how to achieve the healing results that he performed and imparted to his followers.

> . . . *I will pray the Father, and he shall give you another Comforter, that he may abide with you for ever; Even the Spirit of truth; whom the world cannot receive, because it seeth him not, neither knoweth him: but ye know him; for he dwelleth with you, and shall be in you. I will not leave you comfortless: I will come to you. Yet a little while, and the world seeth me no more; but ye see me: because I live, ye shall live also.* John 14:16-19

Christ Jesus said he would send *another* Comforter, the *Spirit of truth*—a different representative, from God. Had he meant himself personally returning, he would have indicated unequivocally that he would return in the flesh. However, the Christ is "without beginning of days," eternal, the "Spirit of truth."

"We read that in Jesus' ascension he was 'taken up, and a cloud received him out of their sight,' and that his return would be 'in like manner as ye have seen him go.' (Acts 1:11) Here the word 'manner' in the original Greek text was 'tropos,' and not 'morphe' which might have indicated a human reappearing. How did he go? In this event Jesus' body was dematerialized and *dis*appeared. The 'cloud' symbolises [sic] the etherealising [sic] that took place— the mental nature of the disappearing, and consequently the mental nature of the expected reappearing. Any reappearing of the Christ would therefore be expected to be in the *manner* in which Jesus finally *dis*appeared—a non-material return in the form of the divine Science of Mind, Spirit (corresponding with Jesus' prophecy in John 14:17)."[28] (See Amplified Version)

The Jewish thought rejected the Christ then, they weren't ready for it (*seeth it not*), they were too materially minded—they crucified him—so this "Comforter" had to be for a different time and a different people, when thought was more receptive to the spiritual idea, to the idea of God as Love. In talking to the Jews, Jesus said to them:

> ". . . *Did ye never read in the scriptures, The stone which the builders rejected, the same is become the head of the corner: this is the Lord's doing, and it is marvellous in our eyes? Therefore say I unto you, The kingdom of God shall be taken from you, and given to a nation bringing forth the fruits thereof.*" Matt. 21:42,43

The word "nation" is translated (in Strong's), a non-Jewish people, Gentile, heathen. The Gentiles had a more receptive thought than the Pharisees or Sadducees. The promised kingdom (of God) was to be taken from the unworthy (the Pharisees and Saduccees), and given to that people "bringing forth the fruits thereof," (the Gentiles) through the Holy Ghost, or Comforter. However, because of the gross materialism of the age, it was necessary for a period of suffering to take place before Israel's thought would be receptive to the Christ idea, and could be blessed. (Note: Israel, as God's chosen people, is not exclusively the Jews, as is conventionally thought today. It is only within the past fifty years that Israel, as a nation-state was formed, and, the Jewish people as a whole were thought of as the State of Israel. Israel as a people have always been God's chosen, but have not always been exclusively Jews, nor are they today.)

"Jesus had just told his disciples that the Second Coming would be accompanied by the resurgence of spiritual power: 'Ye shall recieve power, after that the Holy Ghost is come upon you.' Also in Matthew 24:30 we read regarding the Second Coming: 'Then shall appear the sign of the Son of man in *heaven*,' which again suggests a mental reappearing. When Jesus said 'the kingdom of heaven is within you' (Luke 17:21) he was indicating it to be a conscious realisation [sic] of its presence. The 'clouds' again indicate the transcendent nature of the reappearance."[29]

This "Comforter" would necessarily be the "Spirit of Truth," the Holy Ghost, but would be in a different appearing than that of the personal Jesus returning in the flesh. In Strong's Bible Dictionary we find that the original words translated, "Spirit of Truth," are literally: "The Science of Truth." So Christ Jesus prophesied of Christian Science. The only place in the gospel of John that Jesus mentions he is personally coming again is John 14:28. Is he not referring here to his crucifixion and resurrection? All other references are to the "Spirit of Truth," in the line of prophetic utterances.

A hundred years ago Mary Baker Eddy discovered and brought forth this divinely demonstrable principle of metaphysics that enables all to heal and be healed as the Master practiced in his sojourns. Her demonstrations, as also his, were not due to erudition, but rather inspiration, the divine anointing of one chosen by God

197

to deliver suffering mankind out of sinful sense and into the glories of the kingdom here and now. Then and today these messengers were rejected, spat upon and crucified. Why is this? Has not mankind suffered enough? History does repeat itself. Whenever mankind has had enough suffering they finally turn to God, but always as the last resort. Reception of spiritual truth has always met with the same response, whether it is 4000 years ago, 2000 years ago or today, because "the carnal mind is enmity against God." It is amazing that God is as patient with us as He is.

Prophecy is one of the most enigmatic topics for the average layperson. The greatest value in understanding the Bible comes through inspiration. The literal interpretation of the Scriptures divulges little as to the true meaning and virtually nothing with regard to prophecy, as prophecy is generally couched in symbols. The book of Revelation was written in the format of Hebrew vision literature, resplendent in allusions to Old Testament prophecy and symbology. Christ Jesus, as one chosen by God, a "witness" for Truth, was prophesied and referred to throughout the Bible from Genesis to Revelation. As any honest investigation of the Scriptures will affirm, there is prophesied and referenced, a second "light," a second "witness," uniformly from Genesis to Revelation, paralleling that of the first, our Master, in virtually every instance. (see Gen., Isa., Ezek., Dan., Mic., Zech., Matt., John, Rev.,) Is not this second "light" or "witness," the second advent of the Christ, the "Comforter," or Holy Ghost, of which Christ Jesus spoke? Most Bible scholars agree this is so.

It is quite interesting that the discovery of Christian Science and the advent of *Science and Health with key to the Scriptures*, concurs precisely with the dates prophesied by Daniel of 1866 and 1875. Coincidentally, the major dates of prophetic fulfillment are also corroborated in the design and construction of the Great Pyramid, long believed to have significance in the line of Biblical prophecy. (see *The Great Pyramid* by Piazzi Smyth)

> ... the Comforter, which is the Holy Ghost, whom the Father will send in my name, he shall teach you all things, and bring all things to your remembrance, whatsoever I have said unto you.
> John 14:26

> Our Master said, "But the Comforter ... shall teach you all things." When the Science of Christianity appears, it will lead

you into all truth. The Sermon on the Mount is the essence of this Science, and the eternal life, not the death of Jesus, is its outcome.   *Science and Health* 271:20

> *. . . when the Comforter is come, whom I will send unto you from the Father, even the Spirit of truth, which proceedeth from the Father, he shall testify of me:*   John 15:26

> The term CHRISTIAN SCIENCE was introduced by the author to designate the scientific system of divine healing.
> The revelation consists of two parts:
> 1. The discovery of this divine Science of Mind-healing, through a spiritual sense of the Scriptures and through the teachings of the Comforter, as promised by the Master.
> 2. The proof, by present demonstration, that the so-called miracles of Jesus did not specially belong to a dispensation now ended, but that they illustrated an ever-operative divine Principle. The operation of this Principle indicates the eternality of the scientific order and continuity of being.   *Science and Health* 123:16-29

Mary Baker Eddy discovered this practical truth and healed a multitude of sufferers through her demonstration of divine law, and then established her discovery in a form that would enable millions to accomplish similar results.

> "After intensive study of the Scriptures to discover and understand more of this law, she put her findings to the test, and healed cases of disease as they had not been healed since the days of Jesus and the apostles. Next she undertook the laborious task of committing to the pages of a book her sublime discovery; and thus. . . .today in her revelation of provable, spiritual law may we find the realization of Isaiah's dreams, of Jeremiah's vision, and John's apocalyptic promise."

It was her fidelity to our Master and her spirituality that enabled her to effect so many instantaneous cures. She remarked that as Christians we owe "endless homage" to Christ Jesus for his marvelous example to mankind.

The following several paragraphs are taken from the writings of Paul R. Smillie. (See Bibliography.)

"God told John and Daniel that they could not write the revelation of the book, Science and Health, that they saw in visions. (Dan. 12:4, 9 & Rev. 10:2, 4) God told them it was not time and that they were not the ones to write it. If God knew they were not the ones and it was not the right time, then obviously God knew exactly who was in Mind to do that work. If anyone could have discovered Christian Science, then why didn't these men do it? They were certainly more spiritually minded than the Christian Scientists of our generation. God had special tasks for them but it was not to write the book. Mrs. Eddy said, "To one 'born of the flesh,' however, divine Science must be a discovery. Woman must give it birth." (*Retrospection and Introspection* 26:23) Mrs. Eddy said it must be in the latter days of the 19th century. She even tells us that 1866 was the date of its discovery, the fulfillment of Daniel's dates and John's Apocalypse. It had to be a woman in her time. Many men love to think themselves as spiritual equals with Mrs. Eddy and even greater than the greatest woman who ever lived, as intelligent and wise as she, and more so.

"Mrs. [Flavia] Knapp related to a group of Christian Scientists what Mrs. Eddy had told her household about how she, Mrs. Eddy, had written *Science and Health*. She would write as fast as she could throwing the written sheets on the floor as she finished them. Then after a while she would gather up the sheets, number them and re-write them. One of the group listening to Mrs. Eddy asked her, 'Why, Mother, if God dictated Science and Health to you, why did you re-write the pages?' Mrs. Eddy answered to the effect that she had to re-write the pages so that we could understand them. She had to translate them from the pure language of Spirit to a language that the human mind could understand. Could just anyone have done this? Mrs. Emilie B. Hulin, CSD, while she was living in Brookline, said that one day while she was visiting at Pleasant View, she and Laura Sargent were in the room with Mrs. Eddy and Mrs. Eddy said, 'Girls, would you like me to talk absolute Christian Science to you?' They eagerly answered, 'Yes, Mother.' Then Mrs. Eddy began to talk, and they could not understand one single word which she said, although they were seasoned workers and teachers of Christian Science. (See *S&H* 114:32)

"The statement, anyone could have discovered Christian Science or written *Science and Health,* is a lie. It is the red dragon in operation; it is hatred of womanhood; it is scholastic theology saying that men only can interpret spiritual things. It is an attempt of M.A.M. (malicious animal magnetism) to reverse God's promise
200

in Genesis 3:15. It is intellectualism, Jesuitism attempting to rob her of her place and put power in the hands of those claiming to sit in her seat of teaching and authority.

"The Jewish people were destroyed by the Romans after they rejected our Lord. The nation of Judah went into captivity for not listening to Jeremiah and Ezekiel. The Egyptians suffered plagues for resisting Moses. Rejection of Elijah brought drought and famine for the entire nation. We forfeit the influence of divine Love, as a nation and as a church, when we reject God's messenger. Who do we think we are that we can reject God's representative and escape the punishment for this original sin?

"This nation's great eastern harbor has its lady with a lamp, but there is another harbor, a harbor of refuge from every form of evil, standing at the gateway of the land of Christian Science. Here too stands a lady with a lamp. Her work is without parallel in human history.

"In the minds of many Christian Scientists these sentiments are misconstrued as deification. But this is not possible when we realize we are speaking about the greatest woman who ever lived on this planet. She is the greatest example of womanhood and motherhood the world has ever known." (end of quotes from Paul Smillie)

> When God called the author to proclaim His Gospel to this age, there came also the charge to plant and water His vineyard.
> *Science and Health xi:22*

> By thousands of well-authenticated cases of healing, she and her students have proved the worth of her teachings. These cases for the most part have been abandoned as hopeless by regular medical attendants. Few invalids will turn to God till all physical supports have failed, because there is so little faith in His disposition and power to heal disease.
> *Science and Health x:15*

> Beyond the frail premises of human beliefs, above the loosening grasp of creeds, the demonstration of Christian Mind-healing stands a revealed and practical Science. It is imperious throughout all ages as Christ's revelation of Truth, of Life, and of Love, which remains inviolate for every man to understand and to practise. *Science and Health 98:15*

The physical healing of Christian Science results now, as in Jesus' time, from the operation of divine Principle, before which sin and disease lose their reality in human consciousness and disappear as naturally and as necessarily as darkness gives place to light and sin to reformation. Now, as then, these mighty works are not supernatural, but supremely natural. They are the sign of Immanuel, or "God with us,"—a divine influence ever present in human consciousness and repeating itself, coming now as was promised aforetime,

> To preach deliverance to the captives [of sense],
> And recovering of sight to the blind,
> To set at liberty them that are bruised.　　S & H xi:9

. . . be ye doers of the word, and not hearers only, deceiving your own selves. For if any be a hearer of the word, and not a doer, he is like unto a man beholding his natural face in a glass: For he beholdeth himself, and goeth his way, and straightway forgetteth what manner of man he was. But whoso looketh into the perfect law of liberty, and continueth therein, he being not a forgetful hearer, but a doer of the work, this man shall be blessed in his deed. James 1:22-25

I tell you the truth; It is expedient for you that I go away: for if I go not away, the Comforter will not come unto you; but if I depart, I will send him unto you. And when he is come, he will reprove the world of sin, and of righteousness, and of judgment: Of sin, because they believe not on me; Of righteousness, because I go to my Father, and ye see me no more; Of judgment, because the prince of this world is judged. I have yet many things to say unto you, but ye cannot bear them now. Howbeit when he, the Spirit of truth, is come, he will guide you into all truth: for he shall not speak of himself; but whatsoever he shall hear, that shall he speak: and he will shew you things to come. He shall glorify me: for he shall receive of mine, and shall shew it unto you. John 16:7-14

This book is a testimony to what *can* be accomplished by putting off self, handling the resistance to the Christ consciousness, and putting on the spirit of love, holiness—being a transparency for Truth—then the healing follows naturally, effortlessly when one is aligned with God. During her sojourn here, the sick, the sinful, the dying—one and all—came to her to be healed and she healed them all. It was as natural for Mrs. Eddy to heal as it was for us to breathe, as you have seen in the pages previous.

Dr. John M. Tutt made the following comments at the Annual Meeting of The Mother Church in 1964.

"[Her] discovery of Christian Science through divine revelation was complementary to Christ Jesus' teaching and practice. She was herself a humble disciple of Christ Jesus, and she told her students to follow her only as she followed Christ. In following this leader Christian Scientists find themselves in complete harmony with their Master and the scheme of salvation. Throughout his mission and ministry Christ Jesus suited action to his words. He said, 'If you <u>know</u> these things, happy are ye if ye <u>do</u> them.' Mrs. Eddy subjected her discovery of Christian Science to almost ten years of proof in healing the sick and saving the sinner before she published *Science and Health*."[30]

Science is an emanation of divine Mind, and is alone able to interpret God aright. It has a spiritual, and not a material origin. It is a divine utterance,—the Comforter which leadeth into all truth.   *Science and Health 127:26*

In the words of St. John: "He shall give you another Comforter, that he may abide with you forever." This Comforter I understand to be Divine Science.   *Science and Health 55:27*

Should the reader be interested in reading the inspiring and uplifting book, Science and Health with Key to the Scriptures by Mary Baker Eddy the following organi-zations, other than the church, have it available for sale.

Aequus Institute (800)-441-1963
250 W. First Street, Suite 330, Claremont, Calif. 91711
The Bookmark (800) 220-7767
P.O. Box 801143, Santa Clarita, Calif. 91380
Rare Book Co. (908) 364-8043
P.O. Box 6957, Freehold, New Jersey 07728
The Gethsemane Foundation (208) 245-4087
P.O. Box 583, St. Maries, Idaho 83861

APPENDIX ONE

To my sense the most imminent dangers confronting the coming century are robbing people of life and liberty under warrant of the Scriptures, the rights of politics and human power, industrial slavery, insufficient freedom of honest competition, ritual, creed, and trusts in place of the Golden Rule: "Whatsoever ye would that men should do to you, do ye even so to them."   Mary B. Eddy, 1900

The following sixteen testimonies are selected from pp. 431-456 of *Miscellaneous Writings* and pp. 603-650 of *Science and Health with Key to the Scriptures* by Mary Baker Eddy and illustrate the efficacy of Mrs. Eddy's seminal work. The individuals healed of various problems were healed by simply reading the textbook she left as her legacy to mankind, a book which makes practical the inspired truths of the Bible so that the Word is truly made flesh.

1

Four years ago I learned for the first time that there was a way to be healed through Christ. I had always been sick, but found no relief in drugs; still, I thought that if the Bible was true, God could heal me. So, when my attention was called to Christian Science, I at once bought *Science and Health with Key to the Scriptures*, studied it, and began to improve in health. I seemed to see God so near and so dear,—so different from the God I had been taught to fear. I studied alone night and day, until I found I was healed, both physically and mentally.

Then came a desire to tell every one of this wonderful truth. I expected all to feel just as pleased as I did; but to my sorrow none would believe. Some, it is true, took treatment and were helped, but went on in the old way, without a word of thanks. But still I could not give up. I seemed to know that this was the way, and I had rather live it alone than to follow the crowd the other way. But as time passed, I had some good demonstrations of this Love that is our Life.

204

I am the only Scientist in Le Roy, as yet, but the good seed has been sown, and where the people once scoffed at this "silly new idea," they are becoming interested, and many have been healed, and some are asking about it. One dear old lady and I study the Bible Lessons every Tuesday afternoon. She came to call, and as we talked, she told me of her sickness of years' standing; and was healed during our talk, so that she has never felt a touch of the old trouble since.

One lady, whom I had never seen, was healed of consumption in six weeks' treatment. She had not left her bed in four months, and had been given up by many physicians.

MRS. FLORENCE WILLIAMS, Le Roy, Mich.

2

On my arrival in New York, last July, my brother spoke to me of *Science and Health with Key to the Scriptures*; and, coming in contact with a number of Scientists, all wishing me to procure the book, I did so. I read it through in the same manner in which I would read any other book, to find out the contents.

Before I got to the end, having partly understood its meaning, I began to demonstrate over old physical troubles, and they disappeared. A belt that I had worn for over twelve years, I took off, and threw overboard (being a seafaring man).

Up to that time I had been a constant smoker, and chewed tobacco; but I gradually lost all pleasure in it, and now look upon it with disgust.

I was brought up in the Lutheran doctrine, and when a boy received a good knowledge of Scripture; but I never understood it until explained to me in *Science and Health*.

H. F. WITKOV, 27 Needham Road, Liverpool, England

3

For a long time I have felt that I must in some way express my great debt of gratitude for Christian Science. I know no better way to do so than to give an account, through the *Journal*, of some of the many blessings I have received as a result of our Leader's untiring toil and self-sacrificing love for suffering mortals, in giving to us the wonderful book, *Science and Health with Key to the Scriptures*.

When I first heard of Christian Science, about six years ago, I was satisfied that it was the religion of Christ Jesus, because Jesus had so plainly said, "And these signs shall follow them that believe; In my name shall they cast out devils; . . . they shall lay hands on the sick, and they shall recover."

I had been a church-member since my girlhood, but was not satisfied that my belief would take me to heaven, as I did not have these "signs following"—and this had always troubled me; so, when I heard that an old acquaintance living at a distance had not only been raised from a dying condition to health, but her life had been changed and purified through Christian Science, I could hardly wait to know more of this Christlike religion which was casting out evils and healing the sick. I searched every bookstore in the city for *Science and Health*, at last found a copy, and was delighted to get hold of it, but little realized what a treasure it was to be to me and my household.

At first it was like Greek to me, and I could not understand much of it, but gleaned enough to keep on reading, and longed for some one to talk to me of it.

After I had been reading it about a year's time, I suddenly became almost blind. I knew no Scientist to go to, so went to physicians; they told me that my case was hopeless, that it was certain my sight never could be restored, and the probabilities were that I would soon be totally blind.

I felt sure that Christian Science would help me if I could only fully understand it; but there was no one from whom I could ask help, that I knew of. I gave all the time that I could use my eyes to studying *Science and Health*,—which at first was not more than five minutes two, and sometimes three, times a day; gradually my sight returned, until it was fully restored.

During this time God and the "little book" were my only help. My understanding was very limited; but like the prodigal son, I had turned away from the husks, towards my Father's house, and while I "was yet a great way off" my Father came to meet me. When this great cloud of darkness was banished by the light of Truth, could I doubt that Christian Science was indeed the "Comforter" that would lead us "into all truth"?

Again I lay at the point of death; but holding steadfastly to the truth, knowing, from the teaching of this precious book, that God is Life and there is no death, I was raised up to health,—restored to my husband and little children, all of whom I am thankful to say are now with me in Science.

I had no one to talk with on this subject, knew no one of whose understanding I felt sure enough to ask for help; but I was careful from the first not to read or inquire into anything except genuine Christian Science, and how thankful I am for it! Since then, I have been through a class.

I cannot express in words what Christian Science has done for my children, or my gratitude that the light of Truth has come to them in their innocent childhood,—healing all claims of sickness, and showing us how to overcome the more stubborn claims of sin.—L. F. B.

4

It is a little over one year since a very esteemed friend, of this city, invited me to partake of the heavenly manna contained in the revelation of *Science and Health with Key to the Scriptures*. I had, up to that time, been for fifteen years a victim of hip-joint disease; this eventually confining me to my bed, where I had been ten months when the "book of prophecy" was opened for me. I was not long in finding the light I needed,—that gave "feet to the lame," enabling me now to go, move, and walk, where I will, without crutch or support of any description, save the staff of divine Science.

In proportion as my thoughts are occupied with the work in Science, does the peace and joy come inwardly that transforms the blight of error externally.

T. G. K., Tacoma, Wash.

5

I take advantage of the great privilege granted us, to give my testimony for Christian Science through the pages of our much loved *Journal*. The blessing has been so bountiful that words can but poorly express my gratitude.

A little over six years ago, a relative came from Denver, Colorado, to visit us. She was a Christian Scientist, having herself been healed of a severe claim that M. D.'s, drugs, and climate could not relieve; and her husband having been in the drug business, she had had a chance to give them a fair trial.

My sister-in-law did not talk much on the subject, as I remember; but what was better, lived the truth before us as she realized it.

One day (a blessed day to me), I ventured to open *Science and Health*, and read the first sentence in the Preface. I closed the book, wondering what more it could contain, this seeming to cover the whole ground. When my sister-in-law returned to the room, I asked her if I might read it. Her reply was, "Yes; but begin at the first."

That night, after all had retired, I began to read; within forty-eight hours I destroyed all drugs, applications, etc., notwithstanding the fact that my husband had just paid fifty dollars to a travelling specialist for part of a treatment. With the drugs disappeared ailments of nine years' standing, which M. D.'s had failed to relieve.

I now understand that my sudden healing was due to my turning completely away from material methods; for I was convinced I should never use them again. I realized that God was my health, my strength, my Life, therefore All. As I read *Science and Health*, I wondered why others had not discerned this truth,—physicians, ministers, and others who had devoted their lives to benefit mankind. Yes! why? Because they had been seeking in the opposite direction to Truth, namely, for cause and effect in matter, when all cause and effect are mental.

I mention physicians and ministers, because one class claims to heal disease, the other claims to heal sin; but Christian Science heals physically and morally,—it contains all; "its leaves are for the healing of the nations."

L. B. A., Memphis, Tenn.

6

FIBROID TUMOR HEALED IN A FEW DAYS

My gratitude for Christian Science is boundless. I was afflicted with a fibroid tumor which weighed not less than fifty pounds, attended by a continuous hemorrhage for eleven years. The tumor was a growth of eighteen years.

I lived in Fort Worth, Tex., and I had never heard of Christian Science before leaving there for Chicago in the year 1887. I had tried to live near to God, and I feel sure He guided me in all my steps to this healing and saving truth. After being there several weeks I received letters from a Texas lady who had herself been healed, and who wrote urging me to try Christian Science.

Changing my boarding-place, I met a lady who owned a copy of *Science and Health*, and in speaking to her of having seen the book, she informed me she had one, and she got it and told me I could read it. The revelation was marvellous and brought a great spiritual awakening. This awakened sense never left me, and one day when walking alone it came to me very suddenly that I was healed, and I walked the faster declaring every step that I was healed. When I reached my boarding-place, I found my hostess and told her I was healed. She looked the picture of amazement. The tumor began to disappear at once, the hemorrhage ceased, and perfect strength was manifest.

There was no joy ever greater than mine for this Christ-cure, for I was very weary and heavy laden. I thought very little of either sleeping or eating, and my heart was filled with gratitude, since I knew I had touched the hem of his garment.

I must add that the reading of *Science and Health*, and that alone, healed me, and it was the second copy I ever saw.—S. L., Fort Worth, Tex.

7
A CASE OF MENTAL SURGERY

I have felt for some time I should give my experience in mental surgery. In May, 1902, going home for lunch, on a bicycle, and while riding down a hill at a rapid gait, I was thrown from the wheel, and falling on my left side with my arm under my head, the bone was broken about half-way between the shoulder and elbow. While the pain was intense, I lay still in the dust, declaring the truth and denying that there could be a break or accident in the realm of divine Love, until a gentleman came to assist me, saying, he thought I had been stunned. I was only two and a half blocks from home, so I mounted my wheel again and managed to reach it. On arriving there I lay down and asked my little boy to bring me our textbook. He immediately brought *Science and Health*, which I read for about ten minutes, when all pain left.

I said nothing to my family of the accident, but attended to some duties and was about half an hour late in returning to the office, this being my only loss of time from work. My friends claimed that the arm had not been broken, as it would have been impossible for me to continue my work without having it set, and carrying it in a sling until the bone knit together. Their insistence almost persuaded me that I might have been mistaken, until one of my friends invited me to visit a physician's office where they were experimenting with an X-ray machine. The physician was asked to examine my left arm

209

to see if it differed from the ordinary. On looking through it, he said, "Yes, it has been broken, but whoever set it made a perfect job of it, and you will never have any further trouble from that break." My friend then asked the doctor to show how he could tell where the break had been. The doctor pointed out the place as being slightly thicker at that part, like a piece of steel that had been welded. This was the first of several cases of mental surgery that have come under my notice, and it made a deep impression on me.

For the benefit of others who may have something similar to meet, I will say that I have overcome almost constant attacks of sick headaches, extending back to my earliest recollection.—L. C. S., Salt Lake City, Utah.

8

CATARACT QUICKLY CURED

I wish to add my testimony to those of others, and hope that it may be the means of bringing some poor sufferer to health, to happiness, and to God. I was healed through simply reading this wonderful book, *Science and Health*. I had been troubled periodically for many years with sore eyes, and had been to many doctors, who called the disease iritis and cataract. They told me that my eyes would always give me trouble, and that I would eventually lose my sight if I remained in an office, and advised me to go under an operation. Later on I had to wear glasses at my work, also out of doors as I could not bear the winds, and my eyes were gradually becoming worse. I could not read for longer than a few minutes at a time, otherwise they would smart severely. I had to rest my eyes each evening to enable me to use them the next day; in fact gas-light was getting unbearable because of the pain, and I made home miserable. A dear brother told me about Christian Science, and said that if I would read *Science and Health* it would help me. He procured for me the loan of the book. The first night I read it, it so interested me I quite forgot all about my eyes until my wife remarked that it was eleven o'clock. I found that I had been reading this book for nearly four hours, and I remarked immediately after, "I believe my eyes are cured," which was really the case. The next day, on looking at my eyes, my wife noticed that the cataract had disappeared. I put away my outdoor glasses, which I have not required since, and through the understanding gained by studying
210

Christian Science I have been able to do away with my indoor glasses also, and have had no return of pain in my eyes since. This is now a year and a half ago.—G. F. S., Liverpool, England.

9
RELIEF FROM INTENSE SUFFERING

I became interested in Christian Science in 1901. For four or five years I had suffered with severe attacks which nothing but an opiate seemed to relieve. After one which I think was the worst I ever had, I consulted our family physician, who diagnosed my case as a dangerous kidney disease and said that no medicine could help me but that I must undergo a surgical operation. I continued to grow worse and went to see the physician again, and he advised me to consult a doctor who was connected with the city hospital of Augusta. This doctor made an examination and diagnosed the difficulty as something different but quite as serious. Meanwhile a friend offered me a copy of *Science and Health*. I said I did not care to read the book, but she was so urgent that I finally promised to do so. I received the book on Saturday, and on Sunday morning I sat down to read it. When I reached the place where Mrs. Eddy says she found this truth in the Bible, I began comparing the two books. I read passages which looked very reasonable to me, and said to myself, This is nearer to the truth than anything I have ever seen. I continued to read all day, stopping only long enough to eat my dinner. As I read on, everything became clearer to me, and I felt that I was healed. During the evening a neighbor came in, and I said, "I am healed, and that book has healed me." I read on and was certainly healed. Eight days after my healing I did my own washing. This occurred in February, 1901. About six weeks after, I was called to care for my mother, who was under the care of my former physician. I again let him examine my side, as he wished to see if the trouble was still there. He said, "It is certainly gone." I said to him, "Doctor, you told me I would never be a well woman unless I was operated upon; what has healed me?" He replied, "God has healed you."—S. H. L., North Pittston, Me.

10
GRATEFUL FOR MANY BLESSINGS

It is with sincere gratitude for the many blessings Christian

Science has brought me, that I give this testimony. I first heard of Christian Science about fifteen years ago. A friend of mine was taking treatment for physical troubles, and was reading the textbook of Christian Science, *Science and Health* with Key to the Scriptures. The title of the book appealed to me very strongly. I said to my friend, "If that is a Key to the Scriptures, I must have it."

I had long been a member of a Bible class in an orthodox Sabbath school, but I never felt satisfied with that which was taught; there was something lacking, I did not understand then what it was. I purchased a copy of *Science and Health* and began to study it. I wish I could express in words what that book brought me. It illumined the Bible with a glorious light and I began to understand some of the Master's sayings, and tried to apply them.

I had had a longing to live a better Christian life for many years, and often wondered why I failed so utterly to understand the Bible. Now I knew; it was lack of spiritual apprehension.

I did not know at first that people were healed of disease and sin by simply reading *Science and Health*, but found after a while that such was the case. At that time I had many physical troubles, and one after another of these ills simply disappeared and I found that I had no disease,—I was perfectly free. The spiritual uplifting was glorious, too, and as I go on in the study of this blessed Science, I find I am gaining surely an understanding that helps me to overcome both sin and disease in myself and in others. My faith in good is increased and I know I am losing my belief in evil as a power equal to good. The pathway is not wearisome, because each victory over self gives stronger faith and a more earnest desire to press on.—E. J. R., Toledo, Ohio.

11
GRATEFUL FOR MORAL AND SPIRITUAL AWAKENING

About four years ago, after I had tried different ways and means to be relieved from bodily suffering, a faithful friend called my attention to the teaching of Christian Science. After some opposition, I decided to investigate it, with the thought that if this teaching would be helpful, it was meant for me as well as for others; if it did not afford any help, I could put it aside again, but that I would find out and be convinced.

212

After I had read Mrs. Eddy's work, *Science and Health*, a few days, I found that my ailments had disappeared, and a rest had come to me which I had never before known. I had smoked almost incessantly, although I had often determined to use my will power and never smoke again, but had always failed. This desire as well as the desire for drink simply disappeared, and I wish to say here, that I received all these benefits before I had gained much understanding of what I was reading. Like a prisoner, who had been in chains for years, I was suddenly set free. I did not then know how the chain had been removed, but I had to acknowledge that it came through the reading of this book. I then felt an ardent desire to read more, and to know what this power was that had freed me in a few days of that which I had been trying for years to shake off and had failed. It then became clear to me that this was the truth which Jesus Christ taught and preached to free humanity almost two thousand years ago. It did not, however, occur to me to apply it in my business affairs; on the contrary, I first thought that if I continued in my study I would have to retire from business.

This did not happen, however, for I gradually found that the little understanding of this wonderful teaching which I had acquired became a great help to me in my business. I became more friendly, more honest, more loving to my fellow-men; and I also acquired better judgment and was able to do the right thing at the right time. As a natural result my business improved. Before I knew anything of Christian Science my business had often been a burden to me, fear and worry deprived me of my rest. How different it is now! Through the study of the Bible, which now possesses unmeasurable treasures for me, and of our textbook, *Science and Health*, and the other works of our Leader, I receive peace and confidence in God and that insight into character which is necessary for the correct management of any business. —W. H. H., Bloomfield, Neb.

12
HEREDITARY DISEASE OF THE LUNGS CURED

For a long time I have been impelled to contribute a testimony of the healing power of Truth. As I read other testimonies and rejoice in them, some one may rejoice in mine. I was healed by reading *Science and Health*. By applying it, I found it to be the truth that Jesus taught,—the truth that sets free.

From childhood I had never known a well day. I was healed of lung trouble of long standing. Consumption was hereditary in our family, my mother and three brothers having passed on with it. The law of *materia medica* said that in a short time I must follow them. I also had severe stomach trouble of over eight years' standing, during which time I always retired without supper, as the fear of suffering from my food was so great that I denied myself food when hungry. For over twenty years I had ovarian trouble, which was almost unbearable at times. It dated from the birth of my first child, and at one time necessitated an operation. I suffered with about all the ills that flesh is heir to: I had trouble with my eyes from a child; wore glasses for fourteen years, several oculists saying I would go blind, one declaring I would be blind in less than a year if I did not submit to an operation, which I refused to do.

But thanks be to God whose Truth reached me through the study of our textbook. Words fail to express what Christian Science has done for me in various ways, for my children, my home, my all. The physical healing is but a small part; the spiritual unfolding and uplifting is the "pearl of great price," the half that has never been told.—Mrs. J. P. M., Kansas City, Mo.

13
TEXTBOOK APPRECIATED

It has been my privilege to have interviews with representatives of more than sixty per cent of the nations of this earth, under their own vine and fig-tree. I had never heard a principle understandingly advanced that would enable mankind to obey the apostolic command, "prove all things," until *Science and Health with Key to the Scriptures* was placed in my hands. I believe that the honest study of this book in connection with the Bible will enable one to "prove all things."

I make this unqualified statement because of what my eyes have seen and my ears heard from my fellowmen of unquestioned integrity, and the positive proofs I have gained by the study of these books. Many supposed material laws that had been rooted and grounded in my mentality from youth have been overcome. It required some time for me to wake up to our Leader's words in *Miscellaneous Writings*, p. 206: "The advancing stages of Christian Science are gained through growth, not accretion." I had many
214

disappointments and falls before I was willing to do the scientific work required to prove this statement; yet notwithstanding the cost to ourselves, I am convinced that we cannot do much credit to the cause we profess to love until we place ourselves in a position to prove God as He really is to us individually, and our relation to Him, by scientific work.

I wish to express loving gratitude to our Leader for the new edition of *Science and Health*. In studying this new edition one cannot help seeing the wisdom, love, and careful and prayerful thought expressed in the revision. Often the changing of a single word in a sentence makes the scientific thought not only more lucid to him who is familiar with the book, but also to those just coming into the blessed light. All honor to that God-loving, God-fearing woman, Mary Baker G. Eddy, whose only work is the work of love in the helping of mankind to help themselves; who has placed before her fellow-men understandingly, what man's divine rights are, and what God really is.—H. W. B., Hartford, Conn.

14
RUPTURE AND OTHER SERIOUS ILLS HEALED

When I took up the study of Christian Science nearly three years ago, I was suffering from a very bad rupture of thirty-two years' standing. Sometimes the pain was so severe that it seemed as if I could not endure it. These spells would last four or five hours, and while everything was done for me that could be done, no permanent relief came to me until I commenced reading *Science and Health with Key to the Scriptures*. After I had once looked into it I wanted to read all the time. I was so absorbed in the study of the "little book" that I hardly realized when the healing came, but I was healed, not only of the rupture, but also of other troubles,—inflammatory rheumatism, catarrh, corns, and bunions.

I would never part with the book if I could not get another. I am seventy-seven years old, and am enjoying very good health.—Mrs. M. E. P., St. Johnsbury, Vt.

15
MOTHER AND DAUGHTER HEALED

When Christian Science came to me, I had been taking medicine every day for twenty years, on account of constipation. I had been treated by doctors and specialists; had taken magnetic treatments and osteopathy; had tried change of climate; had an operation in a hospital, and when I came out was worse than before. I was so discouraged, after I had tried everything I ever heard of, and was no better but rather grew worse, that it seemed as though I must give up trying to get well, when a friend suggested that I try Christian Science. I had heard that Christian Scientists healed by prayer, and I thought this must be the way Jesus had healed. I felt that this was all there was left for me to try. I sent for the book, *Science and Health*, and commenced to read it out of curiosity, not thinking or knowing that I could be helped by the reading, but thinking I must still take medicine and that I must also have treatment by a Scientist. I, however, dropped my medicine and read for three days; then a light began to shine in the darkness. I was healed of the trouble and have never had to take medicine since. I have studied *Science and Health* faithfully ever since, and other ailments have disappeared. My little daughter has also been healed and has learned to use this knowledge in her school work.—Mrs. O. R., Leadville, Col.

16
LIVER COMPLAINT HEALED

As my thoughts go back to the time when I believed I had nothing to live for, and when each morning's awaking from sleep brought a sense of disappointment to find myself still among the living (for I had hoped each night that I closed my eyes in sleep that it would be the last time), my heart overflows with love and gratitude to God for our dear Leader who discovered this blessed truth and to the dear ones who have helped me so lovingly and patiently over many rough places.

Twelve years ago, I consulted a physician because I had noticed some odd-looking spots on one of my arms. He said they were liver spots, but that it was not worth while prescribing for those few, that I should wait until I was covered with them. About three months later, with the exception of my face and hands, I was covered with them. Then I became alarmed and called on another physician who prescribed for me, but he finally said he could do no more for me. Other physicians were consulted with no better

216

results. Six years ago, friends advised me to see their family physician, and when I called on him he said he was positive he could cure me, so I asked him to prescribe for me. At the end of two years, after prescribing steadily, he said I was so full of medicine that he was afraid to have me take any more, and advised a rest. After having paid out a small fortune, I was no better, and very much discouraged.

Two years ago, having failed in business, I applied to one of my patrons for a furnished room where I could meet the few I still had left. This lady, who is a Christian Scientist, loaned me *Science and Health*, and because she asked me so often how I was getting on with the book, I began reading it. I also attended the Wednesday evening meetings which I found very interesting. After hearing the testimonies at the meetings, I decided to speak to some practitioner about these spots, but not until I had at least a hundred dollars on hand, because I thought I would require that amount for treatments, as I had been accustomed to paying high prices. I had not inquired about prices, and in fact did not speak to any one about my intentions, because I felt sensitive on this subject. When I had read about half of Science and Health, I missed the spots, and upon searching could find no trace of them. They had entirely disappeared without treatment. In a few weeks the reading of that book had accomplished what *materia medica* had failed to accomplish in ten years. It is impossible to express the feeling of relief and happiness which came over me then.—C. K., Astoria, N. Y.

Shortly before Mrs. Eddy passed from the human scene she had written an article titled, *"Principle and Practice."* Although this article was not published by her church until seven years later, it is indicative of her prescience regarding the handling of errors that were at the base of the decline of her church and illustrates the necessity and importance of true Christianly Scientific healing.

> "The nature and position of mortal mind are the opposite of immortal Mind. The so-called mortal mind is belief and not understanding. Christian Science requires understanding instead of belief; it is based on a fixed eternal and divine Principle, wholly apart from mortal conjecture; and it must be understood, otherwise it cannot be correctly accepted and demonstrated.

The inclination of mortal mind is to receive Christian Science through a belief instead of the understanding, and this inclination prevails like an epidemic on the body; it inflames mortal mind and weakens the intellect, but this so-called mortal mind is wholly ignorant of this fact, and so cherishes its mere faith in Christian Science.

The sick, like drowning men, catch at whatever drifts toward them. The sick are told by a faith-Scientist, "I can heal you, for God is all, and you are well, since God creates neither sin, sickness, nor death." Such statements result in the sick either being healed by their faith in what you tell them—which heals only as a drug would heal, through belief—or in no effect whatever. If the faith healer succeeds in securing (kindling) the belief of the patient in his own recovery, the practitioner will have performed a faith-cure which he mistakenly pronounces Christian Science.

In this very manner some students of Christian Science have accepted, through faith, a divine Principle, God, as their saviour, but they have not understood this Principle sufficiently well to fulfill the Scriptural commands, "Go ye into all the world, and preach the gospel." "Heal the sick." It is the healer's understanding of the operation of the divine Principle, and his application thereof, which heals the sick, just as it is one's understanding of the principle of mathematics which enables him to demonstrate its rules.

Christian Science is not a faith-cure, and unless human faith be distinguished from scientific healing, Christian Science will again be lost from the practice of religion as it was soon after the period of our great Master's scientific teaching and practice. Preaching without practice of the divine Principle of man's being has not, in nineteen hundred years, resulted in demonstrating this Principle. Preaching without the truthful and consistent practice of your statements will destroy the success of Christian Science."

The following five section headings are taken from *Retro- spection and Introspection*, pg. 24-39 by Mary Baker Eddy

The Great Discovery

It was in Massachusetts, in February, 1866, and after the death of the magnetic doctor, Mr. P. P. Quimby, whom spiritualists would associate therewith, but who was in no wise connected with this event, that I discovered the Science of divine metaphysical healing which I afterwards named Christian Science. The discovery came to pass in this way. During twenty years prior to my discovery I had been trying to trace all physical effects to a mental cause; and in the latter part of 1866 I gained the scientific certainty that all causation was Mind, and every effect a mental phenomenon.

My immediate recovery from the effects of an injury caused by an accident, an injury that neither medicine nor surgery could reach, was the falling apple that led me to the discovery how to be well myself, and how to make others so.

Even to the homoeopathic physician who attended me, and rejoiced in my recovery, I could not then explain the modus of my relief. I could only assure him that the divine Spirit had wrought the miracle—a miracle which later I found to be in perfect scientific accord with divine law.

I then withdrew from society about three years,—to ponder my mission, to search the Scriptures, to find the Science of Mind that should take the things of God and show them to the creature, and reveal the great curative Principle,—Deity.

The Bible was my textbook. It answered my questions as to how I was healed; but the Scriptures had to me a new meaning, a new tongue. Their spiritual signification appeared; and I apprehended for the first time, in their spiritual meaning, Jesus' teaching and demonstration, and the Principle and rule of spiritual Science and metaphysical healing,—in a word, Christian Science.

I named it Christian, because it is compassionate, helpful, and spiritual. God I called immortal Mind. That which sins, suffers, and dies, I named mortal mind. The physical senses, or sensuous nature, I called error and shadow. Soul I denominated substance, because Soul alone is truly substantial. God I characterized as individual entity, but His corporeality I denied. The real I claimed as eternal; and its antipodes, or the temporal, I described as unreal. Spirit I called the reality; and matter, the unreality.

I knew the human conception of God to be that He was a physically personal being, like unto man; and that the five physical senses are so many witnesses to the physical personality of mind and the real existence of matter; but I learned that these material senses testify falsely, that matter neither sees, hears, nor feels Spirit, and is therefore inadequate to form any proper conception of the infinite Mind. "If I bear witness of myself, my witness is not true." (John v. 31.)

I beheld with ineffable awe our great Master's purpose in not questioning those he healed as to their disease or its symptoms, and his marvellous skill in demanding neither obedience to hygienic laws, nor prescribing drugs to support the divine power which heals. Adoringly I discerned the Principle of his holy heroism and Christian example on the cross, when he refused to drink the "vinegar and gall," a preparation of poppy, or aconite, to allay the tortures of crucifixion.

Our great Way-shower, steadfast to the end in his obedience to God's laws, demonstrated for all time and peoples the supremacy of good over evil, and the superiority of Spirit over matter.

The miracles recorded in the Bible, which had before seemed to me supernatural, grew divinely natural and apprehensible; though uninspired interpreters ignorantly pronounce Christ's healing miraculous, instead of seeing therein the operation of the divine law.

Jesus of Nazareth was a natural and divine Scientist. He was so before the material world saw him. He who antedated Abraham, and gave the world a new date in the Christian era, was a Christian Scientist, who needed no discovery of the Science of being in order to rebuke the evidence. To one "born of the flesh," however, divine Science must be a discovery. Woman must give it birth. It must be begotten of spirituality, since none but the pure in heart can see God,—the Principle of all things pure; and none but the "poor in spirit" could first state this Principle, could know yet more of the nothingness of matter and the allness of Spirit, could utilize Truth, and absolutely reduce the demonstration of being, in Science, to the apprehension of the age.

I wrote also, at this period, comments on the Scriptures, setting forth their spiritual interpretation, the Science of the Bible, and so laid the foundation of my work called Science and Health, published in 1875.

If these notes and comments, which have never been read by any one but myself, were published, it would show that after my discovery of the absolute Science of Mind-healing, like all great truths, this spiritual Science developed itself to me until Science and Health was written. These early comments are valuable to me as waymarks of progress, which I would not have effaced.

Up to that time I had not fully voiced my discovery. Naturally, my first jottings were but efforts to express in feeble diction Truth's ultimate. In Longfellow's language,—

220

> *But the feeble hands and helpless,*
> *Groping blindly in the darkness,*
> *Touch God's right hand in that darkness,*
> *And are lifted up and strengthened.*

As sweet music ripples in one's first thoughts of it like the brooklet in its meandering midst pebbles and rocks, before the mind can duly express it to the ear,—so the harmony of divine Science first broke upon my sense, before gathering experience and confidence to articulate it. Its natural manifestation is beautiful and euphonious, but its written expression increases in power and perfection under the guidance of the great Master.

The divine hand led me into a new world of light and Life, a fresh universe—old to God, but new to His "little one." It became evident that the divine Mind alone must answer, and be found as the Life, or Principle, of all being; and that one must acquaint himself with God, if he would be at peace. He must be ours practically, guiding our every thought and action; else we cannot understand the omnipresence of good sufficiently to demonstrate, even in part, the Science of the perfect Mind and divine healing.

I had learned that thought must be spiritualized, in order to apprehend Spirit. It must become honest, unselfish, and pure, in order to have the least understanding of God in divine Science. The first must become last. Our reliance upon material things must be transferred to a perception of and dependence on spiritual things. For Spirit to be supreme in demonstration, it must be supreme in our affections, and we must be clad with divine power. Purity, self-renunciation, faith, and understanding must reduce all things real to their own mental denomination, Mind, which divides, subdivides, increases, diminishes, constitutes, and sustains, according to the law of God.

I had learned that Mind reconstructed the body, and that nothing else could. How it was done, the spiritual Science of Mind must reveal. It was a mystery to me then, but I have since understood it. All Science is a revelation. Its Principle is divine, not human, reaching higher than the stars of heaven.

Am I a believer in spiritualism? I believe in no ism. This is my endeavor, to be a Christian, to assimilate the character and practice of the anointed; and no motive can cause a surrender of this effort. As I understand it, spiritualism is the antipode of Christian Science.

I esteem all honest people, and love them, and hold to loving our enemies and doing good to them that "despitefully use you and persecute you."

Foundation Work

As the pioneer of Christian Science I stood alone in this conflict, endeavoring to smite error with the falchion of Truth. The rare bequests of Christian Science are costly, and they have won fields of battle from which the dainty borrower would have fled. Ceaseless toil, self-renunciation, and love, have cleared its pathway.

The motive of my earliest labors has never changed. It was to relieve the sufferings of humanity by a sanitary system that should include all moral and religious reform.

It is often asked why Christian Science was revealed to me as one intelligence, analyzing, uncovering, and annihilating the false testimony of the physical senses. Why was this conviction necessary to the right apprehension of the invincible and infinite energies of Truth and Love, as contrasted with the foibles and fables of finite mind and material existence.

The answer is plain. St. Paul declared that the law was the schoolmaster, to bring him to Christ. Even so was I led into the mazes of divine metaphysics through the gospel of suffering, the providence of God, and the cross of Christ. No one else can drain the cup which I have drunk to the dregs as the Discoverer and teacher of Christian Science; neither can its inspiration be gained without tasting this cup.

The loss of material objects of affection sunders the dominant ties of earth and points to heaven. Nothing can compete with Christian Science, and its demonstration, in showing this solemn certainty in growing freedom and vindicating "the ways of God" to man. The absolute proof and self-evident propositions of Truth are immeasurably paramount to rubric and dogma in proving the Christ.

From my very childhood I was impelled, by a hunger and thirst after divine things,—a desire for something higher and better than matter, and apart from it,—to seek diligently for the knowledge of God as the one great and ever-present relief from human woe. The first spontaneous motion of Truth and Love, acting through

222

Christian Science on my roused consciousness, banished at once and forever the fundamental error of faith in things material; for this trust is the unseen sin, the unknown foe,—the heart's untamed desire which breaketh the divine commandments. As says St. James: "Whosoever shall keep the whole law, and yet offend in one point, he is guilty of all."

Into mortal mind's material obliquity I gazed, and stood abashed. Blanched was the cheek of pride. My heart bent low before the omnipotence of Spirit, and a tint of humility, soft as the heart of a moonbeam, mantled the earth. Bethlehem and Bethany, Gethsemane and Calvary, spoke to my chastened sense as by the tearful lips of a babe. Frozen fountains were unsealed. Erudite systems of philosophy and religion melted, for Love unveiled the healing promise and potency of a present spiritual afflatus. It was the gospel of healing, on its divinely appointed human mission, bearing on its white wings, to my apprehension, "the beauty of holiness,"—even the possibilities of spiritual insight, knowledge, and being.

Early had I learned that whatever is loved materially, as mere corporeal personality, is eventually lost. "For whosoever will save his life shall lose it," saith the Master. Exultant hope, if tinged with earthliness, is crushed as the moth.

What is termed mortal and material existence is graphically defined by Calderon, the famous Spanish poet, who wrote,—

> What is life? 'T is but a madness.
>   What is life? A mere illusion,
>   Fleeting pleasure, fond delusion,
> Short-lived joy, that ends in sadness,
>   Whose most constant substance seems
>   But the dream of other dreams.

Medical Experiments

The physical side of this research was aided by hints from homoeopathy, sustaining my final conclusion that mortal belief, instead of the drug, governed the action of material medicine.

I wandered through the dim mazes of materia medica, till I was weary of "scientific guessing," as it has been well called. I sought

223

knowledge from the different schools,—allopathy, homoeopathy, hydropathy, electricity, and from various humbugs,—but without receiving satisfaction.

I found, in the two hundred and sixty-two remedies enumerated by Jahr, one pervading secret; namely, that the less material medicine we have, and the more Mind, the better the work is done; a fact which seems to prove the Principle of Mind-healing. One drop of the thirtieth attenuation of Natrum muriaticum, in a tumbler-full of water, and one teaspoonful of the water mixed with the faith of ages, would cure patients not affected by a larger dose. The drug disappears in the higher attenuations of homoeopathy, and matter is thereby rarefied to its fatal essence, mortal mind; but immortal Mind, the curative Principle, remains, and is found to be even more active.

The mental virtues of the material methods of medicine, when understood, were insufficient to satisfy my doubts as to the honesty or utility of using a material curative. I must know more of the unmixed, unerring source, in order to gain the Science of Mind, the All-in-all of Spirit, in which matter is obsolete. Nothing less could solve the mental problem. If I sought an answer from the medical schools, the reply was dark and contradictory. Neither ancient nor modern philosophy could clear the clouds, or give me one distinct statement of the spiritual Science of Mind-healing. Human reason was not equal to it.

I claim for healing scientifically the following advantages: First: It does away with all material medicines, and recognizes the antidote for all sickness, as well as sin, in the immortal Mind; and mortal mind as the source of all the ills which befall mortals. Second: It is more effectual than drugs, and cures when they fail, or only relieve; thus proving the superiority of metaphysics over physics. Third: A person healed by Christian Science is not only healed of his disease, but he is advanced morally and spiritually. The mortal body being but the objective state of the mortal mind, this mind must be renovated to improve the body.

First Publication

In 1870 I copyrighted the first publication on spirit-ual, scientific Mind-healing, entitled "The Science of Man." This little book is converted into the chapter on Recapitulation in Science and Health. It was so new—the basis it laid down for physical and moral health was so hopelessly original, and men were so unfamiliar with the subject—that I did not venture upon its publication until later, having learned that the merits of Christian Science must be proven before a work on this subject could be profitably published.

The truths of Christian Science are not interpolations of the Scriptures, but the spiritual interpretations thereof. Science is the prism of Truth, which divides its rays and brings out the hues of Deity. Human hypotheses have darkened the glow and grandeur of evangelical religion. When speaking of his true followers in every period, Jesus said, "They shall lay hands on the sick, and they shall recover." There is no authority for querying the authenticity of this declaration, for it already was and is demonstrated as practical, and its claim is substantiated,—a claim too immanent to fall to the ground beneath the stroke of artless workmen.

Though a man were girt with the Urim and Thummim of priestly office, and denied the perpetuity of Jesus' command, "Heal the sick," or its application in all time to those who understand Christ as the Truth and the Life, that man would not expound the gospel according to Jesus.

Five years after taking out my first copyright, I taught the Science of Mind-healing, alias Christian Science, by writing out my manuscripts for students and distributing them unsparingly. This will account for certain published and unpublished manuscripts extant, which the evil-minded would insinuate did not originate with me.

The Precious Volume

The first edition of my most important work, Science and Health, containing the complete statement of Christian Science,—the term employed by me to express the divine, or spiritual, Science of Mind-healing, was published in 1875.

When it was first printed, the critics took pleasure in saying, "This book is indeed wholly original, but it will never be read."

The first edition numbered one thousand copies. In September, 1891, it had reached sixty-two editions.

Those who formerly sneered at it, as foolish and eccentric, now declare Bishop Berkeley, David Hume, Ralph Waldo Emerson, or certain German philosophers, to have been the originators of the Science of Mind-healing as therein stated.

Even the Scriptures gave no direct interpretation of the scientific basis for demonstrating the spiritual Principle of healing, until our heavenly Father saw fit, through the Key to the Scriptures, in Science and Health, to unlock this "mystery of godliness."

My reluctance to give the public, in my first edition of Science and Health, the chapter on Animal Magnetism, and the divine purpose that this should be done, may have an interest for the reader, and will be seen in the following circumstances. I had finished that edition as far as that chapter, when the printer informed me that he could not go on with my work. I had already paid him seven hundred dollars, and yet he stopped my work. All efforts to persuade him to finish my book were in vain.

After months had passed, I yielded to a constant conviction that I must insert in my last chapter a partial history of what I had already observed of mental malpractice. Accordingly, I set to work, contrary to my inclination, to fulfil this painful task, and finished my copy for the book. As it afterwards appeared, although I had not thought of such a result, my printer resumed his work at the same time, finished printing the copy he had on hand, and then started for Lynn to see me. The afternoon that he left Boston for Lynn, I started for Boston with my finished copy. We met at the Eastern depot in Lynn, and were both surprised,—I to learn that he had printed all the copy on hand, and had come to tell me he wanted more,—he to find me en route for Boston, to give him the closing chapter of my first edition of Science and Health. Not a word had passed between us, audibly or mentally, while this went on. I had grown disgusted with my printer, and become silent. He had come to a standstill through motives and circumstances unknown to me.

Science and Health is the textbook of Christian Science. Whosoever learns the letter of this book, must also gain its spiritual significance, in order to demonstrate Christian Science.

When the demand for this book increased, and people were healed simply by reading it, the copyright was infringed. I entered a suit at law, and my copyright was protected.

AN ARCTIC AURORA—from "Tent Life in Siberia by George Kennan

"On the 26th of February [1866] . . . there occurred one of the grandest displays of the Arctic Aurora which had been observed there for more than fifty years, and which exhibited such unusual and extraordinary brilliancy that even the natives were astonished. . . . Late in the evening . . . there burst suddenly upon our startled eyes the grandest exhibition of vivid dazzling light and color of which the mind can conceive. The whole universe seemed to be on fire. A broad arch of brilliant prismatic colors spanned the heavens from east to west like a gigantic rainbow, with a long fringe of crimson and yellow streamers stretching up from its convex edge to the very zenith. At short intervals of one or two seconds, wide, luminous bands, parallel with the arch, rose suddenly out of the northern horizon and swept with a swift, steady majesty across the whole heavens, like long breakers of phophorescent light rolling in from some limitless ocean of space.

"Every portion of the vast arch was momentarily wavering, trembling, and changing color, and the brilliant streamers which fringed its edge swept back and forth in great curves, like the fiery sword of the angel at the gate of Eden. In a moment the vast auroral rainbow, with all its wavering streamers, began to move slowly up toward the zenith, and a second arch of equal brilliancy formed directly under it, shooting up another long serried row of slender colored lances toward the North Star, like a battalion of the celestial host presenting arms to its commanding angel. Every instant the display increased in unearthly grandeur. The luminous bands revolved swiftly, like the spokes of a great wheel of light across the heavens; the streamers hurried back and forth with swift, tremulous motion from the ends of the arches to the center, and now and then a great wave of crimson would surge up from the north and fairly deluge the whole sky with color, tinging the white snowy earth far and wide with its rosy reflection. But as the words of the prophecy, "And the heavens shall be turned to blood," formed themselves upon my lips, the crimson suddenly vanished, and a lightening flash of vivid orange startled us with its wide, all-pervading glare, which extended even to the southern horizon, as if the whole volume of the atmosphere had suddenly taken fire. I even held my breath a moment, as I listened for the tremendous crash of thunder which it seemed to me must follow this sudden burst of vivid light;

but in heaven of earth there was not a sound to break the calm silence of night, save the hastily-muttered prayers of the frightened native at my side, as he crossed himself and kneeled down before the visible majesty of God. I could not imagine any possible addition which even the Almighty power could make to the grandeur of the Aurora as it now appeared. The rapid alternations of crimson, blue, green, and yellow in the sky were reflected so vividly from the white surface or the snow, that the whole world seemed now steeped in blood, and then quivering in an atmosphere of pale, ghastly green, through which shone the unspeakable glories of mighty crimson and yellow arches.

"But the end was not yet. As we watched with upturned faces the swift ebb and flow of these great celestial tides of colored light, the last seal of the glorious revelation was suddenly broken, and both arches were simultaneously shivered into a thousand parallel perpendicular bars, every one of which displayed in regular order, from top to bottom, the seven primary colors of the solar spectrum. From horizon to horizon there now stretched two vast curving bridges of colored bars, across which we almost expected to see, passing and repassing, the bright inhabitants of another world. Amid cries of astonishment and exclamations of 'God have mercy!' from the startled natives, these innumerable bars began to move, with a swift dancing motion, back and forth, along the whole extent of both arches, passing each other from side to side with such bewildering rapidity, that the eye was lost in the attempt to follow them. The whole concave of heaven seemed transformed into one great revloving kaleidoscope of shattered rainbows. Never had I even dreamed of such an *aurora* as this, and I am not ashamed to confess that its magnificence at that moment overawed and frightened me. The whole sky, from zenith to horizon, was 'one molten, mantling sea of color and fire, crimson and purple, and scarlet and green, and colors for which there are no words in language and no ideas in the mind,—things which can only be conceived while they are visible.' The 'signs and portents' in the heavens were grand enough to herald the destruction of a world: flashes of rich quivering color, covering half the sky for an instant and then vanishing like summer lightning; brilliant green streamers shooting swiftly but silently up across the zenith: thousands of variegated bars sweeping past each other in two magnificent arches, and great luminous waves rolling in from the inter-planetary

228

spaces and breaking in long lines of radiant glory upon the shallow atmosphere of a darkened world.

"With the separation of the two arches into component bars it reached its utmost magnificence, and from that time its supernatural beauty slowly but steadily faded. The first arch broke up, and soon after it the second: the flashes of color appeared less and less frequently; the luminous bands ceased to revolve across the zenith; and in an hour nothing remained in the dark starry heavens to remind us of the Aurora, except a few faint Magellan clouds of luminous vapor."

MEETING OF MY DEPARTED MOTHER AND HUSBAND

JOY for thee, happy friend! thy bark
 is past
The dangerous sea, and safely
  moored at last—
    Beyond rough foam.
Soft gales celestial, in sweet music bore—
Spirit emancipate for this far shore—
    Thee to thy home.

"You've traveled long, and far from mortal
 joys,
To Soul's diviner sense, that spurns such toys,
    Brave wrestler, lone.
Now see thy ever-self; Life never fled;
Man is not mortal, never of the dead:
    The dark unknown.

"When hope soared high, and joy was eagle-
 plumed,
Thy pinions drooped; the flesh was weak,
 and doomed
    To pass away.
But faith triumphant round thy death-couch
 shed

Majestic forms; and radiant glory sped
                    The dawning day.

"Intensely grand and glorious life's sphere,—
Beyond the shadow, infinite appear
                    Life, Love divine,—
Where mortal yearnings come not, sighs
        are stilled,
And home and peace and hearts are found
        and filled,
                    Thine, ever thine.

"Bearest thou no tidings from our loved on
        earth,
The toiler tireless for Truth's new birth
                    All-unbeguiled?
Our joy is gathered from her parting sigh:
This hour looks on her heart with pitying
        eye,—
                    What of my child?"

"When, severed by death's dream, I woke
        to Life,
She deemed I died, and could not know the
        strife
                    At first to fill
That waking with a love that steady turns
To God; a hope that ever upward yearns,
                    Bowed to His will.

"Years had passed o'er thy broken household
        band,
When angels beckoned me to this bright land,
                    With thee to meet.
She that has wept o'er thee, kissed my cold
        brow,
Rears the sad marble to our memory now,
                    In lone retreat.

"By the remembrance of her loyal life,

And parting prayer, I only know my wife,
       Thy child, shall come—
Where farewells cloud not o'er our ransomed
    rest—
Hither to reap, with all the crowned and blest,
       Of bliss the sum.

"When Love's rapt sense the heartstrings
    gently sweep
With joy divinely fair, the high and deep,
       To call her home,
She shall mount upward unto purer skies;
We shall be waiting, in what glad surprise,
       Our spirits' own!"

During Mrs. Eddy's establishment of the Christian Science Church there appeared across the civilized world in virtually every major newspaper articles, editorials or other commentaries on Christian Science, *Science and Health*, or Mrs. Eddy herself. One such was from *The New Century*, Boston, of February, 1895.

ONE POINT OF VIEW—THE NEW WOMAN

We all know her—she is simply the woman of the past with an added grace—a newer charm. Some of her dearest ones call her "selfish" because she thinks so much of herself she spends her whole time helping others. She represents the composite beauty, sweetness, and nobility of all those who scorn self for the sake of love and her handmaiden duty—of all those who seek the brightness of truth not as the moth to be destroyed thereby, but as the lark who soars and sings to the great sun. She is of those who have so much to give they want no time to take, and their name is legion. She is as full of beautiful possibilities as a perfect harp, and she realizes that all the harmonies of the universe are in herself, while her own soul plays upon magic strings the unwritten anthems of love. She is the apostle of the true, the beautiful, the good, commissioned to complete all that the twelve have left undone. Hers is the mission of missions—the highest of all—to make the body not the prison, but the palace of the soul, with the brain for its great white throne.

When she comes like the south wind into the cold haunts of sin and sorrow, her words are smiles and her smiles are the sunlight which heals the stricken soul. Her hand is tender—but steel tempered with holy resolve, and as one whom her love had glorified once said—she is soft and gentle, but you could no more turn her from her course than winter could stop the coming of spring. She has long learned with patience, and to-day she knows many things dear to the soul far better than her teachers. In olden times the Jews claimed to be the conservators of the world's morals—they treated woman as a chattel, and said that because she was created after man, she was created solely for man. Too many still are Jews who never called Abraham "Father," while the Jews themselves have long acknowledged woman as man's proper helpmeet. In those days women had few lawful claims and no one to urge them. True, there were Miriam and Esther, but they sang and sacrificed for their people, not for their sex.

To-day there are ten thousand Esthers, and Miriams by the million, who sing best by singing most for their own sex. They are demanding the right to help make the laws, or at least to help enforce the laws upon which depends the welfare of their husbands, their children, and themselves. Why should our selfish self longer remain deaf to their cry? The date is no longer B. C. Might no longer makes right, and in this fair land at least fear has ceased to kiss the iron heel of wrong. Why then should we continue to demand woman's love and woman's help while we recklessly promise as lover and candidate what we never fulfil as husband and office-holder? In our secret heart our better self is shamed and dishonored, and appeals from Philip drunk to Philip sober, but has not yet the moral strength and courage to prosecute the appeal. But the east is rosy, and the sunlight cannot long be delayed. Woman must not and will not be disheartened by a thousand denials or a million of broken pledges. With the assurance of faith she prays, with the certainty of inspiration she works, and with the patience of genius she waits. At last she is becoming "as fair as the morn, as bright as the sun, and as terrible as an army with banners" to those who march under the black flag of oppression and wield the ruthless sword of injustice.

In olden times it was the Amazons who conquered the invincibles, and we must look now to their daughters to overcome our own allied armies of evil and to save us from ourselves. She must and will succeed, for as David sang —"God shall help her, and that right early." When we try to praise her later works it is as if we would pour incense upon the rose. It is the proudest boast of many of us that we are "bound to her by bonds dearer than freedom," and that we live in the reflected royalty which shines from her brow. We rejoice with her that at last we begin to know what John on Patmos meant—"And there appeared a great wonder in heaven, a woman clothed with the sun, and the moon under her feet, and upon her head a crown of twelve stars." She brought to warring men the Prince of Peace, and he, departing, left his scepter not in her hand, but in her soul. "The time of times" is near when "the new woman" shall subdue the whole earth with the weapons of peace. Then shall wrong be robbed of her bitterness and ingratitude of her sting, revenge shall clasp hands with pity, and love shall dwell in the tents of hate; while side by side, equal partners in all that is worth living for, shall stand the new man with the new woman.

APPENDIX TWO

Following is a complete listing of all the books used in the body of this work. They are referenced by the number following each instance of healing. As mentioned in an introductory note, most instances can be found in at least two, and up to fifteen different sources. For sake of brevity only one of the number of available sources has been quoted.

1. Frye, Calvin A., *Diary*, np
2. Shannon, Clara M. Sainsbury, C.S.D., *Golden Memories*, The Gethsemane Foundation, pd-1990, p.2
3. ibid., p.3
4. Grekel, Doris, *The Founding of Christian Science*, Science in Education, 1987, (vol. 2), ltr. to Judge Hanna, p.387
5. Dickey, Adam H., CSD, *Memoirs of Mary Baker Eddy*, Lillian S. Dickey, CSB, 1927, p.45
6. Spencer, Ralph B., *The Overwhelming Evidence Concerning Spiritual Healings through Mary Baker Eddy*, Ralph B. Spencer, 1963, #39
7. Smillie, Paul R., *Mary Baker Eddy: The Prophetic and Historical Perspective*, vol. 1, The Gethsemane Foundation, 1979, p.182
8. Dickey, *Memoirs of Mary Baker Eddy*, op. cit., p.46
9. Eddy, Mary Baker (and other authors, compiled by Gilbert C. Carpenter, Jr., CSB), *Miscellaneous Documents relating to Christian Science and Mary Baker Eddy*, Gilbert C. Carpenter, Jr., CSB and Gilbert C. Carpenter, Sr., CSB, 1936, p.190
10. Dickey, *Memoirs of Mary Baker Eddy*, op. cit., p.46
11. Eddy, *Miscellaneous Documents*, op. cit., p.190
12. ibid., p.191
13. Smillie, *Mary Baker Eddy. . .*, op. cit., p.188
14. Shannon, *Golden Memories*, op. cit., p.4
15. Eddy, *Miscellaneous Documents*, op. cit., p.134
16. Johnston, Julia Michael, *Mary Baker Eddy: Her Mission and Triumph* Christian Science Publishing Society, 1946, p.6
17. Wilbur, Sibyl, *The Life of Mary Baker Eddy*, Christian Science Publishing Society, 1907, p.33-4
18. Smillie, *Mary Baker Eddy. . .*, op. cit., p.192
19. Shannon, *Golden Memories*, op. cit., p.5
20. Grekel, Doris, *The Discovery of The Science of Man*, Science in Education, 1978, (vol. 1), p.20

21.   Fosbury, Arthur F., CS, *Healings Done by Mrs. Eddy*, Arthur F. Fosbury, CS, np

22.   Eddy, Mary Baker, *Footprints Fadeless*, Joseph Armstrong, 1902, p.6

23.   Shannon, *Golden Memories*, op. cit., p.9

24.   ibid., p.9

25.   Fosbury, *Healings Done by Mrs. Eddy*, op. cit., np

26.   Shannon, *Golden Memories*, op. cit., p.10

27.   Eddy, Mary Baker, *Science and Health with Key to the Scriptures*, Allison V. Stewart, 1906

28.   Glover (Eddy), Mary Baker, *Science and Health*, Christian Scientist Publishing Company, 1875, p.351

29.   Shannon, *Golden Memories*, op. cit., p.10-11

30.   Carpenter, Gilbert C., Jr., CSB, *On the First Evening in February of 1866. . .* , The Carpenter Foundation, np

31.   Oakes, Richard, CS, *Mary Baker Eddy's Six Days of Revelation*, Christian Science Research Library, 1981, p.26-7

32.   *The Lynn Reporter*, February 7, 1866

33.   Smillie, Paul R., *An Analysis of the Film: Mary Baker Eddy; A Heart in Protest*, The Gethsemane Foundation, 1990, p.53

34.   Eddy, Mary Baker, (Richard Oakes, CS, compiler), *Divinity Course and General Collectanea of Items by and about Mary Baker Eddy*, Rare Book Company, p.14

35.   Grekel, *The Discovery of The Science of Man*, op. cit., p.80

36.   Wilbur, Sibyl, *The Life of Mary Baker Eddy*, op. cit., p.140-1

37.   Shannon, *Golden Memories*, op. cit., p.29

38.   Grekel, *The Discovery of The Science of Man*, op. cit., p.82

39.   Smith, Clifford P., *Historical and Biographical Papers; Second Series*, Christian Science Publishing Society, 1934, p.54-5

40.   Wilbur, Sibyl, *The Life of Mary Baker Eddy*, op. cit., p.148-9

41.   Eddy, Mary Baker, *Science and Health*, op. cit., 19th edition, p.180

42.   Hufford, Kenneth, *Mary Baker Eddy: The Stoughton Years*, Longyear Foundation, Brookline Mass., 1963, p.4

43.   Eddy, Mary Baker G., *Retrospection and Introspection*, Joseph Armstrong, Boston, Mass., 1891, 1892, p.40-1

44.   Tomlinson, Rev. Irving C., M.A., CSB, *Twelve Years with Mary Baker Eddy: Recollections and Experiences*, Christian Science Publishing Society, Boston, Mass., 1945, p.54-5

45.   Beasley, Norman, *The Cross and The Crown*, Duell, Sloan & Pierce, N.Y. and Little Brown & Co., Boston, 1952*The Cross and TheCrown*, p.17

46.   Eddy, *Miscellaneous Documents*, op. cit., p.200

47.   Fosbury, *Healings Done by Mrs. Eddy*, op. cit., np

48.   ibid., np

49.   Glover, Mary Baker, *Science and Health*, op. cit., 1st edition, p.338

50.   Spencer, *The Overwhelming Evidence. . .* , op. cit., #2

51.   Smith, *Historical and Biographical Papers. . .* , op. cit., p.51-2

52.   Wilbur, Sibyl, *The Life of Mary Baker Eddy*, op. cit., p.143-4

53.   Grekel, *The Discovery of The Science of Man*, op. cit., p.95

54.   Grekel, *The Discovery of The Science of Man*, op. cit., p.99

55. ibid., p.97
56. Eddy, Mary Baker, *First Church of Christ, Scientist and Miscellany*, Allison V. Stewart, Boston, Mass., 1913, p.105
57. Grekel, *The Discovery of The Science of Man*, op. cit., p.312-13
58. Smith, *Historical and Biographical Papers. . .* , op. cit., p.48-9
59. ibid., 1941, p.81
60. Eddy, *Miscellaneous Documents*, op. cit., p.139
61. Jones, Elizabeth Earl, CSB, *Reminiscences of Mary Baker Eddy*, np
62. Fosbury, *Healings Done by Mrs. Eddy*, op. cit., np
63. ibid., np
64. ibid., np
65. Smith, *Historical and Biographical Papers. . .* , op. cit., p.63
66. Grekel,*The Founding of Christian Science*, op. cit., p.104-5 & 362
67. Beasley, *The Cross and The Crown*, op. cit.,p.307-8
68. Glover, Mary Baker, *Science and Health*, op. cit., 1st edition, p.353
69. ibid., p.352
70. ibid., p.352
71. ibid., p.352
72. Grekel, *The Discovery of The Science of Man*, op. cit., p.274-5
73. Eddy, Mary Baker, *Science and Health*, op. cit., 124th edition, p.193
74. Grekel, *The Discovery of The Science of Man*, op. cit.,p. 141
75. Fosbury, *Healings Done by Mrs. Eddy*, op. cit., np
76. ibid., np
77. Eddy, (Oakes, compiler), *Divinity Course,* op. cit., p.247
78. ibid., p.244
79. ibid., p.260
80. Eddy, *Footprints Fadeless*, op. cit., p.19
81. Spencer, *The Overwhelming Evidence. . .* , op. cit.
82. Smith, *Historical and Biographical Papers. . .* , op. cit., p.
83. Eddy, Mary Baker, *Science and Health with Key to the Scriptures*, op. cit., 391st edition
84. Shannon, *Golden Memories*, op. cit., p.25
85. Eddy, *Miscellaneous Documents*, op. cit., p.5
86. ibid., p.145
87. ibid., p.140
88. *Christian Science Sentinel*, vol. 46, July 18, 1908
89. Eddy, *Miscellaneous Documents*, op. cit., p.140-1
90. Fosbury, *Healings Done by Mrs. Eddy*, op. cit., np
91. Peel, Robert, *Mary Baker Eddy: The Years of Trial, 1876-1891*, Holt, Rhinehart and Winston of Canada, 1971 (vol. 2), p.315
92. Jones, *Reminiscences. . .* , op. cit., np
93. Grekel, *The Discovery of The Science of Man*, op. cit., p.151
94. Eddy, *Miscellaneous Documents*, op. cit., p.
95. Eddy, (Oakes, compiler), *Divinity Course*, op. cit., p.239
96. *We Knew Mary Baker Eddy* (Series), Christian Science Publishing Society, 1972, (vol. 4), p.16-17
97. ibid., p. 9
98. ibid., p.14-16

99. Smith, *Historical and Biographical Papers. . .* , op. cit., p.57
100. Eddy, *Miscellaneous Documents*, op. cit., p.139
101. Spencer, *The Overwhelming Evidence. . .* , op. cit., #34
102. Oakes, *Mary Baker Eddy's Six Days of Revelation*, op. cit., p.81
103. Peel, *Mary Baker Eddy: The Years of Trial*, op. cit., p.13
104. ibid., p.22
105. ibid., p.58
106. Shannon, *Golden Memories*, op. cit.
107. Eddy, Mary Baker G., *Retrospection and Introspection*, op. cit., p.16
108. Fosbury, *Healings Done by Mrs. Eddy*, op. cit., np
109. Eddy, (Oakes, compiler), *Divinity Course*, op. cit., p.239
110. Eddy, *Miscellaneous Documents*, op. cit., p.21
111. Smith, *Historical and Biographical Papers. . .* , 1941, op. cit., p.70
112. Oakes, *Mary Baker Eddy's Six Days of Revelation*, op. cit., p.96-7
113. Eddy, (Oakes, compiler), *Divinity Course*, op. cit., p.114
114. Smith, *Historical and Biographical Papers. . .* , op. cit., p.58-9
115. Grekel, *The Discovery of The Science of Man*, op. cit., p.208
116. Fosbury, *Healings Done by Mrs. Eddy*, op. cit., np
117. Smith, *Historical and Biographical Papers. . .* , 1941, op. cit., p.83
118. Grekel, *The Discovery of The Science of Man*, op. cit., p.218
119. Eddy, *Miscellaneous Writings*, op. cit.
120. Fosbury, *Healings Done by Mrs. Eddy*, op. cit., np
121. *We Knew Mary Baker Eddy* (Series), Christian Science Publishing Society, 1972, (vol. 4), p.53
122. Beasley, The Cross and The Crown, op. cit., p.104
123. Oakes, *Mary Baker Eddy's Six Days of Revelation*, op. cit., p.124-5
124. ibid., p.125
125. Peel, *Mary Baker Eddy: The Years of Trial*, op. cit., p.340
126. Oakes, *Mary Baker Eddy's Six Days of Revelation*, op. cit., p.125
127. Tomlinson, *Twelve Years with Mary Baker Eddy:* op.cit., p.70-1
128. Eddy, *Miscellaneous Writings*, op. cit., p.112
129. Putnam, Robert C., CS, *Notes on Association Meetings*, 1977, p.8
130. Fosbury, *Healings Done by Mrs. Eddy*, op. cit., np
131. Oakes, *Mary Baker Eddy's Six Days of Revelation*, op. cit., p.121
132. ibid., p.121
133. Eddy, *Miscellaneous Documents*, op. cit., p.43-5
134. Eddy, Rev. Mary Baker, *Pulpit and Press*, Mary B. Eddy, 1895, p.69
135. Spencer, *The Overwhelming Evidence. . .* , op. cit.
136. Eddy, (Oakes, compiler), *Divinity Course*, op. cit., p.3-4
137. Frye, *Diary*, op. cit., np
138. Smith, *Historical and Biographical Papers. . .* , op. cit., p.39-40
139. ibid., p.37-8
140. ibid., 1941, p.71-2
141 Eddy, *Miscellaneous Documents*, op. cit., p.198-9
142. ibid., p.200-1
143. ibid., p.210
144. Smith, *Historical and Biographical Papers. . .* , op. cit., 1941, p.79-80
145. Oakes, *Mary Baker Eddy's Six Days of Revelation*, op. cit., p.224-5

146. ibid., p.183
147. Wright, Helen, *Mary Baker Eddy: God's Great Scientist*—Volume 1, Helen Wright, 1984, p.15-16
148. Peel, *Mary Baker Eddy: The Years of Trial*, op. cit., p.154
149. ibid., p.159
150. Grekel, *The Founding of Christian Science*, op. cit., p.318-9
151. Putnam, *Notes on Association Meetings*, op. cit., p.158
152. Shannon, *Golden Memories*, op. cit., p.30
153. Smith, *Historical and Biographical Papers. . .* , op. cit., p.53
154. ibid., p.53-4
155. Spencer, *The Overwhelming Evidence. . .* , op. cit., #19
156. ibid., #46
157. Young, Alan, *Mary Baker Eddy—Her Pleasant View and Infinit Vision*, The Bookmark, p.20-21
158. Smith, *Historical and Biographical Papers. . .* , op. cit., p.62-3
159. Peel, *Mary Baker Eddy: The Years of Trial*, op. cit., p.371
160. ibid., p.371
161. Jones, *Reminiscences*, op. cit., np
162. Tomlinson, *Twelve Years with Mary Baker Eddy. . .* , op. cit., p.55-6
163. *Christian Science Journal*, vol. XXII, no.9, December, 1905
164. Shannon, *Golden Memories*, op. cit., p.29-30
165. Eddy, (Oakes, compiler), *Divinity Course*, op. cit., p.247
166. Wright, Helen, *God's Great Scientist*—Volume 3, Helen Wright, 1987, p.134-5
167. Smith, *Historical and Biographical Papers. . .* , 1941, op. cit., p.74
168. Eddy, Mary Baker, *Collectanea of Items by and about Mary Baker Eddy*, (compiled & published by Gilbert C. Carpenter Jr., CSB), 1938
169. Eddy, *Miscellaneous Documents*, op. cit., p.53-4
170. Peel, *Mary Baker Eddy: The Years of Trial*, op. cit., p.368
171. ibid., p.368
172. Putnam, Robert C., CS, *The Science of Life*, Robert C. Putnam, 1976
173. Eddy, *Collectanea. . .* , op. cit.,p.60
174. Eddy, (Oakes, compiler), *Divinity Course*, op. cit., p.245
175. Wright, *God's Great Scientist*—Volume 3, op. cit., p.123
176. Smith, *Historical and Biographical Papers. . .* , op. cit., p.67
177. Eddy, (Oakes, compiler), *Divinity Course*, op. cit., p.234
178. Putnam, *Notes on Association Meetings*, op. cit., p.108
179. Wright, *God's Great Scientist*—Volume 3, op. cit.
180. Chanfrau, Henrietta, *Reminiscences of Mary Baker Eddy*, The Gethsemane Foundation, pd-1994, p.3
181. Tomlinson, *Twelve Years with Mary Baker Eddy. . .* , op. cit., p.51
182. Grekel, *The Founding of Christian Science*, op. cit., p.62
183. Fosbury, *Healings Done by Mrs. Eddy*, op. cit., np
184. Oakes, *Mary Baker Eddy's Six Days of Revelation*, op. cit., p.368
185. Eddy, (Oakes, compiler), *Divinity Course*, op. cit., p.242-3
186. Gilman, James F., *Recollections of Mary Baker Eddy*, Gilbert C. Carpenter, Jr., CSB, 1934, 1935, 1937, p.145
187. Shannon, *Golden Memories*, op. cit., p.15

188. Gilman, *Recollections of Mary Baker Eddy*, op. cit., p.x
189. Bates, Edward P., *Reminiscences concerning the Construction of The Mother Church. . .* , The Gethsemane Foundation, pd-1989, p.20
190. Smillie, Paul R., *Loving Our Leader*, The Gethsemane Foundation, 1988, p.40
191. Bates, *Reminiscences . . . of The Mother Church. . .* , op. cit., p.23
192. Shannon, Clara M. Sainsbury, CSD, *In the Service of Mary Baker Eddy—Reminiscences by Clara M. Shannon*, Longyear Foundation, Brookline Mass., 1958
193. Norwood, Edward Everett, *Reminiscences of Mary Baker Eddy*, The Bookmark, p.2-3
194. Eddy, (Oakes, compiler), *Divinity Course*, op. cit., p.246-7
195. Shannon, *Golden Memories*, op. cit., p.40-1
196. Bates, *Reminiscences . . . of The Mother Church. . .* , op. cit., p.38
197. Shannon, *Golden Memories*, op. cit., p.38
198. Fosbury, *Healings Done by Mrs. Eddy*, op. cit., np
199. Bates, *Reminiscences . . . of The Mother Church. . .* , op. cit., p.30
200. *Christian Science Journal*, vol. XIV, p.550
201. Eddy, (Oakes, compiler), *Divinity Course*, op. cit., p.248
202. Grekel, *The Discovery of The Science of Man*, op. cit., p.282
203. Shannon, *Golden Memories*, op. cit., p.22-3
204. ibid., p.24
205. Spencer, *The Overwhelming Evidence. . .* , op. cit., #8
206. Fosbury, *Healings Done by Mrs. Eddy*, op. cit., np
207. Chanfrau, *Reminiscences of Mary Baker Eddy*, op. cit., p.6
208. Grekel, *The Founding of Christian Science*, op. cit., p.304
209. ibid., p.325
210. Eddy, *First Church of Christ, Scientist and Miscellany*, op. cit., p.145
211. Grekel, *The Founding of Christian Science*, op. cit., p.329
212. ibid., p.331
213. ibid., p.344-5
214. Eddy, *Miscellaneous Documents*, op. cit., p.112-13
215. *Letters of Augusta Stetson*, p.29
216. Peel, *Mary Baker Eddy: The Years of Trial*, op. cit., p.194
217. Shannon, *Golden Memories*, op. cit., p.31
218. Eddy, *Miscellaneous Documents*, op. cit.
219. Shannon, *Golden Memories*, op. cit., p.41-2
220. Putnam, *The Science of Life*, op. cit., p.88
221. Spencer, *The Overwhelming Evidence. . .* , op. cit., #16
222. Shannon, *Golden Memories*, op. cit., p.38-9
223. Fosbury, *Healings Done by Mrs. Eddy*, op. cit., np
224. Grekel, *The Founding of Christian Science*, op. cit., p.359
225. Spencer, *The Overwhelming Evidence. . .* , op. cit., #10
226. ibid., #11
227. Eddy, (Oakes, compiler), *Divinity Course*, op. cit., p.255
228. Shannon, *Golden Memories*, op. cit., p.42-3
229. Jones, *Reminiscences*, op. cit., np
230. Eddy, (Oakes, compiler), *Divinity Course*, op. cit., p.253-4

231. Jones, *Reminiscences*, op. cit., np
232. Frye, *Diary*, op. cit., np
233. Spencer, *The Overwhelming Evidence. . .* , op. cit., #12
234. Frye, *Diary*, op. cit., np
235. Grekel, Doris, *The Forever Leader*, Science in Education, 1990, (vol. 3), p.5-6
236. ibid., p.33
237. ibid., p.18-19
238. Shannon, *Golden Memories*, op. cit., p.25
239. ibid., p.40
240. Fosbury, *Healings Done by Mrs. Eddy*, op. cit., np
241. ibid., np
242. Grekel, *The Founding of Christian Science*, op. cit., p.262
243. ibid., p.262
244. ibid., p.262
245. Fosbury, *Healings Done by Mrs. Eddy*, op. cit., np
246. Henty, Doris Dufour, CS, *Addresses and Other Writings on Christian Science*, Mulberry Press, 1990
247. Putnam, *Notes on Association Meetings*, op. cit., p.115
248. Smillie *An Analysis of the Film: Mary Baker Eddy. . .* , op. cit., p.52-3
249. Smith, *Historical and Biographical Papers. . .* , op. cit., p.61-2
250. ibid., np
251. Spencer, *The Overwhelming Evidence. . .* , op. cit., #1
252. Jones, *Reminiscences*, op. cit., np
253. Grekel, *The Forever Leader*, op. cit., p.133
254. Eddy, (Oakes, compiler), *Divinity Course*, op. cit., p.13
255. Spencer, *The Overwhelming Evidence. . .* , op. cit., #3
256. Peel, Robert, *Mary Baker Eddy, The Years of Authority*, Holt, Rhinehart and Winston of Canada, 1977, p.469
257. Wright, *God's Great Scientist*—Volume 3, op. cit., p.206-7
258. Grekel, *The Forever Leader*, op. cit., p.174-5
259. Smillie *An Analysis of the Film: Mary Baker Eddy. . .* , op. cit.
260. Eddy, (Oakes, compiler), *Divinity Course*, op. cit., p.256
261. ibid., p.249-50
262. Grekel, *The Forever Leader*, op. cit., p.180
263. Eddy, *Miscellaneous Documents*, op. cit., p.126-7
264. Jones, *Reminiscences*, op. cit., np
265. Peel, *Mary Baker Eddy, The Years of Authority*, op. cit., p.279
266. Tomlinson, *Twelve Years with Mary Baker Eddy. . .* , op. cit., p.62-5
267. Eddy, *Miscellaneous Documents*, op. cit., p.35-6
268. Powell, Lyman P., *Mary Baker Eddy: A Life Size Portrait*, The MacMillan Company, New York, 1930, p.253-4
269. Eddy, (Oakes, compiler), *Divinity Course*, op. cit., p.262
270. Dickey, *Memoirs of Mary Baker Eddy*, op. cit.
271. ibid., p.38-9
272. Jones, *Reminiscences*, op. cit., np
273. Eddy, (Oakes, compiler), *Divinity Course*, op. cit., p.242
274. ibid., p.114

275. Smillie, Paul R., *The Father, the Prodigal, and the Citizen*, The Gethsemane Foundation, 1988, p.17
276. Grekel, *The Forever Leader*, op. cit., p.568, 575
277. Smillie, *The Father, the Prodigal, and the Citizen*, op. cit., p.17
278. Frye, *Diary*, op. cit., np
279. Eddy, *Miscellaneous Documents*, op. cit., p.136
280. Oakes, Richard, CS, compiler, *Mary Baker Eddy's Lessons of The Seventh Day*, Christian Science Research Library, Christian Science Foundation, 1989, p.307
281. Oakes, *Mary Baker Eddy's Six Days of Revelation*, op. cit., p.113
282. Grekel, *The Forever Leader*, op. cit., p.574
283. Smillie, *The Father, the Prodigal, and the Citizen*, op. cit.
284. ibid., p.18
285. Grekel, *The Forever Leader*, op. cit., p.570
286. Putnam, *Notes on Association Meetings*, op. cit., p.150
287. ibid., p.91
288. Grekel, *The Forever Leader*, op. cit., p.589-90
289. ibid., p.590-91
290. Grekel, Doris, *The Independent Christian Scientist*, vol. 4, No. 4, Science in Education, 1990
291. Bates, Ernest Sutherland, *Mrs. Eddy's Right-Hand Man*, Harper and Brothers, 1931, pamphlet
292. Oakes, *Mary Baker Eddy's Lessons of The Seventh Day*, op. cit., p.307
293. Peel, *Mary Baker Eddy, The Years of Authority*, op. cit., p.513
294. Putnam, *Notes on Association Meetings*, p.151

APPENDIX THREE

FOOTNOTES

1 Mark 16:17, 18

2 Matt. 28:20

3 Elizabeth Earl Jones, CSB, *Reminiscences*, n.p.

* Today's Merriam-Webster Dictionary bears little resemblance to the inspired work accomplished by Noah Webster on behalf of the American people. The current publisher of this dictionary has confirmed that Noah Webster's work was never revised, but in fact completely replaced! The definitions are completely different in many cases. This 1828 version maintains the integrity of his work.

† Christian Scientists take these Biblical synonyms (Life, Truth, Love, Mind, Soul, Spirit, Principle) for God and capitalize them.

‡ "Leader" is the title given Mary Baker Eddy by all adherents of the Christian Science faith.

4 *Personal Knowledge of Mary Baker Eddy* by Elizabeth Earl Jones, CSB
"I am going to tell you many things I have personal knowledge of concerning our beloved Leader. Some important things,—some just 'homey ' little things, as I remember them. *I feel it is the duty of those of us who had personal knowledge of the Discoverer and Founder of Christian Science and of those very closely associated with her, to share our 'first hand' knowledge with others.* It is a great joy to do this. (emphasis added) ..." I have had the privilege of reading many letters our dear Leader wrote her students. These letters were shown me by the students to whom they were written. I did not get them from copied statements circulated among Scientists. If I had, I would not quote them. (lesson 7:20)

5 Mary Baker Eddy, *Science and Health with Key to the Scriptures*, vide p. 138:20-22

6 *We Knew Mary Baker Eddy, First Series*, pp. 68-9

7 Mary Baker Eddy, *Mary Baker Eddy's Lessons of The Seventh Day*, Richard Oakes, compiler, p. 338

8 Clifford Smith, *Historical Sketches*, pp.70-71

9 Julia M. Johnston, *Mary Baker Eddy: Her Mission and Triumph, pp.,78-9*

10 Tomlinson, op. cit., pp. 136-7

11 Arthur Brisbane, *What Mrs. Eddy Said to Arthur Brisbane*, pp. 42-45

12 Reverend Severin E. Simonsen, *From the Methodist Pulpit Into Christian Science*, pp. 155-156

13 *Miscellaneous Documents*, op. cit., p. 17-18

14 Jones, *Ibid.*

15 Mary Baker Eddy,*Divinity Course and General Collectanea*, Richard Oakes, p.224.

* The appellation 'Mother' was given Mrs. Eddy by many of her students because of the natural motherlove she constantly expressed to all those around her.

16 Jones, op. cit., n.p.

17 *We Knew Mary Baker Eddy*, Fourth Series, p. 72

18 Jones, op. cit., n.p.

19 Mary Baker Eddy,*Divinity Course and General Collectanea*, Richard Oakes

20 Jones, op. cit., Lesson XII:25

21 Reminiscence contained in a letter to Bliss Knapp from Ira Knapp, as related by Dr. Robert C. Putnam (member of Bliss Knapp's Association) to the compiler.

22 Jones, op. cit., n.p.

23 *Miscellaneous Documents*, op. cit., p. 141

24 *Divinity Course and General Collectanea*, op. cit., p. 252

25 see Wright, Helen, *God's Great Scientist, vol. III*, p. 76

26 Jones, op. cit.

27 *The Christian Science Standard*, Vol. 5, No. 3, July 1, 1994, p.10

28 Jones, op. cit. & *Divinity Course and General Collectanea*, op. cit.

29 *Miscellaneous Documents*, op. cit., p. 40-1

30 Tomlinson, Irving C., *Twelve Years with Mary Baker Eddy*

31 Oakes, Richard, *Lessons of the Seventh Day*

32 *Divinity Course and General Collectanea*, op. cit., p. 25

33 Jones, op. cit., n.p.

34 ibid.

35 Haw, Richard C., *Mindpower and the Spiritual Dimension*, p.126

36 Ibid

37 John Randall Dunn, *The Woman God-crowned*, Christian Science Sentinel of Sept. 18, 1943, p. 1609

38 Mary Baker Eddy, *Science and Health with Key to the Scriptures*, vide p. 18

39 Paul R. Smillie, *The Father, the Prodigal and the Citizen*, p.20

40 Carpenter, Gilbert C., *Mary Baker Eddy: Her Spiritual Footsteps*

41 Jones, op. cit., n.p.

42 Mary Baker Eddy,*Divinity Course and General Collectanea*, Richard Oakes, compiler, p. 260

3 Diary *of Calvin Frye, CSD*

43 Irving C. Tomlinson, *Twelve Years with Mary Baker Eddy*, p.135

44 Ralph Spencer, *The Overwhelming Evidence*, p. 36

45 Tomlinson, op. cit., p. 212

46 Tomlinson, op. cit., p.51

47 *Miscellaneous Documents*, op. cit., p. 142

48 *Divinity Course and General Collectanea*, op. cit., pp. 257-258

49 *Miscellaneous Documents*, op. cit., p. 136

50 *Ibid.*, p. 258

BIBLIOGRAPHY

To the interested student wanting to learn more about Mary Baker Eddy and Christian Science it is helpful to read those volumes that portray the most accurate picture of Mrs. Eddy and her discovery. Naturally, those books written by those students who knew Mrs. Eddy or worked in her home would certainly provide the most accurate, and usually the most inspiring, accounts of her life and character.

"The Christian world accepts as infallible, statements which were made by our Lord and Master, which were not recorded for from thirty to sixty years after he made them. The statements recorded by Mrs. Eddy's students were written down within a few moments after they were made, a fact which should weigh on the side of proving their accuracy and correctness...." (p. viii, *Divinity Course and General Collectanea*)

Of course, the reader is safe with any of Mrs. Eddy's (also Glover) writings and is heartily recommended to them.

Your local library may have some of the better known volumes. Certainly the nearby Christian Science Reading Room will be able to provide many of the items listed. For many older volumes the only available place to find them is in used book stores. Several organizations that sell works on C. S. and Mary Baker Eddy are listed below. Please write them for a catalog of their current offerings.

Aequus Institute, (800) 441-1963
250 W. First St., Suite 330, Claremont, CA 91711
The Bookmark, Ann Beals, (805) 298-7767
P. O. Box 801143, Santa Clarita, CA 91380
Rare Book Company, Jerry Lupo, (908) 364-8043
P. O. Box 957, Freehold, NJ 07728
The Gethsemane Foundation (208) 245-4087
P.O. Box 583, St. Maries, Idaho 83861

Some of the books listed are wonderful inspiring accounts of Mrs. Eddy as Discoverer, Founder and Leader of the Christian Science church, revealing precious insights into her life work and continuous healing ministry. Other volumes may have accurate historical information but are negligent in their ability to portray Mary Baker Eddy's life in a spiritual light. In the realm of intellectual scholarly exercise one or another of the books listed are accorded significant accolades and position in the arena of known and "authorized" literature about this great woman. However, a merely scholastic recitation, although comprehensive in historical fact, is insufficient to present even a half-way proper account of one of history's greatest religious lights and inspired leaders.

It was not a comprehensive accounting of every fact of Christ Jesus' material existence which has made him the inspired example that has commanded the world's allegiance—it is however, his spiritual stature, his nearness or oneness with his Father-Mother God, his practical demonstration of divine law in the human condition, that has elevated him to Master of all mankind.

To gain a proper understanding of a spiritual idea, or one who is spiritually near God, the preparation and composition must be from an inspired viewpoint, the standpoint of spiritual sense, not material conceptions.

Armstrong, Joseph, *The Mother Church*
    Christian Science Publishing Society, © 1897, vols., 103 pp., second edition

Baker, Alfred E., M.D., C.S.D., *Instruction in Metaphysics*
    Carpenter, Gilbert C., Jr., C.S.B., ©, vols., 45 pp., first edition

Bancroft, Samuel Putnam, *Mrs. Eddy As I Knew Her In 1870*
    Longyear Foundation, © 1923, vols., 127 pp., first edition

Bates, Edward P., *Reminiscences concerning the Construction of The Mother Church ...*
    The Gethsemane Foundation, St. Maries, Idaho, © pub.-1989, vols., 40 pp., second edition

Bates, Ernest Sutherland, P.H.D. & John V. Dittemore, *Mary Baker Eddy, The Truth and the Tradition*
    Alfred A. Knopf, © 1932, vols., 476+36 pp., first edition

Beals, Ann, *Crisis in the Christian Science Church*
    Ann Beals, P.O. Box 4184, Pasadena, California 91106, © 1978, vols., 145 pp., first edition

Beasley, Norman, *The Continuing SPIRIT*
    Duell, Sloan and Pierce, N.Y., © 1956, vols., 403 pp., first edition

Beasley, Norman, *The Cross and The Crown*
    Duell, Sloan & Pierce, N.Y. and Little, Brown & Co., Boston, © 1952, vols., 664 pp., first edition

Beasley, Norman, (© by Meredith Publishing Co.), *Mary Baker Eddy*
    Duell, Sloan & Pierce, N.Y., © 1963, vols., 371 pp., first edition

Braden, Charles S., *Christian Science Today; Power, Policy, Practice*
    Southern Methodist University Press, Dallas, © 1958 SMU, vols., 432 pp., first edition

Brisbane, Arthur, *Mary Baker G. Eddy*
    The Ball Publishing Company, Boston, © 1908, vols., 64 pp., first edition

Brisbane, Arthur, *What Mrs. Eddy Said to Arthur Brisbane*
    M. E. Paige, Publisher, 33 W. 42nd St., NewYork, © 1930, vols., 64 pp., edition

Brosang, Ernest J., *A Christian Science Library*
    Ernest J. Brosang, © 1990, vols., 214 pp., first edition

Byrum, E. E., *Miracles and Healing*
    Gospel Trumpet Company, © 1919, vols., 302 pp., first edition

Caldwell, Sallie Bowman, *Mary Baker Eddy*
    Christian Science Publishing Society, © 1936, 1942, vols., 20 pp., first edition

Canham, Erwin D., *The Christian Science Monitor: "To injure no man, but to bless all mankind."*
    The Newcomen Society in North America, 1954, © 1954, vols., 28 pp., first edition

Carpenter, Gilbert C., C.S.B., & GCC, Jr., C.S.B., *Mary Baker Eddy, Her Spiritual Footsteps*
    Carpenter, Gilbert C., Jr., C.S.B., © 1934, vols., 432 pp., first edition

Carpenter, Gilbert C., Jr., C.S.B., *On the First Evening in February of 1866 ...*
    The Carpenter Foundation, ©, vols., 2 pp., first edition

Carpenter, Gilbert C., Jr., C.S.B., COP-Rhode Island, *Questions and Answers on Christian Science*
    Newport County Sentinel, Tiverton, R.I., © 1932, vols., 128 pp., first edition

Carpenter, Gilbert Congdon, C.S.B., G. C. C., Jr., C.S.B., *Poems of Spiritual Thought*
    Gilbert C. Carpenter, Jr., C.S.B., © 1933, vols., 30 pp., first edition

Carpenter, Jr., Gilbert C., C.S.B., *500 Watching Points for advancing students of Christian Science*
    Gilbert C. Carpenter, Jr., C.S.B., © 1942, vols., 317 pp., first edition

Carpenter, Jr., Gilbert C., C.S.B., *Address on Christian Science*
The Newport County Sentinel, Tiverton, Rhode Island, © 1932 , vols., 32 pp., first edition

Chanfrau, Henrietta, *Reminiscences of Mary Baker Eddy*
The Gethsemane Foundation, St. Maries, Idaho, © 1994 , vols., 12 pp., second edition

Christian Science Publishing Society, *Editorial Comments on the Life and Work of Mary Baker Eddy*
Christian Science Publishing Society, © 1911 , vols., 132 pp., first edition

Christian Science Publishing Society, *Landmarks from Bow to Boston*
Christian Science Publishing Society, © 1948 , vols., N.P. pp., fourth+ edition

Christian Science Publishing Society, *Mary Baker Eddy Mentioned Them*
Christian Science Publishing Society, © 1961 , vols., 239 pp., first edition

Christian Science Publishing Society, *Permanancy of The Mother Church and Its Manual—Revised Edition*
Christian Science Publishing Society, © 1954 , vols., 28 pp. Revised edition

Christian Science Publishing Society, *We Knew Mary Baker Eddy—Volume I*
Christian Science Publishing Society, © 1943 , 1/4 vols., 87 pp., first edition

Christian Science Publishing Society, *We Knew Mary Baker Eddy—Volume II*
Christian Science Publishing Society, © 1950 , 2/4 vols., 75 pp., first edition

Christian Science Publishing Society, *We Knew Mary Baker Eddy—Volume III*
Christian Science Publishing Society, © 1953 , 3/4 vols., 96 pp., first edition

Christian Science Publishing Society, *We Knew Mary Baker Eddy—Volume IV*
Christian Science Publishing Society, © 1972 , 4/4 vols., 110 pp., first edition

Christian Science Publishing Society - 12 authors, *Mary Baker Eddy, A centennial appreciation*
Christian Science Publishing Society, © 1965 , vols., 115 pp., first edition

Compilation from Ladies Home Jour. & C.S. Monitor, *America's Twelve Great Women Leaders during the Last ...*
Associated Authors Service, 222 West Adams St., Chicago, IL, © 1933 , vols., 55 pp. ,of Prog. edition

Covington, Benjamin N., *A Clarion Call*
Benjamin N. Covington, Atlanta, Georgia, © 1985 , vols., 53 pp., first edition

d'Humy, Fernand E., *Mary Baker Eddy Fulills Prophecy*
Library Publishers, New York, © 1953 , vols., 217 pp., first edition

d'Humy, Fernand E., *Mary Baker Eddy, in a new light*
Library Publishers, New York, © 1952 , vols., 181 pp., first edition

Dakin, Edwin Franden, *MRS. EDDY, The Biography of a Virginal Mind*
Charles Scribner's Sons, N.Y., London, © 1929 , vols., 553 pp., first edition

Dickey, Adam H., C.S.D., *Memoirs of Mary Baker Eddy*
Lillian S. Dickey, C.S.B., Brookline, Mass., © 1927 , vols., 141 pp., first edition

Eddy, Mary Baker, *Collectanea of Items by and about Mary Baker Eddy*
Carpenter, Gilbert C., Jr., C.S.B., © 1938 , vols. ,175+73 pp., first edition

Eddy, Mary Baker, *Essays on Christian Science ascribed to Mary Baker Eddy*
Carpenter, Gilbert C., Jr. C.S.B., © , vols., 158 pp., first edition

Eddy, Mary Baker, *First Church of Christ, Scientist and Miscellany*
Allison V. Stewart, Boston, Mass., © 1913 , vols., 364 pp. ,edition

Eddy, Mary Baker, *Footprints Fadeless*
Joseph Armstrong, 95 Falmouth St. (orig.), GCC, Jr., © 1902 , vols., 67 pp. ,imited) edition

Eddy, Mary Baker, *Fragments Gathered From Unpublished Items*
Gilbert C. Carpenter, Jr., C.S.B., © 1947, vols., 208 pp., first edition

Eddy, Mary Baker, *Instruction in Metaphysics*
Gilbert C. Carpenter, Jr., C.S.B., ©, vols., 45 pp., first edition

Eddy, Mary Baker, *Items by and about Mary Baker Eddy culled from the press*
Carpenter, Gilbert C., Jr. C.S.B., © 1961, vols., 116+40 pp., first edition

Eddy, Mary Baker, *Notes on the Course in Divinity recorded by Lida Fitzpatrick, 1903,4,7*
Carpenter, Gilbert C., Jr. C.S.B., ©, vols., **** pp., second edition

Eddy, Mary Baker, *Poems*
Mary Baker Eddy (privately printed), © 1910, vols., 79 pp. ;ntation edition

Eddy, Mary Baker, *Repaid Pages*
Mary Baker Eddy, Concord, N.H., © 1896, vols., • pp. ,imited) edition

Eddy, Mary Baker, *Retrospection and Introspection*
Trustees under the Will of Mary Baker Eddy, © 1891, 1892, vols., 95 pp. ,edition

Eddy, Mary Baker, *Rudimental Divine Science/No and Yes*
Trustees under the Will of Mary Baker Eddy, © 1891, 1908, vols., 46 pp. ,edition

Eddy, Mary Baker, *Science and Health*
, ©, vols., pp., 124th edition

Eddy, Mary Baker, *Science and Health with Key to the Scriptures*
Eric William Winston Taylor, © 1906, vols., 700 pp. ,edition

Eddy, Mary Baker, *Science and Health with Key to the Scriptures*
Allison V. StewartFalmouth and St. Paul Streets, Boston, Mass., © 1875, 1906, vols., 700 pp., 1910 edition

Eddy, Mary Baker, *Stetson Letters*
Ann Beals, The Bookmark, ©, vols., pp. ,edition

Eddy, Mary Baker, *Unity of Good*
Trustees under the Will of Mary Baker Eddy, © 1887, 91, 08, vols., 64 pp. ,edition

Eddy, Mary Baker, *Visions of Mary Baker Eddy as recorded by her secretary, Calvin A. Frye*
Carpenter, Gilbert C., Jr., C.S.B., © 1935, vols., 89 pp., second edition

Eddy, Mary Baker, *What is Nearest and Dearest to My Heart*
The Harmony Shop, 38 West St., Boston, © 1907, vols., 1 pp., first edition

Eddy, Mary Baker (many authors about MBE), *Miscellaneous Documents relating to Christian Science & MBE*
Carpenter, Gilbert C., Jr. C.S.B., ©, vols., 232 pp., first edition

Eddy, Mary Baker as prepared by Alfred E. Baker, *Notes on Metaphysical Obstetrics, Obstetrics Class of June, 1900*
Carpenter, Gilbert C., Jr., C.S.B., © 1930, vols., 41 pp., first edition

Eddy, Mary Baker G., *Historical Sketch of Metaphysical Healing.*
Eddy, Mary Baker G., © 1885, 1 vols., 21 pp., first edition

Eddy, Mary Baker G., *Mind-Healing: Historical Sketch.*
Eddy, Mary Baker G., © 1886, 1 vols., 24 pp., first edition

Eddy, Mary Baker G., *Miscellaneous Writings 1883-1896*
Trustees under the Will of Mary Baker Eddy, © 1896, vols., 471 pp. ,edition

Eddy, Mary Baker G., *Retrospection and Introspection*
Joseph Armstrong, 250, Huntington Ave., Boston, Mass., 1907, © 1891, 1892, vols., 130 pp. ,edition

Eddy, Mary Baker G., *Rudimental Divine Science*
    Joseph Armstrong, CSD, 95 Falmouth St., Boston, Mass., 1897, © 1891, vols.,   35 pp.,   tenth edition

Eddy, Mary Baker with commentary by GCC, Sr., & Jr., *Mary Baker Eddy, Her Spiritual Precepts, volumes I-V*
    Gilbert C. Carpenter, C.S.B., & Gilbert C. Carpenter, Jr., C.S.B., © 1942, 5 vols.,   np pp.,   first edition

Eddy, Mary Baker, compiled by G. C. Carpenter, Jr., *Fragments Gathered from Unpublished Items ascribed to Mrs. Eddy*
    Carpenter, Gilbert C., Jr., C.S.B., © 1947, vols., 208 pp.,   first edition

Eddy, Mary Baker, compiled by G. C. Carpenter, Jr., *Watches • Prayers • Arguments*
    Carpenter, Gilbert C., Jr., C.S.B., © 1950, vols., 114 pp.,   final edition

Eddy, Mary Baker—©James Neal & Thomas Hatten, *Church Manual of The First Church of Christ, Scientist*
    Christian Science Publishing Society, 95 Falmouth St., Boston, Mass., © 1897, vols.,   76 pp., edition

Eddy, Rev. Mary Baker, *Christ and Christmas*
    Mary Baker Eddy, © 1897, vols.,   53 pp.,   third edition

Eddy, Rev. Mary Baker, *Pulpit and Press*
    Mary Baker Eddy, © 1895, vols.,   131 pp.,   first edition

Eisen, Gustavus A., *The Great Chalice of Antioch*
    Fahim Kouchakji, New York, © 1933, vols.,   22 pp., edition

Ernest Sutherland Bates, *Mrs. Eddy's Right-Hand Man*
    Harper and Brothers, © 1931, 162 vols.,   12 pp., edition

F. A. Moore, editor, *Gems for You*
    William H. Fisk, Manchester, NH, © 1850, vols.,   312 pp.,   first edition

F. E. H., *The Latter Days with Evidence from The Great Pyramid*
    London: Robert Banks & Son, Racquet Court, Fleet Street, E.C., © 1895, vols.,   40 pp.,   first edition

Fisher, H. A. L., *Our New Religion*
    Jonathan Cape & Harrison Smith, New York, © 1930, vols.,   201 pp.,   first edition

Flower, B. O., *Christian Science as a Religious Belief and a Therapeutic Agent*
    20th Century Company, © 1909, vols.,   158 pp.,   first edition

Fosbery, Arthur F., C.S., *Healings Done by Mrs. Eddy*
    Arthur F. Fosbury, C.S., ©, vols., pp., edition

Frye, Calvin A., *Diary*
    Calvin A. Frye, © n/a, vols.,   n.p. pp., photost edition

Gilman, James F., *Recollections of Mary Baker Eddy*
    Gilbert C. Carpenter, Jr., C.S.B., © 1937?, vols.,   92 pp.,   second edition

Glover, Mary Baker, *Science and Health*
    Christian Scientist Publishing Company, © 1875, vols.,   456 pp.,   first edition

Glover, Mary Baker, *Science and Health*
    Asa G. Eddy, Lynn, No. 8 Broad Street, © 1876, 2nd vols.,   167 pp.,   second edition

Glover, Mary Baker, *Science and Health*
    , ©, vols., pp.,   19th edition

Glover, Mary Baker, *The Science of Man by which the sick are healed embracing Q's & A's . . .*
    Mary Baker Glover, © 1870, vols.,   22 pp.,   second edition

Glover, Mary Baker (Mary Baker Eddy), *Science and Health*
    Winifred W. Gatling, Mizpah, Jaffa Road, Jerusalem, Israel, © 1874, vols.,   456 pp.,   first edition

Grekel, Doris, *The Discovery of The Science of Man* (Volume I)
Science in Education, Oakhurst, California, 1978, © 1978, 1/3 vols.,   390 pp.,   first edition

Grekel, Doris, *The Forever Leader* (Volume III)
Science in Education, 1990, © 1990, 3/3 vols.,   661 pp.,   first edition

Grekel, Doris, *The Founding of Christian Science* (Volume II)
Science in Education, 1987, © 1987, 2/3 vols.,   526 pp.,   first edition

Grekel, Doris, *The Individual Christian Scientist—vol. 4, no. 4*
Science in Education, 1990, ©, vols.,   661 pp.,   first edition

Hanna, Septimus J., *Christian Science History*
Christian Science Publishing Society, © 1899,   1 vols.,   44 pp.,   first edition

Hanna, Septimus J., *The Christian Science Case*
Ernest J. Brosang, 4 Glen Rd., Bound Brook, NJ (republished), ©, vols.,   21 pp., edition

Hanna, Septimus J.-orig. published by CSPS, *Healing through Christian Science. Discourses and Editorials*
Ernest J. Brosang, 4 Glen Rd., Bound Brook, NJ (republished), © 1898, 1902, vols.,   36 pp., edition

Harper's Magazine, *vol. 162, 2/31*
, ©, vols., pp., edition

Hartsook, Andrew, *Christian Science after 1910*
Andrew Hartsook, Zanesville, Ohio, © 1993, vols.,   215 pp.,   first edition

Hay, Ella H., *A Child's Life of Mary Baker Eddy*
Christian Science Publishing Society, One Norway Street, Boston, Mass., © 1942, vols.,   120 pp., edition

Henry, Edward L., *The Birthplace of Mary Baker Eddy—Bow, New Hampshire*
The Woodbury E. Hunt Company, Concord, New Hampshire, © 1914, vols., np(12) pp.,   first edition

Henty, Doris Dufour, C.S., *Addresses and Other Writings on Christian Science*
Mulberry Press, Box 461, Carmel, Calif. 93921, © 1990, vols.,   346 pp.,   first edition

Houpt, Charles Theodore, *Bliss Knapp, Christian Scientist*
Charles Theodore Houpt, © 1976, 1979, vols.,   417 pp.,   first edition

Hufford, Kenneth, *Mary Baker Eddy: The Stoughton Years*
Longyear Foundation, 120 Seaver St., Brookline, MA, © 1963, vols.,   41+2 pp.,   first edition

Irving C. Tomlinson, M.A., C.S.B., *Twelve Years with Mary Baker Eddy; Recollections and Experiences*
Christian Science Publishing Society, Boston, Mass., USA, © 1945, vols.,   227 pp., edition

Johnson, William Lyman, *From Hawthorne Hall*
The Homewood Press, (Dorchester) Boston, Mass., © 1922, vols.,   421 pp., edition

Johnson, William Lyman, *The History of the Christian Science Movement*
The Zion Research Foundation, © 1926,   2 vols.,   958 pp.,   first edition

Johnston, Julia Michael, *Mary Baker Eddy: Her mission and Triumph*
Christian Science Publishing Society, © 1946, 1974, vols.,   195 pp.,   ? edition

Jones, Elizabeth Earl, *Reminiscences of Mary Baker Eddy*
Elizabeth Earl Jones, © ?, vols., pp., edition

Jones, Elizabeth Earl, *The Language of Color*
Hackney & Mcale Co., Asheville, © 1903, vols.,   76 pp.,   first edition

Joseph S. Robinson, *Waymarks . . in the life of Mary Baker Eddy*
The Pond-Ekberg Company, Springfield, Mass., © 1942, vols.,   108 pp., De Luxe edition

Kathrens, R. D., (compiler), *Sidelights on Mary Baker Eddy-Glover-Science Church Trustees Controvers*
    Kathrens, R. D., © 1907 ̗ vols.,   88 pp.,   first edition

Keene, John Henry, *Christian Science and its Enemies.*
    W. E. C. Harrison & Sons, Baltimore, © 1902 ̗ vols.,   49 pp.,   first edition

Kimball, Edward A., *Lectures and Articles on Christian Science*
    Edna Kimball Wait, Chesterton, Indiana, © 1921 ̗ vols.,   486 pp.,   first edition

Kimball, Edward A.–edited by Frank Baker Smith, *Teaching and Addresses of Edward A. Kimball, C.S.D.*
    Metaphysical Science Association, Los Angeles, California, © 1917 ̗ vols.,   382 pp., edition

Knapp, Bliss, *Ira Oscar Knapp and Flavia Stickney Knapp: A Biographical Sketch*
    Plimpton Press, © 1925 ̗ vols., pp.,   xerox edition

Knapp, Bliss, *The Destiny of The Mother Church*
    Bliss Knapp, © 1947 ̗ vols.,   234 pp.,   first edition

Kratzer, Rev. G.A., *Dominion Within*
    Kratzer, Rev. G.A., © 1913 ̗ vols.,   224 pp.,   sixth edition

Kratzer, Rev. G.A., *Revelation Interpreted*
    The Central Christian Science Institute, Chicago, © 1915 ̗ vols.,   396 pp.,   first edition

Lambert, Rev. L. A., *Christian Science • Before the Bar of Reason*
    Christian Press Association Publishing Company, © 1908 ̗ vols.,   212 pp., edition

Longyear, Mary Beecher, *The Genealogy and Life of Asa Gilbert Eddy*
    Mary Beecher Longyear, © 1922 ̗ vols.,   140 pp.,   first edition

Longyear, Mary Beecher, *The History of a House • Its Founder, Family and Guests*
    The Zion Research Foundation, Brookline, Mass., © 1925 ̗ vols.,   69 pp.,   first edition

Lord, Myra B., *Mary Baker Eddy*
    Davis & Bond, Boston, © 1918 ̗ vols.,   62 pp.,   first edition

Meehan, Michael, *Mrs. Eddy and the Late Suit in Equity*
    Meehan, Michael, © 1908 ̗ vols.,   371 pp. ̗ horized edition

Milmine, Georgine, *Mary Baker G. Eddy; The story of her life & the history of C.S.*
    S. S. McClure Co. (and originalholder of copyright), © 1906 ̗   4 vols.,   ? pp.,   xerox edition

Milmine, Georgine, *The Life of Mary Baker G. Eddy and The History of Christian Science*
    Doubleday, Page & Company, New York, © 1907,8,9 ̗ vols.,   495 pp.,   first edition

Norton, Carol, *The Christian Science Church; Its Organization and Polity*
    Christian Science Publishing Society, © 1904 ̗ vols.,   38 pp.,   first edition

Norton, Carol, NCSA copyright holder, *The New World*
    Christian Science Publishing Society, © 1894 ̗ vols.,   np pp.,   second edition

Norwood, Edward Everett, *Reminiscences of Mary Baker Eddy*
    Edward Everett Norwood, © ̗ vols., pp., edition

Nowell, Ames, C.S.B., D.D., Th.D., *Mary Baker Eddy, Her Revelation of Divine Egoism*
    Veritas Institute, Inc., New York, © 1963, 1965 ̗ vols.,   264 pp.,   first edition

Oakes, Richard F., C.S., *Discerning the Rights of Man*
    Richard F. Oakes, © 1971 ̗ vols.,   42 pp., edition

Oakes, Richard, C.S., compiler, *Divinity Course and General Collectanea of Items By & About MBE*
    Rare Book Company, © ̗ vols.,   286 pp. ̗ second edition

251

Oakes, Richard, C.S., compiler, *Essays and other Footprints*
　　Rare Book Company, ©, vols., 　280 pp., ed book edition

Oakes, Richard, C.S., compiler, *Mary Baker Eddy's Lessons of The Seventh Day*
　　Christian Science Research Library, Christian Science Found., © 1989, vols., 　377 pp., vn book edition

Oakes, Richard, C.S., compiler, *Mary Baker Eddy's Published Writings—(other than Prose) 1895-1910*
　　Christian Science Research Library, Christian Science Found., © 1987, vols., 　535 pp., w book edition

Oakes, Richard, C.S., compiler, *Mary Baker Eddy's Six Days of Revelation*
　　Christian Science Research Library, © 1981, vols., 　561 pp., en book edition

Oakes, Richard, C.S., compiler, *The Story of The Chicago Addresses of Mary Baker Eddy*
　　Richard Oakes, © 1988, vols., 　70 pp., Revised edition

Orcutt, William Dana, *Mary Baker Eddy and her books*
　　Christian Science Publishing Society, © 1950, vols., 　198 pp., 　first edition

Orgain, Alice, *Distinguishing Characteristics of MBE's Progressive Revisions of S & H*
　　Rare Book Company, 99 Nassau Street, New York, NY, © 1933, vols., 　80 pp., edition

Orgain, Alice, *Story of the Christian Science Manual • Proving its immortality*
　　Rare Book Company, © 1934, vols., 　331 pp., 　first edition

Orgain, Alice L., *The Detached Branch, The Olive Branch of Peace*
　　The Detached Branch, © 1931, vols., 　503 pp., 　first edition

Orgain, Alice L., "A Loyal Christian Scientist", *As It Is*
　　Alice L. Orgain, © 1929, vols., 　949 pp., 　first edition

Peel, Robert, *Mary Baker Eddy, The Years of Authority, 1892-1910*
　　Holt, Rhinehart and Winston of Canada, © 1977, 3/3 vols., 　528 pp., 　first edition

Peel, Robert, *Mary Baker Eddy, The Years of Discovery, 1821-1875*
　　Holt, Rhinehart and Winston of Canada, © 1966, 1/3 vols., 　370 pp., 　first edition

Peel, Robert, *Mary Baker Eddy: The Years of Trial, 1876-1891*
　　Holt, Rhinehart and Winston of Canada, © 1971, 2/3 vols., 　391 pp., 　first edition

Powell, Lyman P., *Mary Baker Eddy: A Life Size Portrait*
　　The MacMillan Company, New York, 1930, © 1930, vols., 　364 pp., 　first edition

Putnam, Robert C., C.S., *Items on The Science of Life*
　　Robert C. Putnam, Mountain Lakes, New Jersey 1981, © 1977, vols., 　74 pp., 　first edition

Putnam, Robert C., C.S., *Items on The Science of Life—Volume II*
　　Robert C. Putnam, Mountain Lakes, New Jersey 1988, © 1988, vols., 　234 pp., 　first edition

Putnam, Robert C., C.S., *Notes on Association Meetings*
　　Robert C. Putnam, Mountain Lakes, New Jersey, © 1977, vols., 　161 pp., 　first edition

Putnam, Robert C., C.S., *Notes on Association Meetings—Supplement*
　　Robert C. Putnam, Mountain Lakes, New Jersey, © 1987, vols., 　129* pp., mental edition

Putnam, Robert C., C.S., *The Science of Life*
　　Robert C. Putnam, Mountain Lakes, NJ, © 1976, vols., 255+2c pp., 　first edition

Quimby, Phineas P./ ed. by Horatio W. Dresser, *The Quimby Manuscripts*
　　Thomas Y. Crowell Company, New York, © 1921, vols., 　462 pp., 　first edition

Ramsay, E. Mary, *Christian Science and its Discoverer*
　　Christian Science Publishing Society, © 1923, 1935c, vols., 　118 pp., 　second edition

Richard Southall Grant, *Landmarks for Christian Scientists from Bow to Boston*
 Rand Avery Co., Boston, Mass., © 1937, vols., 174 pp., third edition

Salchow, John G., *Souvenir Album of the Home of Rev. Mary Baker Eddy, Chestnut Hill,...*
 John G. Salchow, © 1911, vols., np pp., first edition

Sargent, Laura and Victoria, *Reminiscences of Mary Baker Eddy*
 , ©, vols., pp., edition

Sass, Karin with illustrations by Christa Kieffer, *Mary Baker Eddy: A Special Friend*
 Christian Science Publishing Society, © 1983, vols., np pp., second edition

Seal, Frances Thurber, *Christian Science in Germany*
 Longyear Historical Society, 120 Seaver St., Brookline, MA 02146, © 1931, vols., 83 pp., third edition

Searle, George M., *The Truth about Christian Science*
 The Paulist Press, New York, © 1916, vols., 305 pp., edition

Shannon, Clara M. Sainsbury, C.S.D., *Golden Memories*
 The Gethsemane Foundation, St. Maries, Idaho, © pub.-1990, vols., 36 pp., second edition

Shannon, Clara M. Sainsbury, C.S.D., *In the Service of Mary Baker Eddy-Reminiscences by Clara M. Shannon*
 Longyear Foundation, Brookline, Mass., © 1958, vols., pp., edition

Simonsen, Reverend Severin E., *From The Methodist Pulpit into Christian Science & How I Demonstrated ..*
 M. Simonsen, P. O. Box 487, Fair Oaks, CA 95628, © 1928, vols., 294 pp., ninth edition

Smaus, Jewel Spangler, *Mary Baker Eddy, The Golden Days*
 Christian Science Publishing Society, © 1966 CSPS, vols., 193 pp., first edition

Smillie, Paul R., *An Analysis of the Film: Mary Baker Eddy: A Heart in Protest*
 The Gethsemane Foundation, St. Maries, Idaho, © 1990, vols., 53 pp., first edition

Smillie, Paul R., *Christian Scientists and the Child Court Cases*
 The Gethsemane Foundation, St. Maries, Idaho, © 1986, vols., 14 pp., first edition

Smillie, Paul R., *Does God Know Mary Baker Eddy and Christ Jesus?*
 The Gethsemane Foundation, St. Maries, Idaho, © 1987, vols., 16 pp., first edition

Smillie, Paul R., *Gratitude or Indifference; Love or Deification*
 The Gethsemane Foundation, St. Maries, Idaho, © 1986, vols., 14 pp., first edition

Smillie, Paul R., *Loving Our Leader*
 The Gethsemane Foundation, St. Maries, Idaho, © 1988, vols., 52 pp., first edition

Smillie, Paul R., *Mary Baker Eddy: The Prophetic and Historical Perspective—Vol. I*
 The Gethsemane Foundation, St. Maries, Idaho, © 1979, 1/3 vols., 320 pp., second edition

Smillie, Paul R., *Our Leader's Demonstration of Generic Man*
 The Gethsemane Foundation, St. Maries, Idaho, © 1987, vols., 12 pp., first edition

Smillie, Paul R., *The Father, the Prodigal, and the Citizen*
 The Gethsemane Foundation, St. Maries, Idaho, © 1988, vols., 52 pp., first edition

Smillie, Paul R., *What Did Mrs. Eddy Say?*
 The Gethsemane Foundation, St. Maries, Idaho, © 1991, vols., 20 pp., first edition

Smith, Clifford P., *Historical and Biographical Papers; First Series*
 Christian Science Publishing Society, © 1934, 1/2 vols., 103 pp., first edition

Smith, Clifford P., *Historical and Biographical Papers; Second Series*
 Christian Science Publishing Society, © 1934, vols., 268 pp. (2 or 3rd) edition

Smith, Judge Clifford P., *Christian Science and Legislation*
 Christian Science Publishing Society, © 1905,1909 ̖ vols., 128 pp., second edition

Smith, Judge Clifford P., *Christian Science: Its Legal Status, A Defence of Human Rights*
 Christian Science Publishing Society, © 1914 ̖ vols., 127 pp., first edition

Smith, Judge Clifford P., *Historical and Biographical Papers*
 Christian Science Publishing Society, © 1934 ̖ vols., 127 pp., first edition

Smith, Karl N., and Walter H. Wilson, *Support for the Christian Science Board of Directors*
 Plainfield Community Church, Plaifield, NJ, © 1945 ̖ vols., ̖p. con. pp., edition

Smith, Louise A., *Mary Baker Eddy: Discoverer and Founder of Christian Science*
 Christian Science Publishing Society, © 1990 ̖ vols., 198 pp., century edition

Spencer, Ralph B., *The Overwhelming Evidence Concerning Spiritual Healings thru MBE*
 Ralph B. Spencer, 90 Noble St., Seekonk, Mass. 02771, © 1963, 1976 ̖ vols., 68 pp., Fourth edition

Springer, Fleta Campbell, *According to the Flesh; a biography of Mary Baker Eddy*
 Coward-McCann, Inc., New York, © 1930 CMcC ̖ vols., 497 pp., first edition

Stetson, Augusta E., C.S.D., *Reminiscences, Sermons and Correspondence / 1884-1913*
 G. P. Putnam's Sons, New York and London, © 1913 ̖ vols., 1200 pp., first edition

Stetson, Augusta E., C.S.D., *Sermons Which Spiritually Interpret the Scriptures and Other Writings*
 G. P. Putnam's Sons, New York and London, © 1924 ̖ vols., 1277 pp., first edition

Stewart, Myrtle, *The 1910 Coup*
 Stewart, Myrtle, © 1972 ̖ vols., 58 pp., first edition

Still, M. Adelaide, *Reminiscences of Mary Baker Eddy*
 M. Adelaide Still, © ̖ vols., pp., photost edition

Studdert Kennedy, Hugh A. (Anketell), *Christian Science and Organized Religion*
 The Farallon Press, © 1930 ̖ vols., 335 pp., first edition

Studdert Kennedy, Hugh A. (Anketell), *Mrs. Eddy*
 The Farallon Press, San Francisco, © 1947 ̖ vols., 507 pp., first edition

Swain, Richard L., *The Real Key to Christian Science*
 Fleming H. Revell Company, © 1917 ̖ vols., 95 pp., fifth edition

Tomlinson, Rev. Irving C., M.A., C.S.B., *Twelve Years with Mary Baker Eddy: Recollections and Experiences*
 ©1945,1966,renewed 1973, Christian Science Board of Directors:All rights reserved, © CSPS ̖ vols., 227 pp.,

Twain, Mark, *Christian Science with notes containing corrections to date*
 Harper & Brothers Publishers, New York & London, © 1899 ̖ vols., 362 pp., edition

Walter, William W., *The Unfoldment*
 William W. Walter, © 1921 ̖ vols., 206 pp., first edition

Wilbur, Sibyl, *Cradled Obscurity or The Finding of the Christ*
 The Bookmark, © ̖ vols., 11 pp., xerox edition

Wilbur, Sibyl, *The Life of Mary Baker Eddy*
 Christian Science Publishing Society, © 1907 ̖ vols., 384 pp., first edition

Williamson, Margaret, *The Mother Church Extension*
 Christian Science Publishing Society, © 1939, 1968 ̖ 2/2 vols., 109 pp., edition

Winslow, Wentworth Byron, *God Can Do It*
 Dodd, Mead Company, New York, © 1939 ̖ vols., 145 pp., first edition

Winslow, Wentworth Byron, *God Is Doing It*
Dodd, Mead Company, New York, © 1941 , vols. ,   101 pp. ,   first edition

Winslow, Wentworth Byron, *God Will Do It*
Dodge Publishing Company, New York, © 1940 , vols. ,   138 pp. ,   first edition

Winslow, Wentworth Byron, *Let God Do It*
Dodge Publishing Co., New York, © 1937 , vols. ,   146 pp. ,   first edition

Wright, Helen, *Mary Baker Eddy: God's Great Scientist—Volume I*
Helen Wright, © 1984 , 1/3 vols. ,   255 pp. ,   first edition

Wright, Helen, *Mary Baker Eddy: God's Great Scientist—Volume II*
Helen Wright, © 1984 , 2/3 vols. ,   133 pp. ,   first edition

Wright, Helen, *Mary Baker Eddy: God's Great Scientist—Volume III*
Helen Wright, © 1987 , 3/3 vols. ,   265 pp. ,   first edition

Wright, Helen M., *If Mary Baker Eddy's Manual were Obeyed—Enlarged Edition*
Helen Wright, © 1986 , vols. ,   231 pp. ,nlarged edition

Wright, Helen M., *Mary Baker Eddy Reveals Your Divinity*
Hearthstone Book, © 1991 , vols. ,   271 pp. ,   first edition

Wright, Helen M., *Mary Baker Eddy's Church Manual and "Church Universal Triumphant"*
Helen Wright, © 1981 , vols. ,   319 pp. ,   first edition

Young, Alan, *MBE-Her Pleasant View and Infinite Vision*
The Bookmark, © , vols. ,   9 pp. ,   xerox edition